REPENTANCE RITUAL
of the Emperor of Liang

A complete translation of
REPENTANCE DHARMA OF KINDNESS
AND COMPASSION IN THE BODHIMANDA

REPENTANCE
RITUAL
of the Emperor of Liang

A complete translation of
REPENTANCE DHARMA OF KINDNESS
AND COMPASSION IN THE BODHIMANDA

Buddhist Text Translation Society
Dharma Realm Buddhist University
Dharma Realm Buddhist Association
Ukiah, California, USA

Repentance Ritual of the Emperor of Liang
A complete translation of Repentance Dharma of Kindness and Compassion in the Bodhimanda

© 2016 Buddhist Text Translation Society
          Dharma Realm Buddhist University
          Dharma Realm Buddhist Association

All rights reserved. No part of this book may be reproduced in any form or by any electronic or mechanical means including information storage and retrieval systems without permission in writing from the publisher, except by a reviewer, who may quote brief passages in a review.

For more information contact:
Buddhist Text Translation Society
4951 Bodhi Way
Ukiah, CA 95482
www.buddhisttexts.org
email: info@buddhisttexts.org

ISBN 978-1-60103-087-0 paperback
ISBN 978-1-60103-086-3 ebook

Cataloging-in-Publication Data is available from the Library of Congress

Pinyin is used for the romanization of Chinese words, except for proper names which retain familiar romanizations.

TABLE OF CONTENTS

FOREWORD

Bowing the Repentance of Emperor Liang has always been a special event for me during my life as a Buddhist monastic—now in its forty-seventh year. I have participated in many such ceremonies. One occasion stands out as most memorable.

This occasion unfolded a couple of decades ago when my teacher, Master Hua, named *me* as a potential Repentance Host. It had never occurred to me that I, housed in a female body this life, might presume to be a host of anything! That gender-prejudiced view I held harkened back to a childhood dominated by the strict father, an education dispensed by male teachers and administrators, and church-going experiences where religious rituals were always conducted by men-only.

So, when I stood for the first time at the center of the Repentance of Emperor Liang assembly fulfilling the role of Repentance Host, I personally experienced an aspect of the extraordinary equality of Buddhism, as presented to us by our Master, a bright-eyed sage!

More than that, as Host, I quickly became aware of the power of the collective energy that is generated by a gathering of sincere practitioners performing a ritual together. This strong and positive energy that surges and spreads was palpable to me from my vantage point at the Host's post in the middle of the assembly.

As the Repentance of Emperor Liang unfolds, this powerful energy can be channelled into severing doubts, repenting for deeds done, bringing forth the resolve for bodhi, making significant vows, aiding beings in many realms, and dedicating the merit of all this to peace for the world and well-being for all inhabitants of it.

As this energy created by the performance of the Repentance pulsates outward and onward, repentance participants are invigorated and the effectiveness of repentance becomes a practical reality, not only within the confines of the assembly, but extending throughout the cosmos as far as the minds of the participants can reach-- for the betterment of all. Thus, the actual experience of bowing the Repentance provides the very best affirmation of faith possible! I trust you will join one soon and see for yourselves.

Bhikshuni Heng Chih
On Ullambana and the Buddhas' Happy Day
August 17, 2016

PREFACE

The Liang Dynasty of China (502–587) is not well known in the West. It was short-lived, during the chaotic period of small warring kingdoms that sprang up after the fall of the Han Dynasty. However, the Liang Dynasty is important in the history of Chinese Buddhism due to the patronage of Emperor Wu (464–549) and the mind-transmission of Patriarch Bodhidharma.

Emperor Wu was an early imperial patron of Buddhism. He built temples and was magnanimous in his support of the monastic community.

When Bodhidharma, the 28th Indian Patriarch in direct lineage from Shakyamuni Buddha, saw that the timing and potential were right for propagating Buddhism, he resolved to bring the Dharma to China. He personally met with Emperor Wu in Nanjing. Thereafter, he went into seclusion in a cave near the Shaolin Temple in the Song Mountains, meditating in front of a wall for nine years.

Bodhidharma is the first patriarch of Buddhism in China.He transmitted the mind-seal Dharma to the venerable Chinese monk Hui Ke, who became the second patriarch in China. Thus the Buddhist lineage of mind-transmission which started in India, continued and flourished in China.

One of Emperor Wu's legacies in Buddhism is this repentance text in ten chapters that bears his name. In order to save his deceased empress from the retributions of the animal realm, he sought the help of National Master Baozhi, who compiled this Dharma of Repentance. This text is commonly known as *Emperor of Liang Repentance* and continues to be practiced today, inspiring many with the many testimonials of its effectiveness.

Bowing repentance is not a well-known or popular form of cultivation in the West. It is also not often practiced in the Theravada tradition. However repentance is emphasized in Mahayana Buddhism, in texts such as the *Avatamsaka Sutra*. This Dharma exhorts everyone to repent of all offenses and reform in order to eradicate karma, thus clearing obstructions and paving the way for advancement in the spiritual path.

This particular repentance was designed to be practiced in a monastery with bhikshus or bhikshunis (monks or nuns) leading the assembly to repent in a week-long ceremony.

The repentance text is divided into forty sections grouped into ten chapters. Each chapter starts with a verse of praise, the cantor (bhikshu or bhikshuni that leads the chanting) exhorting the assembly to listen respectfully and a formal commencement of the repentance by bowing to the six Buddhas of the past, Shakyamuni Buddha, and the future Maitreya Buddha. The main part of each chapter contains sections of texts explaining the principles of repentance interspersed with bowing in full prostration (head, hands and knees to the ground) to various Buddhas and Bodhisattvas. Each chapter concludes with a verse of praise, text for concluding the chapter and a final verse to end the chapter.

The main points of each chapter are as follows:

Chapter One explains the necessity of repentance.

Chapter Two extols the virtue of bringing forth the bodhi resolve (the intention to become enlightened) and exhorts everyone to make vows and to dedicate merit.

Chapter Three explains how current suffering is due to an individual's previous deeds.

Chapter Four describes the various hells and the deeds that cause beings to fall into the hells.

Chapter Five and Six explain how to dispel enmity and resolve animosity by emulating bodhisattvas (enlightened beings).

Chapter Seven encourages everyone to cultivate by relying on the Three Treasures - the Buddha, the Dharma and the Sangha.

Participants also start bowing to the the Buddhas on behalf of heavenly beings, ascetic masters and Brahma kings.

In Chapter Eight participants continue bowing to the Buddhas on behalf of asuras, dragon kings, demon kings, human kings, and other in the human realm.

In Chapter Nine participants continue bowing to the Buddhas on behalf of those in the various hells, the realm of hungry ghosts and those in the animal realm.

In Chapter Ten participants learn about the bodhisattva's Dharma of dedicating merit and virtue to living beings, sincerely wishing that their vows will be fulfilled and that they will accomplish bodhi.

During the past 70 years, Buddhism has become increasingly popular in the West. Many Chan/Zen texts have been translated into English, but translations of repentance liturgy are almost non-existent. This is the first complete English language translation of **Liang Huang Bao Chan**, *The Repentance Dharma of Kindness and Compassion of the Bodhimanda,* more widely known as Emperor of Liang Repentance.

Bhikshuni Heng Jen started the English translation over fifteen years ago for her master's thesis for the Dharma Realm Buddhist University. She passed away after translating the first six rolls of the Repentance. Bhikshuni Heng Tyan completed the four remaining rolls of text, thus, completing the primary translation. In 2014, the translation team under the leadership of Bhikshu Jin Yan undertook the review and editing of this work, aided by the commentary of Great Master Dixian (諦閑大師). The Buddhist Text Translation Society is pleased to offer English readers this text to use as a practice manual and source of reference.

Emperor of Liang Repentance Translation Team
On the Buddha's 3043 Birthday (May 2016)

The Eight Guidelines of
The Buddhist Text Translation Society

1. A volunteer must free him/herself from the motives of personal fame and profit.
2. A volunteer must cultivate a respectful and sincere attitude free from arrogance and conceit.
3. A volunteer must refrain from aggrandizing his/her work and denigrating that of others.
4. A volunteer must not establish him/herself as the standard of correctness and suppress the work of others with his or her fault-finding.
5. A volunteer must take the Buddha-mind as his/her own mind.
6. A volunteer must use the wisdom of Dharma-selecting vision to determine true principles.
7. A volunteer must request virtuous elders in the ten directions to certify his/her translations.
8. A volunteer must endeavor to propagate the teachings by printing and distributing *sutras*, *shastra* texts, and *vinaya* texts when the translations are certified as being correct.

ROLL ONE

Namo Buddhas and Bodhisattvas of the Dragon Flower Assembly
(*bow three times*)

The origin

This Repentance Dharma of Kindness and Compassion in the Bodhimanda was compiled by ten eminent monks led by Chan Master Baozhi.
It has been commonly known as the *Emperor of Liang Repentance* because
it was compiled at the request of Emperor Wu of the Liang Dynasty.

Emperor Wu (464 C.E. - 549 C.E.), whose surname was Xiao, given
name Yan, and courtesy name Shuda, was born in Lanling, (Jiangsu
Province). He served as a government official in the Qi Dynasty, and
was appointed as Duke of Liang. Later, he forced the abdication of
Emperor Qi and ascended the throne. He named his dynasty "Liang."
He reigned for 46 years until his death at the age of 86.

His wife, Empress Chi, died a premature death at the age of thirty.
She was intensely jealousy of and hated the Emperor's consorts and
concubines. Her words and thoughts were as vicious as that of a poisonous snake. Because she harbored so much hatred and anger while
alive, she was consequently reborn as a python.

As a python, her spiritual nature was not entirely clouded, and she
knew of her karmic causes. In the second year of Emperor Wu's reign,
she appeared in the palace in the form of a python and told the
emperor of her suffering as well as her evil karma. She beseeched the
emperor to rescue her from her misery. Accordingly the emperor
requested the assistance of Chan Master Baozhi and other monks who
then compiled this *Repentance*. This text consists of ten rolls and is
based on the essentials of bowing repentances taught in the sutras

and *vinaya* texts. With this text, an assembly of monks set up the Bodhimanda and conducted the Repentance on her behalf.

At the conclusion of the repentance, a person attired in red robes and wearing a high hat suddenly appeared and expressed profound gratitude to the Emperor, "By the power of the Buddhas, I have been liberated from the body of a python. I am about to be reborn in the heavens. Before going, I have come to express my gratitude."

After that, the person disappeared. From this we can conclude the merit and virtue accrued from this repentance is inconceivable. Since then, the *Emperor of Liang Jeweled Repentance* has spread throughout the world and is still practiced today.

Prologue

This Repentance was compiled at the request of Emperor Wu of Liang on behalf of the deceased Empress Chi. The Emperor had been mourning her death for several months, pining for her during the day and suffering from insomnia at night. One evening when the Emperor was in his bedroom, he heard a rustling sound outside. Upon taking a closer look, he saw a python curled up in the main hall, staring at him with its eyes blinking and mouth wide open. The emperor was extremely frightened, tried to escape but had no place to hide.

Being cornered, he stood up tensely and said to the python, "This palace is tightly guarded; there should not be a snake here. Are you a demon trying to haunt me?"

The python answered with a human voice, "I was your wife Chi, and am now in the form of a python. When I was alive, I was very jealous of your concubines. I had a ferocious temper and a vicious nature. Once my anger erupted, it was like blazing fire or darting arrows, harming people and destroying things. Due to such offenses, I was reborn in a lower realm as a python. Without food and shelter, I suffer unbearable hunger and misery.

"Moreover, there are many parasites underneath each of my scales and they gnaw at my flesh. The pain is like sharp knives stabbing my skin. I became a python, and unlike an ordinary snake, can tranform my body and come here unhindered into your royal palace, a restricted place. Mindful of your Majesty's deep affection for me in the past, I now reveal myself before you in this grotesque form. I pray that you can create some merit on my behalf so that I can be rescued from this predicament."

Upon hearing this, Emperor Wu of Liang deeply lamented, but when he sought to interact further, the python had already disappeared!

The following day, the Emperor gathered a large group of monks in the palace, explained what had happened, and asked them the best method to liberate the python from its suffering.

Venerable Baozhi said, "The only way is to bow to the Buddhas and repent sincerely on behalf of the empress."

The Emperor agreed to the advice. The monks then searched the sutras, gathered the names of Buddhas, extracted passages, and compiled the Repentance. The Emperor himself gave invaluable input, helping edit and embellish the writing of the Repentance text, including removing extraneous words. With the actual Repentance proper based on the words of the Buddhas, this text then became the Repentance Dharma in ten rolls that the assembly used to repent on the behalf of the empress.

One day, a rare fragrance permeated the palace and lingered for a long time. At first, no one knew where it came from. But when the Emperor looked up, he saw an adorned heavenly being, who said to him, "I was the python that you saw previously. Because of the merit and virtue accrued from the Repentance, I was reborn in the Trayas-trimsha Heaven. I am here to give testimony to your repentance effort." Having expressed heart-felt gratitude, the heavenly being disappeared.

Although it has been more than a thousand years since the Liang Dynasty, people still use this text to conduct repentances. Whoever bows or prays sincerely will obtain an invisible response. I, as editor of this reprint, was afraid that such knowledge concerning the

Emperor of Liang Repentance would be lost in the future or would not be understood clearly, thus, I, as editor of this reprint, have tried to explain it in simple words for everyone's benefit.

Summer of 1889, 15th Year of the Guangxu Reign, Qing Dynasty
A preface by Jinling (Nanking) Sutra Texts Publishing House
before republishing the *Repentance.*

Listen Attentively

The Emperor of Liang initiates this Repentance;
Maitreya Bodhisattva names it.
Venerable Baozhi compiles it from the sacred Flower Treasury,
With names of Buddhas gathered from the sutras;
Monastics assemble and conduct the Repentance.
This Dharma of Repentance is proclaimed vastly.
The Repentance originates from a dreamlike encounter by the Emperor of Liang,
And it results in clouds of auspiciousness welling forth around the palace.
Within the Bodhimanda,

> Glittering lanterns shining everywhere;
> Golden flames ever illuminating;
> Fragrant incense enveloping the palace;
> Exquisite flowers adorning in many layers.
> In the white clouds and blue sky, appears an adorned celestial being,
> Before the white jade staircase, Chi is liberated from her suffering.
> By the merit and virtue of this Repentance,
> Calamities are quelled and offenses eradicated.
> Calamities quelled, auspiciousness descends;
> Offenses eradicated, blessings sprout forth.
> A good medicine it is, curing illnesses;
> A bright light it is, dispelling darkness.
> Benefitting the nine states of existence,
> Blessing the four kinds of birth.
> Boundless is its merit and virtue,
> Beyond praise or exaltation!

To commence this Repentance, we with utmost sincerity:

> Bow respectfully to Samantabhadra, King of Great Conduct Bodhisattva,

Contemplate that this incense and flowers are offered to all
Buddhas of the ten directions,
Recite the sacred mantra phrases to purify this Repentance
Bodhimanda,
Cause the "flower of offenses" to wither away and fall so as to
achieve the perfect and abundant fruition.

We again reverently bow to the Greatly Compassionate One, wishing
that he will bless us with efficacious responses.

Namo Samantabhadra Bodhisattva Mahasattva (*three times*)

Verse in Praise of Samantabhadra[1] Bodhisattva

There exists a Bodhisattva,
Seated in full-lotus posture,
Known as Samantabhadra,
With a body of white jade.
From the back of his neck
Emanates fifty kinds of light
Made of fifty different colors.
From every pore,
Golden light comes pouring forth;
At each tip of golden light,
Appear countless transformation Buddhas
And countless transformation Bodhisattvas
All as his retinue.
Together they stroll around peacefully,
As precious flowers shower down.
Samantabhadra descends before the cultivator.
His elephant trumpets
And on top of its tusks,
Appear many jade maidens in ponds,
Singing and playing melodious music.
Their voices and sounds wonderful and subtle,

In praise of the Great Vehicle,
And the Path of One Reality.
Seeing this, the cultivator rejoices and bows in worship.
He further reads and recites,
The profound sutras.
Universally bow to the ten-direction
Myriad transformation Buddhas,
Stupa of Many Jewels Tathagata,
Shakyamuni Buddha,
Samantabhadra Bodhisattva,
And all great Bodhisattvas.
I now make this vow:
If I have planted blessings,
I can surely see Samantabhadra Bodhisattva.
So may this Venerable Universally Auspicious One
Manifest before me.

Namo Samantabhadra Bodhisattva   (*chant ten times*)

Let us all be respectful and reverent.
Single-mindedly, we bow to the eternally abiding Buddhas of the
Dharma Realm of the ten directions.
Single-mindedly, we bow to the eternally abiding Dharma of the
Dharma Realm of the ten directions.
Single-mindedly, we bow to the eternally abiding Sangha of the
Dharma Realm of the ten directions.

The cantor chants:

All in this assembly, each one kneeling and solemn, holding incense
and flowers, in accord with Dharma, make offerings to the Three
Treasures of the Dharma Realm of the ten directions.

May this incense and flower pervade the ten directions,
Making a tower of subtle, wonderful light.
All heavenly music, jeweled heavenly incense,

Rare heavenly delicacies, and jeweled heavenly garments,
All inconceivably wonderful dharma objects,
Each object emitting all objects,
Each object emitting all dharmas,
Revolving unobstructed and adorning each other,
Are offered everywhere to the Three Treasures of the ten directions.
Before the Three Treasures of the Dharma Realm of the ten directions,
My body everywhere makes offerings.
Each one entirely pervades the Dharma Realm,
Each one unalloyed and unimpeded,
Exhausting the bounds of the future, doing the Buddhas' work.
May the fragrances permeate living beings throughout the Dharma Realm.
Having been permeated, may they all bring forth the resolve for bodhi.
May this cloud of incense and flowers fully pervade the ten directions,
As an offering to all Buddhas, all Dharmas, and all Bodhisattvas,
As well as to the multitudes of Hearers, Pratyekabuddhas, and devas,
Making a tower of subtle, wonderful light that extends boundlessly
into all realms.
May beings in boundless Buddhalands
Enjoy them and do the Buddhas' work.
May the fragrances permeate all beings,
So they bring forth the resolve for bodhi.
        (Assembly rises and bows to the following Bodhisattva)

Namo Precious *Udumbara* Flower Bodhisattva, Mahasattva (*three times*)

His appearance, how wonderful and rare,
His light, illumining all ten directions!
To whom I had made offerings in the past,
To whom I am now drawing near.
A sage leader he is, a king, a heaven among heavens,
With the voice of kalavinkas,
Taking great pity on all beings,
To him we now pay reverence.

Commencement of the Repentance

Listen respectfully

One body transforms and responds universally to the lands of the ten directions.

One sound proclaims the Dharma; all beings hear it – humans, heavenly beings, and the rest of the three realms.

One path and *One* gateway enable all, unobstructed, to transcend oceans of samsara.

One Attribute and *One* Flavor enable one to ascend the summit of Nirvana on the Perfect and Direct Teaching of the *One* Vehicle.

Like the moon reflecting in a thousand rivers, the Dharma is taught according to the capacities of beings.

Like spring returning to earth, sages respond to beings accordingly.

They universally engage all beings throughout the Dharma Realm, while seated in each and every Bodhimanda.

We hope you will witness this with your enlightened eye, and verify our sincerity and humility.

[Dharma Host]: On behalf of _____ [those who seek to repent], we practice this Repentance Dharma of Kindness and Compassion in the Bodhimanda. We now come to Roll One. With all conditions fulfilled, we now enter the Repentance Platform. May we all reverently and wholeheartedly purify our three karmas and chant the text accordingly. We burn incense and present flowers as an offering to the Three Treasures in the ten directions. We chant and praise the sacred names of Buddhas. We bow to them in full prostration and take refuge in them. We confess our mistakes and seek to eradicate our karmic obstacles. We are earnestly mindful that, from time without beginning until now, due to our confusion in the One Nature, the Buddha-Nature, we have turned our backs on the Dharma of the One Vehicle.

One small defect in our diseased eyes causes us to see a labyrinth of flowers in empty space. One small bubble in the ocean causes waves to roll and churn in the stormy ocean of delusion. We have long been going against the samadhi of One Reality. Our single thought of ignorance has let loose all reins, causing our minds to be filled with the three poisons, resulting in our creating myriad forms of karma. This opens up the doors to the eighty-four thousand defiling passions, and gives rise to the hundreds of thousands of obstacles of afflictions. Like a wild and unrestrained elephant, we indulge in desires. Like a moth flying into fire, we chase after illusory conditions. Our offenses accumulate as high as mountains and our karma runs as deep as the ocean. With such scant roots of goodness, we fear we will not be able to escape our evil retributions.

Let us now be diligent in our mindfulness and rectify our thoughts. Externally, we rely on the sublime conditions of this wonderful bowing ceremony; internally, we feel deep shame and remorse. We gather together in this present pure assembly to chant this efficacious repentance. By relying on the awesome light of thousands of Buddhas, we cleanse our offenses of defilements which we have accumulated through many lives. We pray all Buddhas will take pity on us. We now respectfully bow to the Greatly Compassionate One to invisibly protect us.

By the Repentance Host

In the heavens above and all that is below,
Nothing compares with a Buddha
Throughout the worlds of the ten directions he is matchless
Of all I have seen in the world,
There is nothing at all like a Buddha.

We now begin the Repentance Dharma of Kindness and Compassion in the Bodhimanda. Together in this assembly, we single-mindedly return to and rely on all Buddhas of the three periods of time.

Namo Buddhas of the past, Vipashyin Buddha

Namo Shikhin Buddha

Namo Vishvabhu Buddha

Namo Krakucchanda Buddha

Namo Kanakamuni Buddha

Namo Kashyapa Buddha
Namo our Fundamental Teacher Shakyamuni Buddha
Namo Honored Future Buddha, Maitreya

Verse for Opening a Sutra

The unsurpassed, profound, and wonderful Dharma,
Is difficult to encounter in hundreds of millions of eons,
I now see and hear it, receive and uphold it,
And I vow to fathom the Tathagata's true meaning.

The words "Kindness and Compassion in the Bodhimanda" were chosen for the title of this repentance due to a response in a dream. Maitreya, the World-Honored, replete with great kindness and compassion extending to the end of time, bequeathed the title of this repentance. This was how the title was established. We do not dare change the title.

Relying on the strength of the kindness of the World-Honored One, we resolve to protect the Three Treasures, eclipse the power of demons, and humble those with arrogance and overweening pride. We also resolve to cause those who have not planted roots of goodness to do so, and cause the roots of goodness already planted to flourish. We further resolve to cause those who cling to the notion of attainment and who dwell in various views to aspire for transcendence. Finally, we resolve to enable those who delight in the Small Vehicle not to doubt the Mahayana, and to cause those who delight in the Mahayana to be joyous.

Furthermore, compassion reigns supreme among all goodness and serves as the sanctuary for all living beings. Like the sun which lights up the day and the moon which illuminates the night, it guides us like eyes or teachers, and cares for us like parents or siblings. Drawing all of us back to the Bodhimanda, it serves as a true spiritual mentor. Kindness and compassion connect with us in a way deeper than that of the relationship with our blood relatives. It accompanies us life after life and never leaves us even after death. Therefore, we take it to heart and use "Kindness and Compassion" as the title of this Repentance.

Today in this Bodhimanda, we, both visible and invisible beings, gather to establish this Repentance and bring forth the resolve for bodhi. There are twelve major reasons for this. What are the twelve?

1. With limitless resolve, we vow to transform all beings in the six paths.
2. With limitless vigor, we vow to repay kindness and compassion.
3. We vow this power of goodness will enable all beings to uphold the Buddhas' precepts without thoughts of violating them.
4. By the power of this goodness, we vow that all beings will not give rise to thoughts of arrogance towards teachers and elders.
5. By the power of this goodness, we vow that all beings will not give rise to thoughts of anger or hatred with regard to their position in life.
6. By the power of this goodness, we vow all beings will not envy others' fine appearance.
7. We vow this power of goodness will enable us not to be stingy with the giving of wealth, both internal and external.
8. By this power of goodness, we vow all beings will cultivate blessings, not for themselves, but for all those lacking support and protection.
9. With this power of goodness, we vow all beings practice the four dharmas of attraction[2], not for themselves, but for others.
10. With this power of goodness, we vow all beings resolve to care for the orphaned the solitary, the sick, and the imprisoned so they can attain peace and happiness.
11. With this power of goodness, we vow to subdue and gather in whoever needs to be subdued and gathered.
12. With this power of goodness, we vow all beings everywhere will constantly be mindful to bring forth and sustain the resolve for bodhi.

May all sages and ordinary beings, both visible and invisible, come to protect and help us return to purity through our repentance and fulfill all our wishes, so that our minds will be the same as all Buddhas', and that we make the same vows as all Buddhas. May all beings of the four births and the six paths accomplish bodhi.

Section 1 Taking Refuge with the Three Treasures

Today, we are here in this Bodhimanda due to our shared karma. We should bring forth the resolve for awakening. Always be mindful of impermanence. Our bodies do not last long, our youthful vitality slowly but definitely fades. Thus we should refrain from indulging in defiled conduct and realize that our fine appearance or graceful demeanor has no lasting reliability.

Nothing is permanent; everything eventually drifts towards ruin. Be it in heaven or on earth, who can live forever? When we are young, our muscles may be supple and our skin lustrous, with an aura of vitality. However, the body can retain none of this. This body that comes into being due to conditions will surely wither and perish. It goes through birth, aging, sickness, and death, which comes anytime unannounced! Who can rid us of these miseries? When calamities suddenly hit, we are unable to escape, and we perish, regardless of our status or rank. Our bodies bloat and stink, and the stench is unbearable. So what is the purpose of lavishing so much care on our bodies? If we do not vigorously cultivate meritorious deeds, how can we escape this suffering?

[The Dharma Host makes the following exhortation to the great assembly:] I _____ now contemplate that life is as impermanent as the morning dew; as fleeting as the setting sun. Having lived a life of meager virtue, I have neither the brilliant wisdom of the great ones, nor the insightful knowledge of the sages. My speech lacks gentleness, humaneness, trustworthiness, and kindness. I do not know when to advance and when to retreat, when to lead and when to follow. However, with great apprehension, I humbly take on this task of leading the repentance and exhort everyone to vigorously apply effort in this repentance. This session is finite. When it ends, no amount of longing can bring it back. You will no longer encounter this session again. It is my earnest wish that after the conclusion, each of you will continue to work diligently with a focused mind to personally make daily offerings to the Three Treasures and spur yourself on with vigor. You ought to joyfully follow this virtuous path. I also wish that you will wear the armor of patience and deeply enter this Dharma-door.

Today, we are here in this Bodhimanda due to our shared karma. We should, with utmost earnestness and reverence, bring forth a courageous mind, a mind that never becomes lax, a mind of dwelling peacefully, an expansive mind, a supreme mind, a mind of great kindness and compassion, a mind that delights in giving, a joyful mind, a mind of gratefully repaying kindness, a mind of liberating beings, a mind of protecting all beings, a mind of rescuing all beings, and a mind equal to that of Bodhisattvas and the Tathagatas.

With single-minded concentration, we respectfully bow in full prostration on behalf of the heads of state, leaders, people of all nations, parents, elders, teachers, monastics of the three seniorities[3], good and bad advisors, heavenly beings, ascetic masters, the four world-protecting heavenly kings, spiritual beings who bless the good and punish the evil, spiritual beings who guard and protect those who uphold mantras, the dragon kings of the five directions, dragons and the rest of the eightfold division, as well as the limitless sentient beings in water, air, or on land throughout the ten directions.

> I take refuge with all the Buddhas of the ten directions to the ends of empty space. (*bow*)
> I take refuge with all the venerable Dharmas of the ten directions to the ends of empty space. (*bow*)
> I take refuge with the Sangha of all sages and worthies of the ten directions to the ends of empty space. (*bow*)

Today, we are here in this Bodhimanda due to our shared karma. We should reflect on why we take refuge with the Three Treasures. It is because Buddhas and Bodhisattvas, with their infinite compassion, rescue all beings; with their infinite kindness, they bring comfort to all beings. They are constantly mindful of all beings in the same way parents are attentive to their only child. With their great kindness and compassion, they never weary in constantly doing good and benefiting all beings. They vow to extinguish the fire of the three poisons in all living beings, teaching and transforming them, so that they can attain *Anuttara-samyak-sambodhi*. If living beings fail to become Buddhas, they themselves will not enter Proper Enlightenment. That is why we should take refuge with the Three Treasures.

Furthermore, the Buddhas' compassionate and mindful regard for all living beings surpasses that of one's own parents. As it is said in the sutras, "Parents' love and care for their children are limited to only one lifetime. However, the Buddhas' kindness and compassion towards all living beings is eternal."

Moreover, when parents see their children become ungrateful, behaving unethically and rebelliously, they react with anger or displeasure, becoming less compassionate. Whereas, Buddhas and Bodhisattvas are never like that; not only are they always compassionate but also have increasing concern and care for such beings. They are even willing to enter the *Avici* Hell[4] on behalf of beings to undergo limitless suffering such as being burned by the great wheels of fire. From this, we know that the compassionate regard all Buddhas and great Bodhisattvas have for beings exceeds that of our own parents.

Moreover, living beings' wisdom is covered by ignorance. Our minds are shrouded by afflictions, and we fail to turn to the Buddhas and Bodhisattvas for refuge and reliance. When we hear the teachings of the Buddhas and Bodhisattvas, we do not have faith or accept such teachings, or even worse, we may utter harsh or slanderous speech.

We living beings are not aware, much less mindful, of the kindness and grace bestowed upon us. Due to this disbelief in the basic law of karma, beings fall into and revolve within the three evil destinies of hells, hungry ghosts, and animals, undergoing limitless suffering.

After karmic retributions are resolved, beings are temporarily reborn in the human realm, hindered by incomplete or defective sense faculties, lacking dhyana samadhi and the strength of wisdom. All such obstructions are caused by our lack of faith.

Today, we are here in this Bodhimanda due to our shared karma. We should know that the lack of faith is the worst of all defects. It will continuously prevent us from seeing the Buddhas. Each one of us should now zealously subdue our emotional mind. We must all strengthen and enhance our resolve and bring forth a sense of shame and remorse. We bow with utmost sincerity and ask for forgiveness as we repent and reform of our past offenses. When accumulated karma is eradicated, our bodies and minds will be pure. Only then can we contemplate entering deeply the gateway of true faith. If we do not bring forth such a resolve and do not contemplate in this way, we are afraid that our faith will be hindered by obstacles. If we lack proper faith, we will be lost in the darkness and unable to find our way back.

For this reason, all of us in this Assembly should single-mindedly renew our faith and free ourselves of any doubt. With earnestness and humility, we bow in full prostration like a mountain collapsing before the Buddhas and Bodhisattvas. Now, based on the strength of the kindness and compassion of all Buddhas and Bodhisattvas, we come to such an awakening and bring forth a sense of shame and remorse. May the Buddhas help us to eradicate all offenses that we have created. May we dare not create any offenses we have not yet committed. From now until we accomplish bodhi, we shall bring forth a solid resolve of faith and never retreat.

When this life ends, we may be reborn in the realm of hells, the realm of hungry ghosts, the realm of animals, the realm of human beings, or the realm of heavens. We may be reborn in the three realms in the form of males, females, non-males, non-females. We may be born big or little, and rise or fall in the realms of rebirth. We may suffer unbearable oppression and affliction, yet we vow never to lose the faith that we have established today. We may undergo this suffering for hundreds of thousands of kalpas, yet we vow never to lose this faith. We hope all Buddhas and great Bodhisattvas will guard, protect, and gather us in, enabling us to sustain firm faith that demons and externalists cannot destroy. May our minds and vows be identical with that of all Buddhas. With utmost, heartfelt sincerity, we make this vow together and bow in full prostration.

> We take refuge with all the Buddhas of the ten directions to the ends of empty space. (*bow*)
> We take refuge with all the venerable Dharmas of the ten directions to the ends of empty space. (*bow*)
> We take refuge with the Sangha of all sages and worthies of the ten directions to the ends of empty space. (*bow*)

Today, we who are here in this Bodhimanda due to our shared karma should listen attentively. Beings such as devas and humans are deluded, and the worlds are illusory. Because everything is illusory and not real, there is no real fruition among the mundane existences. Since all things are illusory, fragile, and drifting along with the currents of karma, boundless changes and transmigrations take place. Having no real fruition among the mundane existences, we have been caught in the flow of birth and death for a long time. Because of changes and transmigrations, we have long been adrift in the sea of suffering and emotional love.

That is why sages pity such living beings. According to the *Flowers of Compassion Sutra*, each Bodhisattva becomes a Buddha according to his respective fundamental vows. Shakyamuni Buddha did not manifest a long lifespan, but a short one. He felt deep sympathy for beings living an ephemeral and ever-changing life, adrift in the sea of suffering without being able to transcend it. Because of that, he came to this world to rescue beings prone to being evil and wicked and painstakingly educating obstinate ones, without retreating from his resolve to save all, regardless of the hardships encountered. He constantly applied expedient means to vastly benefit all living beings.

The *Sutra of Samadhi* states, "The mind of all Buddhas is that of great kindness and great compassion. All suffering beings are the subject of this kindness and compassion."

Upon seeing living beings undergoing suffering, Buddhas grieve and weep without a moment of peace and feel as if arrows were piercing their hearts or poking their eyes. They long to eradicate the suffering of living beings and help them attain bliss and happiness. Moreover, all Buddhas teach and transform everyone equally with the wisdom of impartiality. Shakyamuni Buddha was particularly renowned for his courageous vigor. He was able to endure all manner of suffering to take across living beings. Thus we should be aware that we are indebted to our fundamental teacher's deep and profound kindness. He was able to speak different Dharmas for afflicted living beings to benefit each one of them.

But why have we not been liberated by his teaching? Did we not receive the Buddha's teaching in person when he was alive? Did we not witness his Nirvana at Twin-Tree Grove? Our karmic obstacles cause our mind to separate from the Buddhas' kindness. Therefore today in this assembly, we long for the Tathagata. Due to this yearning, our mind will be enriched with goodness. Although we are suffering, we should still be mindful of the Tathagata's kindness. Weeping and fretting, and choked with deep shame and remorse, we bring forth heartfelt earnestness as we bow in full prostration. We take refuge with the Three Treasures on behalf of heads of nations, people of all nations, parents, teachers, elders, faithful donors, good and bad advisors, heavenly beings and ascetic masters, the intelligent and righteous spirits, celestial spirits, earth spirits, empty space spirits, the four world-protecting heavenly kings, spirits who bless the good and punish the evil, spirits who guard and protect those who uphold mantras, dragon kings of the five directions and their retinues, as well as the dragons and the rest of the eightfold division, extending to and including the boundless living beings of the ten directions.

On their behalf, we take refuge with all the Buddhas of the ten
directions to the ends of empty space.(*bow*)
We take refuge with all the venerable Dharmas of the ten
directions to the ends of empty space. (*bow*)
We take refuge with the Sangha of all sages and worthies of the
ten directions to the ends of empty space. (*bow*)

With earnest resolve, we now kneel, put our palms together, and
mindfully chant:

All Buddhas, great honored sages,
Are completely awakened to all dharmas, and
Are unsurpassed teachers of people and heavenly beings;
Thus we should take refuge with them.
Dharma that eternally abides,
The sutras that purify,
Can cure illnesses of body and mind.
Thus, we take refuge in them.
Great Bodhisattvas of all sagely grounds,
Unattached shramanas of the Four Fruitions,
Are able to rescue us from suffering.
Thus we take refuge in them.
The Three Treasures protect the world.
We now respectfully bow to them.
Living beings in the six paths,
We now take refuge on behalf of them all.
"Great Bodhisattvas' kindness and compassion gather in all,
And cause everyone to attain peace and bliss.
They have deep sympathy for living beings.
Thus, together we all take refuge in them.

We bow in full prostration. Each of us now recite: We pray to the
Three Treasures of the ten directions. May they enable all living
beings to attain awakening with their power of kindness and compassion, power of their original vows, their great spiritual powers,

inconceivable powers, boundless power of self-mastery, power to rescue beings, power to protect beings, and power to comfort beings.
May all living beings know that today we have taken refuge on their
behalf; and with the power of the merit and virtue of taking refuge,
may all of them have their wishes fulfilled. May heavenly beings and
ascetic masters extinguish all outflows. May asuras renounce their
ingrained arrogance. May humans no longer have any suffering. May
hell beings, hungry ghosts and animals immediately be freed and
transcend the evil paths. Moreover, today, regardless of whether or
not living beings have heard the name of the Three Treasures, may
the spiritual power of the Buddhas enable living beings to be liberated, ultimately accomplish unsurpassed bodhi, and attain Proper
Enlightenment like all Bodhisattvas.

Section 2 Severing Doubt

Today, we who are here in this Bodhimanda due to our shared karma
should single-mindedly listen. The law of cause and effect operates
like a shadow following form, or an echo following sound, with the
response arising naturally. That is the way things are, and its principle will not be off by the slightest. However, living beings' karma is
complicated, with a mixture of good and evil. Because our karma is
complex, we receive different rewards and retributions, such as being
noble or servile, wholesome or unwholesome, which vary in myriad
possibilities. Due to such vast diversities, we do not understand our
own karma. Without such understanding, we become greatly confused
and give rise to doubt.

Some may question why a person who vigorously upholds the precepts lives a short life instead of a long one; or why a butcher lives a
long life rather than a short one; or why an honest official who should
be wealthy ends up in poverty; or why a greedy thief who should suffer poverty turns out enjoying a life of abundance. Who could be
without such doubts? These doubts arise in people because they fail to

recognize that these retributions are caused by their past karma, which can be likened to seeds planted in the past.

As clearly stated in the *Prajna Sutra*, "If a person who reads and recites this sutra is slighted or humiliated by others, that person's karmic offenses from previous lives which would have destined him for the evil paths, are now eradicated."

However, living beings do not have deep faith in the Sutra text. Their doubts are caused by their ignorance and delusion, which lead to such inverted thinking."

Furthermore, we do not realize the three realms are full of suffering, and what is beyond the three realms is full of bliss. Most of us take pleasure in experiences that are actually defiling. Why does that supposed pleasure cause us suffereing? If we eat too much, we become sick, gasp and have a stomach ache. Clothing causes even more trouble. In cold weather, we do not appreciate light, thin clothing. In warm weather, we are afflicted just by the sight of a thick fur coat. If we regard food and clothing as bringing us happiness, then why do they cause us affliction? From this we know neither food nor clothes can really bring us happiness.

Furthermore, if we regard family and relatives as bringing us happiness, then we should be able to forever enjoy their company, continuously singing and laughing. Why is it that before we realize it, impermanence sets in and our happiness perishes after a short time? What was there before has now suddenly vanished. When our loved ones depart, we feel extreme sorrow and heartbreak. We wail to heaven and stomp the earth. Yet we do not know where our loved ones came from and where they will go after passing. All we can do is to mournfully see them off to their place of burial. At the final moment of separation, we bid them farewell for what we think is eternity. All this brings us endless suffering.

We living beings are deluded by our views and regard worldly things as happiness. We regard the causes that bring world-transcending happiness as suffering – for example, disciplining the body, eating simple and plain vegetarian food, eating at proper times only, and wearing rags instead of fine clothes. We regard all these as needless self-imposed mortification. Actually, we fail to understand that these practices lead to the path of liberation.

We consider diligence in giving, upholding precepts, patience, vigor, bowing, and chanting sutras as suffering. We do not understand that all these are are practices that focus the mind on transcendental Dharmas Upon seeing those cultivators who encounter sickness or death, we may give rise to doubt and think, "All day long these people are just torturing their body and mind without any break. How can our human body handle all this? If they were not so industrious, they would not have to suffer so much. Such strenuous efforts bring no benefit and they may even die in vain."

We further hold onto our own views, insisting them to be true. Failing to understand the actual causes behind these effects, we harbor such deluded views. If we encounter a good mentor, then our improper views can be corrected. But if we encounter a bad advisor, we will become more confused due to our doubts and delusion and will fall into the three evil paths. Then it will be too late for regret.

Today, we are here in this Bodhimanda due to our shared karma. We should understand that all such doubts are due to limitless causes and conditions. Even those who have transcended the three realms may not have completely rid themselves of habitual doubt and delusion. How can we mere mortals ever hope to quickly get rid of ours? If we do not severe these doubts and delusions in this lifetime, they will become increasingly worse in future lives. We are just embarking on a long spiritual journey. Thus we should practice rigorously in accord with the Buddha's teaching. We must not harbor any doubt or retreat because of hardship. It is because of accumulated goodness and merit that Buddhas and sages have transcended birth and death, arrived at the other shore, and attained non-obstruction, self-mastery, and liberation.

It is a pity that all of us are still trapped in the cycle of birth and death. How can we continue to indulge ourselves in such an evil world? We are fortunate that our bodies, comprised of the four elements, have not yet declined, our five organs are still healthy, and we are able to move about freely and comfortably. If we do not cultivate diligently now, then what are we waiting for?

During our past lives, we failed to realize the Truth. In this life, if we pass our time in vain without any spiritual attainment, how will we save ourselves in the future? If we deeply reflect within, we should truly be remorseful and pity ourselves.

Great assembly, deeply contemplate this matter, be diligent in cultivation and not lazy. Knowing that the road to sagehood is long and difficult and cannot be accomplished in one day, we should not use that as an excuse to seek rest and recreation. Otherwise, we may never attain realization because day after day, time flies by. We may already have started to recite sutras, or sit in meditation, or hold ascetic practices, but sometimes when we run into a small illness, we think that the cause of the sickness is due to our diligence in reciting sutras or sitting in meditation. We do not realize that if we had not practiced in this way, we might have died already. Because we put effort in our practice, we are able to continue living. It is natural that our body, which is composed of the four elements, goes through the processes of illness, old age, and death. It is unavoidable. Everything in this world will eventually perish. If we wish to attain the Way, we must accord with the Buddhas' teaching. It is impossible to attain the Way without following the Buddhas' teaching. Because living beings turn away from the teaching of the Buddhas, we revolve in the three evil paths and go through all types of suffering. If we want to follow the Buddhas' teaching, then we should diligently practice all Dharmas, as if our own heads are at stake. We should not live our life in vain without accomplishment in the Way.

Now each one of us should bring forth utmost sincerity and bow in full prostration, like a great mountain collapsing. From the time we first had consciousness until now, on behalf of our present parents and all parents from past lives, all our families and relatives of kalpas past, teachers of Dharma, acharyas, and the ordination certifying masters, monastics of the three seniorities, faithful donors, good and bad advisors, all heavenly beings and ascetic masters, the four world-protecting heavenly kings, spirits who bless the good and punish the evil, spirits who guard and protect those who uphold mantras, dragon kings of the five directions, dragons and the rest of the eightfold division, extending to and including the limitless beings of the ten directions, we bow and take refuge with the Greatly Kind and Compassionate Ones who are like fathers to those of us in this world.

Namo Maitreya Buddha
Namo Vipashyin Buddha
Namo Shikhin Buddha
Namo Visvabhu Buddha
Namo Krakucchanda Buddha
Namo Kanakamuni Buddha
Namo Kashyapa Buddha
Namo Shakyamuni Buddha
Namo Boundless Body Bodhisattva
Namo Guan Shi Yin[5] Bodhisattva

Again we take refuge with the Three Treasures of the ten directions to the ends of empty space. We beseech the Three Treasures to gather us in with their power of kindness and compassion, and protect us with the strength of their spiritual powers. We vow that henceforth until we attain bodhi, we will always be mindful of the four limitless minds and practice the six paramitas, attain as-you-wish mastery of the four unobstructed wisdoms and the six spiritual powers. We shall always practice the Bodhisattva path, enter the Buddhas' wisdom, and teach and transform beings throughout the ten directions so that all will eventually realize Proper Enlightenment.

Today, we are here in this Bodhimanda due to our shared karma. Once again, with utmost sincerity, we focus our minds. Now that we have entered the gateway of faith, we must persevere in our resolve, aspire for the ultimate goal of bodhi, and never again be obstructed by whatever dharmas we are practicing, be they internal or external. If we are not clear about the fundamental working of karma, we will not know how to plant blessings. Now when seeing others plant blessings, we should exhort and encourage them in their good deeds by applauding them or joining our palms. We should not even think of impeding them, causing them to retreat. Whether we succeed in obstructing their practice or not, either way our attempt to do so will certainly harm ourselves.

How could we benefiting from making things up and gossiping about others' rights and wrongs? If we are kind and do not create obstruction for others, then we are in accordance with the Way and is the behavior of a great person. But if we obstruct others, then in the future how can we progress smoothly on the path of bodhi? If we investigate this principle, we will realize the grave harm we have been doing. Thus, obstructing others from planting roots of goodness is a really heavy offense.

The *Sutra of Guarding One's Speech* relates the story of a hungry ghost with a grotesque and frightening appearance. All who saw him were so frightened that their hair stood on end. The searing flames that the ghost emitted were like a conflagration. From his mouth spewed forth uncountable worms. Filth such as pus and oozing blood covered his body. His stench kept everyone at a distance. His mouth also spewed forth a flame of fire, and flames even blazed forth from his limbs and joints, so that he ran about and cried for help.

At that time an Arhat named Full and Perfect asked him, "What did you do in the past to receive such terrible suffering?"

The ghost replied, "When I was a *shramana* in the past, I craved offerings, was greedy, stingy, and refused to practice renunciation. I also failed to observe proper deportment and often spoke harsh or vulgar words. I further reviled and looked with hate and contempt upon those who diligently upheld the precepts or who practiced vigorously. Counting on being strong and healthy, I assumed that I would live a long life and would not die anytime soon. Consequently, I committed limitless unwholesome karma. Looking back now, I am filled with regret, but to no avail. I would rather use a sharp knife to cut off my own tongue and undergo suffering for kalpa after kalpa than to utter a single word of slander about those who perform meritorious deeds.

"Venerable One, after you return to Jambudvipa, I beg you to use my misery and grosteque appearance as an example to teach and admonish all bhikshus and other disciples of the Buddha to carefully guard their mouth from committing any speech offense and to avoid casual or reckless speech. When they see others upholding the precepts or those who are not, they should just be mindful of and praise those people's virtues. Day and night I am suffering miserably the retribution of being a ghost throughout thousands of kalpas. When my retribution of being a ghost ends, I will then fall into the hells."

After explaining these causes and conditions, the ghost threw itself on the ground, collasping like a mountain, and wailed with great grief.

Today, we who are here in this Bodhimanda due to our shared karma should be greatly terrified and fearful about what was mentioned in the Sutra text. Just the offense of speech karma can cause a person to suffer for so many kalpas, how much the more suffering when we include the offenses from committing other unwholesome karma! Losing a human body and undergoing suffering all have to do with the karma we create.

If there is no cause, how can the effect possibly come about? If we create the causes, then we will definitely receive the retributions or rewards. Both offenses and blessings are not far apart from us, and we will have to face them in person. They follow us just like a shadow or an echo. Because of ignorance, we are born; because of ignorance, we die. Throughout all time – the past, present, and future – whoever is self-indulgent or lax in cultivation will never attain liberation. Only by guarding and protecting our cultivation can we receive endless blessings.

All of us gathered here today should bring forth a sense of shame and remorse and purify our body and mind. We should repent and reform of our past mistakes and vow not to commit new offenses. This is lauded and praised by all Buddhas. Henceforth, we should not be judgmental about but rejoice in the good deeds of others, whether or not the deeds can be accomplished, and whether or not those doing them will persevere in their good deeds. Whatever good others do, whether only lasting the duration of a thought, a minute, an hour, a day, a month, six months, or a year, is much better than not doing any good at all.

The *Dharma Flower Sutra* states, "Even if a person with a scattered mind enters a stupa or temple and recites only once 'Namo Buddha,' that person will certainly become a Buddha."

How much more so for someone who brings forth a great resolve and diligently plants blessing or practices good deeds. Sages pity those who fail to rejoice in the good deeds of others.

We disciples should now reflect and contemplate, since time without beginning until the present, undergoing cycles of birth and death, we have had countless evil thoughts about obstructing others when they perform good deeds. How do we know that? If we had not committed such offenses, why are we encountering many obstacles when practicing meritorious dharmas. We have difficulty applying effort in meditation or in cultivating wisdom. We complain it is suffering after bowing for awhile. We easily feel tired and bored after practicing according to a sutra for a short while. All day long, we occupy ourselves with mundane activities and are vexed and distressed by a multitude of afflictions, creating various evil karma that prevents us from liberation.

We are like a silkworm that spins its own cacoon, or a moth that flies toward a lamp and burns itself. With these infinitely many obstacles, we hinder our own bodhi resolve, our bodhi vows, and our bodhi practices. These are all because of our evil thoughts of slandering the good deeds of others. Now that we realize our mistakes, we should bring forth a sense of shame and remorse, pray for forgiveness, and repent and reform of our offenses. May all the Buddhas and Bodhisattvas aid us with their power of kindness, compassion and spiritual penetrations and enable us to eradicate our offenses and return to purity. Through this repentance, may all obstacles and offenses be completely eradicated. Now each one of us should bring forth utmost and heartfelt sincerity and bow in full prostration to take refuge in the Greatly Kind and Compassionate Ones who are like fathers to those of us in this world.

Namo Maitreya Buddha
Namo Shakyamuni Buddha
Namo Meritorious Virtue Buddha
Namo Worry-free and Virtuous Buddha
Namo Chandana Virtue Buddha
Namo Precious Giving Buddha
Namo Infinite Light Buddha
Namo Blossoming Virtue Buddha
Namo Appearance of Virtue Buddha
Namo Practicing the Three Vehicle Buddha
Namo Pervasively Accumulating Virtue Buddha
Namo Bright Virtue Buddha
Namo Lion Playfully Roaming Bodhisattva
Namo Lion Swiftness and Vigor Bodhisattva
Namo Boundless Body Bodhisattva
Namo Guan Shi Yin Bodhisattva

Again we take refuge with the Three Treasures of the ten directions to the ends of empty space. We kneel, place our palms together, and mindfully recite "From time without beginning until now, we have not been able to accomplish the Way. Instead we are now burdened with a retribution body that relies on the four necessities of life, and we do not have a moment of freedom. Meanwhile, our minds are plagued by three blazing poisons of greed, anger, and jealousy, causing us to commit all kinds of offenses."

When we see people giving or upholding precepts, we not only fail to practice them ourselves, but we also do not rejoice in their deeds. When we see others cultivating patience or vigor, we not only fail to practice them ourselves, but we also do not rejoice in their deeds. When we see people sitting in *chan* meditation and cultivating wisdom, we not only fail to practice them ourselves, but we also do not rejoice in their deeds. The above offenses are countless and boundless. We now repent and reform of them all, and beseech that they be eradicated.

Furthermore, from time without beginning until now, we have failed to rejoice when we see others practicing good deeds and cultivating merit and virtue. Whether walking, standing, sitting, or reclining, we reveal our shameless arrogance and our lax attitude towards impermanence. We are not aware that when this body meets its end, we might fall into the hells. We have given rise to impure thoughts toward the bodies and appearances of other people. We have obstructed others from establishing, propagating, and making offerings to the Three Treasures. We have hindered those who want to cultivate all types of merit and virtue. The above offenses are countless and boundless. We now repent and reform of them all, and beseech that they be eradicated.

Again, from time without beginning until now, we have not believed that the Three Treasuress are our refuge. We impede others from leaving the householder's life. We obstruct others from upholding their precepts. We hinder others in their practice of giving. We hamper others in their practice of patience. We prevent others from cultivating vigor. We deter others in their practice of meditation. We impede others in their recitation or copying of sutras. We make it difficult for others to host vegetarian offerings to monastics. We impede others from making images of sages. We hamper others from making offerings. We disturb others while they perform ascetic practices. We impede others from cultivating the Way. We obstruct even a hair's breadth of goodness that other people want to practice. We do not believe that leaving the householder's life is the practice for leaving defilement. We do not believe that practicing patience helps us gain peace and bliss. We do not believe that cultivating equanimity is the bodhi Way. We do not realize that cutting off deluded thoughts is practicing transcendental Dharma. Consequently our lives are filled with obstructions. We have committed boundless and limitless offenses, which only the Buddhas and great Bodhisattvas fully know and see. For all the amount of the offenses seen and known by all Buddhas and Bodhisattvas, we now bring forth the mind of shame and remorse to repent of all these offenses. We pray and beseech that the causes of all the offenses and the consequent effects and retributions will all be eradicated.

From now until we attain Buddhahood, we resolve to tirelessly practice the Bodhisattva Path and continuously and endlessly practice the giving of wealth and Dharma. We endeavor to use wisdom and expedient means in all our undertakings so that we do nothing in vain. May everything we see or hear lead us towards liberation. With utmost sincerity, we bow in full prostration and pray that all Buddhas, Bodhisattvas, sages and worthies in the ten directions, out of great kindness and compassion, and with their spiritual powers, bless and help all living beings in the six paths. By the merit of this repentance, we pray you will eradicate all suffering, help us leave conditions of inversion and never give rise to evil thoughts, and lead us to renounce the karma that plunges us into the four lowly paths. May all of us gain wisdom, ceaselessly practice the Bodhisattva Path, accomplish our vows, quickly attain the Ten Grounds[6], gain entry to the vajra mind, and realize Proper and Equal Enlightenment.

Section 3 Repentance

Today, we are here in this Bodhimanda due to our shared karma. We should note that the sutras state, "What ordinary beings perceive as fetters or bondage, sages perceive as freedom."

Bondage refers to the results of evil committed by beings through their three karmas of body, speech, and mind. Freedom refers to the results of goodness derived from the non-obstruction of the sages' three karmas. It is on this freedom that all sages peacefully settle their mind. With their wisdom and spiritual powers, they are able to apply expedient means of various Dharma-doors to thoroughly understand the wholesome and evil karma of all living beings. From a single body they can manifest limitless bodies. From a single form they can change to limitless forms. They can contract one kalpa into a single day, and can extend a single day into an entire kalpa. If they wish to eliminate the restriction of a life span, they manifest non-extinction. If they wish to reveal impermanence, they manifest entering Nirvana. Their spiritual powers and wisdom enable them to appear and disappear as they wish, to fly at will, to sit freely or recline in empty space, to walk on water as if it were solid ground, and not to be troubled by any difficulty or danger. They take the state of ultimate tranquility and emptiness as their home. They thoroughly understand both emptiness and existence, as well as the myriad dharmas. They accomplish eloquence and attain unobstructed wisdom.

All dharmas such as these do not arise from evil karma, greed, hatred, or jealousy. They do not arise from ignorance, deviant views, laziness or laxness. They do not arise from arrogance or self-indulgence. Instead, all these dharmas come from being prudent, refraining from evil, and diligently cultivating wholesome karma.

Those who accord with the Buddhas' teachings and cultivate meritorious deeds will gain positive results that will ensure they avoid ending up poor ugly, sick, disabled, ill-at-ease, bullied and despised because of their lowly status, or distrusted in whatever they say. We, the monks who compiled the Repentance pledge, "If anyone who accords with Dharma and selflessly cultivates merit and virtue ends up receiving evil retribution, we ourselves will enter the *Avici* Hell and receive the myriad suffering. However, there is no possibility of such an eventuality."

Today, we are here in this Bodhimanda due to our shared karma. We should follow the teachings of the Buddhas and cultivate accordingly in order to renounce the mundane to enter the level of sages. We should not become lazy when we encounter hardship. Instead we should diligently strive to repent of all the offenses we have committed so as to eradicate them. The sutras state, "Offenses arise from causes and conditions, and cease due to causes and conditions."

Since we are ordinary people and are constantly confused, if we do not rely on repentance, there is no way we can transcend the mundane. Henceforth, let us all bring forth a courageous mind and a firm resolve for repentance. We should understand that the power of repentance is inconceivable. How do we know that this is true?

In the past, King Ajatasatru committed one of five rebellious acts (patricide), which would have resulted in a severe retribution. However, he was remorseful and repented of his offense, so he received a minor retribution instead. Furthermore, this dharma of repentance helps all cultivators attain peace and happiness. If we can reflect upon ourselves, earnestly bring forth our sincerity, bow in repentance, rely on the Three Treasures, aspire for bodhi without ever retreating, how can we fail to evoke a response from the Buddhas? We should be fearful as retribution from our offenses will never be off by the slightest, just as a shadow follows a form or an echo follows a sound. Therefore, we should painstakingly repent. Let us all bow in full prostration with utmost, heartfelt sincerity. We are mindful as we call out to the Buddhas to take pity on us and to bless us from afar.

> *May you save us who are in distress,*
> *With your all-encompassing great compassion.*
> *May you pervasively radiate pure light,*
> *To dispel our ignorance and darkness.*
> *May you be mindful of us and those*
> *Undergoing suffering in the hells.*
> *May you readily come to us,*
> *Bestowing bliss and peace upon us.*
> *We now bow in full prostration,*
> *Before you who hear and rescue us.*
> *We now all take refuge with you,*
> *Our Greatly Kind and Compassionate Father.*

Namo Maitreya Buddha
Namo Shakyamuni Buddha
Namo Vajra-indestructible Buddha
Namo Jeweled Light Buddha
Namo Venerable Dragon-king Buddha
Namo Vigor's Army Buddha
Namo Vigor and Joy Buddha
Namo Precious Fire Buddha
Namo Jeweled Moonlight Buddha
Namo Manifesting without Delusion Buddha
Namo Jeweled Moon Buddha
Namo Apart from Defilement Buddha
Namo Lion Banner Bodhisattva
Namo Lion Deeds Bodhisattva
Namo Boundless Body Bodhisattva
Namo Guan Shi Yin Bodhisattva

Again we take refuge with the Three Treasures of the ten directions to the ends of empty space. We sincerely wish that you take pity on all of us suffering from the three poisons, enable us to attain peace and bliss, up to our entering parinirvana. May you cleanse our defilements with the water of great compassion, helping us until we attain bodhi, the ultimate purity. We hope all living beings in the six paths and the four births with similar offenses will also attain purity and accomplish *Anuttara-samyak-sambodhi*, ultimate liberation. With utmost, heartfelt sincerity and remorse, we bow in full prostration.

We disciples from time without beginning until now, have been blanketed by the lack of understanding, burdened by the fetters of emotional love, bound by hatred and anger, and trapped in the net of ignorance. Thus we revolve in the three realms, tread on the six paths, drift in the sea of suffering and are unable to free ourselves. We fail to know the causes and conditions of our past karma. We have destroyed our own proper livelihood and that of others. We have ruined our own pure conduct and that of others. We have broken the precepts of purity and caused others to break them. For these boundless offenses that we have created, we now feel shame and remorse, repent and reform of them all, and beseech that they be eradicated.

We disciple again with utmost sincerity, bow in full prostration, repent of all past mistakes, reform, and seek forgiveness. From time without beginning until now, we have committed the ten evil deeds through our body, mouth, and mind. Through our body, we kill, steal, and engage in sexual misconduct. Through our mouth, we commit false speech, frivolous speech, divisive speech, and harsh speech. In our mind, we harbor greed, anger, and delusion. We have done all these ten evils ourselves and have taught others to do them. We have praised the ten evil dharmas and praised others who practice them. Within the space of a single thought, we have committed forty types of evil. For these boundless offenses that we have committed, we now repent and reform of them all and beseech that they be eradicated.

We disciples again sincerely bow in full prostration. From time without beginning until now, we have been relying on the six sense faculties, using our six sense consciousnesses, and grasping at the six sense objects. Our eyes are attached to sights, our ears to sounds, our nose to smells, our tongue to tastes, our body to sensations of touch, and our mind to mental objects of dharmas. With all these attachments, we create various types of karma, up to and including opening the doors of eighty-four thousand types of defiling passions. All these offenses are boundless and limitless. We now repent and reform of them all, and beseech that they be eradicated.

We disciples again sincerely bow in full prostration. From time without beginning until now, we have engaged in discriminating actions with our body, mouth, and mind. We only cared for ourselves, not others; only knew our own suffering, not that of others; only sought our own peace and happiness, but failed to realize that others also seek happiness; only sought liberation for ourselves, but failed to realize that others also seek liberation. We were only concerned about our own family and relatives, not others'. We could not bear any minor pain or itch, but when hurting others, such as flogging or clubbing them, we were only afraid that we did not beat them hard enough. We only fear our present minor suffering, but not the forthcoming misery when our life ends and we fall into the hells and undergo all kinds of suffering due to our evil karma. We do not know the myriad types of suffering in the realm of hungry ghosts, the realm of animals, the realm of *asuras*, the realm of humans, the realm of heavenly beings. Because of discrimination in our mind, we give rise to thoughts of self and others, thoughts of friends and foes. Thus, those who harbor animosity towards us pervade all the six paths. All these offenses are boundless and limitless. We now repent and reform of them all and beseech that they be eradicated.

We disciples again sincerely bow in full prostration. From time without beginning until now, because of our inverted mind, inverted thoughts, and inverted views, we stayed away from good and wise advisors and preferred the company of bad advisors. We turned our back on the eightfold noble path[7] and practiced the eight deviant paths. We spoke of deviant dharma as proper dharma, and spoke of proper dharma as deviant dharma. We took what is evil as good, and took what is good as evil. We raised the banner of arrogance, hoisted the sails of delusion, and drifted along the current of ignorance into the sea of birth and death. All these offenses are boundless and limitless.We now repent and reform of them all and beseech that they be eradicated.

We disciples again bow in full prostration and willingly endure the painstaking rigor of bowing this repentance. From time without beginning until now, through the three unwholesome roots[8], we have continually given rise to the four inversions[9], committed the five rebellious acts[10], and the ten evils[11]. The three poisons blaze forth and exacerbate the eight sufferings[12], creating the causes for the eight freezing hells, and the eight burning hells, as well as the causes for the eighty-four thousand solitary-cell hells. They also create the causes for becoming animals, hungry ghosts, humans, or heavenly beings, who are all subjected to the suffering of birth, aging, sickness, and death, and thus undergo limitless suffering in the six paths, all too agonizing to our eyes and ears. All these offenses are boundless and limitless. We now repent and reform of them all and beseech that they be eradicated.

We disciples again bow in full prostration and willingly endure the painstaking rigor of bowing this repentance. We repent and reform of all past mistakes and humbly seek pity and forgiveness. From time without beginning until now, rooted in the three poisons, we have traversed the three realms of existence[13] undergoing rebirth in the twenty-five planes of existence[14]. In all these places, we have committed all kinds of offenses, and have been unknowingly blown adrift by the winds of karma. We might have obstructed people from upholding precepts, from cultivating samadhi and wisdom, from creating merit and virtue, and from cultivating spiritual powers. These offenses that we have created obstruct our own bodhi resolve, obstruct our own bodhi vows, and obstruct our own bodhi conduct. We now repent and reform of them all and beseech that they be eradicated.

We disciples again bow in full prostration and willingly endure the painstaking rigor of bowing this repentance. From time without beginning until now, driven by thoughts of greed and hatred, our six consciousnesses arise, following and chasing after the sense objects, committing multitudes of offenses. Those offenses may have been committed against living beings or non-living beings. Those offenses may have been committed against someone who has attained the state of non-outflow or in opposition to the dharmas of non-outflow. All such offenses that have arisen from greed and anger, we now repent and reform of them all, and beseech that they be eradicated.

Because of deluded thoughts, our conduct is inverted. We believed in deviant teachers and their instruction. We became attached to views of eternalism and annihilation, to our ego or egoistic views. We conducted ourselves under the influence of delusion and committed limitless offenses. All such causes and conditions obstruct our bodhi resolve, our bodhi vows, and our bodhi conduct. We now repent and reform of them all and beseech that they be eradicated.

We disciples again sincerely bow in full prostration. From time without beginning until now, through our body we created three evil karmas; through our speech, four evil karmas; in our mind, three evil karmas. From time without beginning, we have been hindered by the five grounds of afflictions resulting from ignorance[15], formidable afflictions that number like the Ganges' sand[16], formidable afflictions-[17]during the practice of cessation and contemplation[18], the four dwelling grounds of afflictions[19], the three evils[20], the four graspings[21], the five hindrances[22], the six attachments[23], the seven outflows[24], the eight defilements[25], the nine entanglements[26], and the ten fetters[27]. Because of these afflictions and limitless other obstacles, we have been obstructed in our bodhi resolve, our bodhi vows, and our bodhi conduct. We now repent and reform of them all, and beseech that they be eradicated.

We disciples again sincerely bow in full prostration. From time without beginning until now, we have been unable achieve the mental state of joyful renunciation; we have failed to cultivate *dana paramita*[28], *sila paramita*[29], *ksanti paramit*[30], *virya paramita*[31], *dhyana paramita*[32] and *prajna paramita*[33] or other Dharmas that aid on the path towards Bodhi. Therefore, neither our wisdom nor our expedient means are sufficiently developed, since we have been obstructed in our bodhi resolve, our bodhi vows, and our bodhi conduct. We now repent and reform of them all, and beseech that they be eradicated.

We disciples again bring forth complete sincerity and bow in full prostration. From time without beginning until now, we have revolved in the wheel of the three realms, undergoing the four births in the six paths, sometimes as male, sometimes female, sometimes as non-male, sometimes non-female. In these forms everywhere we have created countless offenses. Sometimes we were born as beings with large bodies, devouring each other, sometimes as beings with small bodies, devouring each other. Thus we have created boundless offenses from the karma of killing and consequently have been obstructed in our bodhi resolve, our bodhi vows, and our bodhi conduct. We now repent and reform of them all and beseech that they be eradicated.

We disciples again sincerely bow in full prostration. From the time we first had consciousness until now, we have been subjected to the four births and the six paths committing limitless offenses. All Buddhas and great Bodhisattvas throughout the ten directions see and know the entirety of our offenses. Now with utmost sincerity, feeling shame and remorse, we repent of our faults. May our past offenses be eradicated completely, and may we resolve not to commit further offenses. We pray that all Buddhas in the ten directions, with your great kindness, will accept our repentance and use the water of great compassion to wash away all our offenses and defilement that hinder the path to bodhi. May all of us attain Buddhahood, the ultimate purity.

We also pray that all Buddhas in the ten directions, with power that is inconceivable, power of fundamental vows, power of rescuing living beings, and power of protecting and supporting living beings enable us to henceforth resolve on bodhi, without ever regressing, until we attain Buddhahood, the ultimate accomplishment. May our vows be identical with that of all Bodhisattvas. We pray all Buddhas and great Bodhisattvas in the ten directions, with your great kindness and compassion, accept and gather us in and enable us to fulfill our vows and our bodhi resolve. May all living beings' wishes be completely fulfilled, and may all perfect the bodhi resolve.

Praise

> Taking refuge with the Three Treasures,
> Cutting off the roots of doubt,
> Reining in emotions and subduing the ego,
> We enter the esoteric gateway.
> Clearly aware of the presence of cause and effect,
> We realize that the merit derived from repenting and reforming is profound.
> Upon us all, Buddhas bestow their kindness.

Namo Bodhisattvas Mahasattvas of the Ground of Happiness
(three times)

Concluding the Repentance

In the heavens above and in this world,
Appears the One Replete with Proper and Universal Knowledge.
His brilliance surpasses the Sun and Moon,
His virtue more encompassing than the Great Void.
Neither coming nor going, he dwells firmly in the Flower Treasury realm
Transcending birth and death, he sits majestically in the city of Nirvana.
He appears appropriately according to conditions.
He responds to beings in accord with their potential,
Like a great bell waiting to be struck or a deep valley waiting to
transmit echoes.
May you shower our Repentance with your great and boundless
compassion,
Witnessing us at this very moment doing the Buddha's work.

[Dharma Host]: On behalf of _____ [those who seek to repent], we practice this Repentance Dharma of Kindness and Compassion in the Bodhimanda. We have now successfully completed Roll One; the merit and virtue is complete and perfect. We have established the Repentance Platform and adorned the altar with Buddha images, with bright lamps ornamenting the tree branches, with the fragrance of sandalwood incense permeating everywhere, with exquisite multi-colored arrays of flowers throughout, and with offerings of wonderful fruit.

Singing hymns of praise and chanting the exalted Buddha names, we cultivate samadhi and recite sutras and mantras. All the merit thus accumulated from these deeds we now dedicate to the ever-abiding and truly kind Three Treasures, the Dharma-protecting devas, spirits and ghosts of all realms, and the innumerable spirits, far or near, who bestow rewards. May they all bear witness to our heartfelt sincerity and be delighted. May their beneficence extend throughout heaven and earth; may their teaching and transforming spread like rays of the sun benefitting all. May they help perfect our Repentance in this Bodhimanda, aiding us in accompling merit and virtue. May they be mindful of us   [those who seek to repent] who are now doing this Repentance, and help us eradicate our offenses, increase our blessings, usher in auspiciousness, and help us all be reborn in the Pure Land.

- May the offenses of all our entire lives melt away like ice;
- May we be purified of our karma and karmic condition;
- May we attain awakening through single-mindedness and tend towards the One Principle of True Suchness;
- May we, within one thought, reflect and return the light to shine within, to advance towards the wondrous path of the One Vehicle;
- May we transform the conditions of suffering into those of happiness and sprinkle water to cool off and wash away all heated afflictions;
- May our ancestors and relatives be assured of rebirth in the Pure Land;
- May every member of our family be blessed with longevity;
- May all our friends and foes alike, equally bathe in the radiance of your kindness, and together, with all other ordinary beings and sages, ascend to the Jeweled Land.

[Dharma host]: Although we have repented according to the Repentance Text, we fear that we have not been fully spared from the retributions of our subtle offenses. Thus I am taking the liberty to request that together, we continue to repent and reform.

Praise

> The meritorious power of the Emperor of Liang Repentance Roll One
> Enables the deceased and the disciples to eradicate their One Offense;
> May all realize the Bodhisattva's Ground of Happiness.
> As the Repentance is chanted our offenses are blown away like flower petals in the wind.
> Offenses repented, enmity resolved,

Wisdom and blessing increase as calamities are dispelled.
Liberated from suffering and reborn in the Trayastrimsha,
May we gather at the Dragon Flower's Three Assemblies
And receive a prediction personally from Maitreya Buddha.

Namo Dragon Flower Assembly of Bodhisattvas Mahasattvas

(three times)

Final praise

Emperor of Liang Repentance Roll One now concludes.
We dedicate its merit to the four benefactors and the three realms.
May all in this assembly enjoy increased longevity and blessings,
May the Dharma water cleanse our offenses.
May the deceased be reborn in the Western Pure Land.
May the Bodhisattvas of the Ground of Happiness compassionately
gather us in.

Namo Ascending the Path to the Clouds Bodhisattva Mahasattva

(three times)

End Notes

1. **Samantabhadra Bodhisattva:** One of the four great Bodhisattvas, he is considered foremost in practice. He rides on an elephant with six tusks. A pond appears in the curves of said tusks, and singing maidens reside in the pond. (Also Universal Worthy Bodhisattva or Puxian Pusa).
2. **Four dharmas of attraction:** a) Charitable deeds or giving, b) kind words, c) beneficial deeds, and d) working together.
3. **Monastics of the three seniorities:** Three tiers of monastic seniority refers to a monastic's ordination age or how long he has held the precepts. Junior Seated Ones are those who have been ordained for 0-9 years, Middle-Seated Ones have 10-19 years, and Senior Seated Ones have 20 or more years.

4. **Avici Hell:** the uninterrupted hell, which means that living beings who fall into such hell will endure endless and severe sufferings without respite.

5. **Guan Shi Yin:** One of the four Bodhisattvas of greatest importance in Mahayana Buddhism, he is foremost in compassion. He is the disciple and future successor of the Buddha Amitabha in the Western Land of Ultimate Bliss. His name in Sanskrit, **Avalokitesvara**, is often translated as Observer of the Sounds of the World. It can also be interpreted as meaning Contemplator of Self-Mastery. (Also Kuanyin).

6. **Ten Grounds:** Ten stages in the development of Mahayana Bodhisattvas.
   i)   Ground of Happiness or Dry Wisdom
   ii)   Ground of Transcending Defilement
   iii) Ground of Emitting Light
   iv)   Ground of Blazing Wisdom
   v)   Ground of Difficult to Surpass
   vi)   Ground of Manifestation
   vii) Ground of Traveling Far
   viii) Ground of No Movement
   ix)   Ground of Perfected Wisdom, and
   x)   Ground of Dharma Clouds.

7. **Eightfold noble path** (or noble eightfold path): right view, right thought, right speech, right behavior, right livelihood, right effort, right mindfulness, right concentration.

8. **Three unwholesome roots:** root of greed, root of hatred, root of stupidity.

9. **Four inversions** (or four distorted deeds or four *viparyaya*): impurity, suffering, impermanence, personality. These are the opposite of purity, joy, permanence and no self.

10. **Five rebellious acts:** killing one's father, killing one's mother, killing an Arhat, causing schisms in the harmonious Sangha, shedding the Buddha's blood.

11. **Ten evils** (or ten evil deeds): killing, stealing, sexual misconduct, lying, divisive speech, harsh speech, frivolous speech, greed, hatred, stupidity.
12. **Eight sufferings**: birth, old age, sickness, death, being apart from those one loves, being together with those one hates, being unable to obtain what one seeks, the raging blaze of the five *skandhas*.
13. **Three realms of existence**: existence of desire, existence of form, existence of formlessness.
14. **Twenty-five planes of existence**
    a) fourteen planes of existence in the desire realm
       i) four evil destinies
          hells
          path of hungry ghosts
          path of animasl
          path of asuras
       ii) four continents
          Jambudvipa in the south
          Purva-videha in the east
          Apara-godaniya in the west
          Uttarakuru in the north
       iii) six desire heavens
          Chaturmaharajika – Heaven of the Four Great Kings
          Trayastrimsha – Heaven of the Tirty-three
          Suyama Heaven
          Tushita Heaven
          Nirmanarati Heaven
          Paranirmitavashavartin Heaven
    b) seven planes of existence in the form realm
       i) four dhyana heavens
       ii) Great Brahma Heaven
       iii) (count as one) Five Heavens of Pure Dwelling
       iv) Heaven of No-Thought

c) four planes of existence in the formless realm
   Four Stations of Emptiness
   station of boundless space
   station of boundless consciousness
   station of nothing whatever
   station of neither perception nor non-perception

15. **Grounds of affliction resulting from ignorance** (or state of ignorance): Ignorance without substance relies on the nature of dharma as its substance. This ignorance is based on the ground of the nature of the dharma.

16. **Afflictions like Ganges'sand**: Afflictions are as many as the number of sand grains in the Ganges River. This is based on wrong views as its substance. It refers to the first mark of wisdom in the six coarse delusions.

17. **Formidable afflictions**: The more intense afflictions among the ten fundamental afflictions. The ten are divided into five sharp and five dull. The five sharp ones are views of self, extreme views, wrong views, views of attachment, views of rigid morality or precepts, and the five dull ones are desire, hate, stupidity, pride, and doubt.

18. **Cessation and contemplating**: This refers to the state of torpor and delusion which those who cultivate the dharma of cessation and contemplating easily fall into and this cultivation obstructs their opening of perfect wisdom.

19. **The four dwelling grounds of afflictions**: This refers to the four dwelling grounds of love based on view, desire, form, and formlessness. Because of this, thought and view delusion come into being and make us live in delusion.

20. **Three evils**: greed, hatred, stupidity.

21. **Four graspings**:
   a) grasping of desire- grasping in the five desires,
   b) grasping of view and knowledge- view of grasping at views,

44

    c) grasping at the view of prohibitions - view of grasping at precepts and prohibitions,

    d) grasping of self- view of self and being arrogant.

22. **Five hindrances**: desire, anger, drowsiness, excitability, and doubts.

23. **Six attachments**: This refers to the attachments when the six organs encounter the six defiled objects.

24. **Seven outflows**: joy, anger, sorrow, thinking, grief, fear, love, and loathing.

25. **Eight defilements**: This refers to eight kinds of false thoughts of desire, view, doubt, arrogance, stinginess, sleep, jealousy, afflictions.

26. **Nine entanglements**: love, anger, arrogance, ignorance, view, grasping, doubt, jealousy, stinginess.

27. **Ten fetters**: greed, hatred, stupidity, arrogance, doubt, view of self, view of extremes, view of grasping at views, view of grasping at precepts, deviant views.

28. *Dana paramita*: giving.

29. *Sila paramita*: precepts.

30. *Ksanti paramita*: patience.

31. *Virya paramita*: vigor.

32. *Dhyana paramita*: samadhi.

33. *Prajna paramita*: wisdom.

ROLL TWO

Namo Buddhas and Bodhisattvas of the Dragon Flower Assembly
(*chant three times*)

Praise

Offerings of flowers are made to
Bodhisattvas Manjushri and Samantabhadra,
Peonies, admirable and exquisite, and
Hundreds more kinds of flowers grace the golden palace;
Lotuses bloom, shed petals and reveal golden pods;
A dark-robed youth holds the flowers before the Honored Compas-
sionate One.

Namo Universal Offering Bodhisattva Mahasattva (*three times*)

Listen respectfully

To realize the *two* emptinesses, emptiness of self and emptiness
of dharmas, we must certify to the ultimate fruition of the *dual*
adornments[1].

To understand the *two* truths, Ultimate Truth and Conventional
Truth, we must put an end to the conditions of delusion that
lead to birth and death.

Dragons and the rest of the eightfold division follow along and
learn, and together with other efficacious beings, visible and
invisible, offer unseen protection.

A symbol for the "myriad virtues" adorns the Buddha's chest;
A wheel with a thousand spokes is imprinted on his soles.
His virtues are inconceivable and beyond praise or exaltation.

He never forgets his fundamental vows to universally benefit sentient beings.

He sits high on the hundred-jeweled lotus platform, witnessing this repentance that we have been conducting day and night.

[Dharma Host]: On behalf of _____ [those who seek to repent], we practice this Repentance Dharma of Kindness and Compassion in the Bodhimanda. We have come to Roll Two. With all conditions fulfilled, we now enter the Repentance Platform. May our three karmas be pure as snow and our six sense faculties clean as ice. We burn *turushka*[2] incense, spread *pundarika*[3] flowers, and respectfully invite the sages of the ten directions, as we praise the Buddhas and chant their exalted names. May we receive the sprinkling of sweet dew to cleanse us of our multifarious karmic offenses.

We are earnestly mindful that from innumerable kalpas past, we have been tightly bound in the entanglements of the *two* karmas[4], and have continuously revolved in the cycle of birth and death. We have not awakened to the *two* emptinesses[5], and have quickly given rise to love and hate. We have been drifting along, holding onto the *two* extreme deviant views[6], as we wander on the *two* paths of happiness and suffering. When ignorance suddenly arises, our thoughts of killing, stealing, lust, and lying, flow forth unabated. Daily, our afflictions grow, and we continuously commit offenses with our body, mouth, and mind. We undergo a mix of good and bad retributions, constantly rising or falling, like an ever-revolving waterwheel. We ought to be aware that karmic retributions are just and never err, just like the three parts of the aksha[7] cluster. Hence, if we do not rely on this Repentance, how can we ever eradicate our offenses and mistakes?

May we therefore give rise to shame and remorse and bring forth our utmost sincerity. May this Repentance that generates immediate blessings serve as an enduring method to effectively eradicate all our offenses. This is the vow we make, and may the Buddhas take pity on us and invisibly bless and protect us.

The Buddha's face is like the pure, full moon,
Radiant like the light of a thousand suns.
His aura universally illumines the ten directions, and
He is replete with kindness, compassion, joy and equanimity.

Commencement of the Repentance

We now begin the Repentance Dharma of Kindness and Compassion in the Bodhimanda. Together in this assembly, we single-mindedly return to and rely on all Buddhas of the three periods of time.

Namo Buddhas of the past, Vipashyin Buddha
Namo Shikhin Buddha
Namo Vishvabhu Buddha
Namo Krakucchanda Buddha
Namo Kanakamuni Buddha
Namo Kashyapa Buddha
Namo our Fundamental Teacher Shakyamuni Buddha
Namo Honored Future Buddha, Maitreya

Section 4 Bringing Forth the Bodhi Resolve[8]

Today, we are here in this Bodhimanda due to our shared karma. We have bowed and repented. Our defilements are now cleansed, and the heavy karmic obstructions from the ten evil deeds are completely removed. The burden of our karma has been lifted; we are now experiencing a pervasive purity. Let us now learn from the Bodhisattvas and practice the straight way, so that we may establish merit, virtue and wisdom. Buddhas have always praised those who bring forth the resolve for bodhi, as the bodhi resolve itself is the Bodhimanda and it will bring us to accomplishment. May all of us in this great assembly, strengthen our resolve and not let our life pass in vain; let us not further waste our time, lest we regret later.

We are gathered here today, and the timing is opportune. Therefore, from morning to night we should not cover ourselves with afflictions, instead, we should exhaust our efforts to bring forth the bodhi resolve. This very resolve for bodhi is the Buddha mind. The merit, virtue, and wisdom that comes from the bodhi resolve are immeasurable, beyond reckoning or calculation. Just a single thought of resolving for bodhi creates incredible merit, virtue, and wisdom, how much the more will many such thoughts. The blessings accumulated from many kalpas of doing good is not even one part in ten thousand of the merit and virtue of resolving for bodhi. It is not comparable, not even by reckoning or analogy.

Moreover, a person who practices meritorious deeds without first bringing forth the unsurpassed resolve for bodhi is like one who ploughs a field without planting seeds. Without seeds and sprouts, how can fruits come forth? Therefore, we must make the resolve for bodhi. The causes and conditions for bringing forth the resolve are stated in the sutras, "Above, we must seek to repay the kindness of the Buddhas; below, we must seek to save and rescue all." Therefore the Buddha once praised the devas, saying, "Good indeed, good indeed! It is as you have said. Bringing forth the bodhi resolve for the sake of benefiting all living beings is the most supreme offering to the Buddhas." It is not sufficient to bring forth the bodhi resolve just once. We need to do so repeatedly, in order for the bodhi resolve to grow without cease.

So the sutras state, "Before the Buddhas, bring forth this great vow of goodness as many time as there are sand grains in *nayutas* of Ganges Rivers." From this, we know that the resolve for bodhi can be brought forth limitless times. Furthermore, it is not that the resolve for bodhi can only be brought forth during the time a Buddha appears in the world, it can also be brought forth upon encountering a good and wise advisor. Manjushri Bodhisattva, for example, brought forth his bodhi resolve due to a woman. There are more ways than one to bring forth the bodhi resolve.

Moreover, we should not look down on the bodhi resolve brought forth by an ordinary person. It is the mind set that is important. Anyone who avidly seeks the Buddhadharma and aspires to the Mahayana can bring forth the resolve. Thus, we should rely on the sutras, apply the principles from the analogies therein to our mundane life, regard friends and foes as the same and equal, and consider all in the six paths to be one, sharing the same attributes. May this goodness of bringing forth the bodhi resolve enable all of us to attain liberation. Those who share our faith and understanding will know that these teachings are not sophistry.

In order to bring forth the resolve for bodhi, we who are here in this Bodhimanda due to our shared karma must begin our contemplation, starting with being mindful of those who are close to us: our parents, teachers, family members and relatives. Next we extend our contemplation to hell beings, hungry ghosts, and animals. Then we expand the scope of our mindfulness to include the heavenly beings, ascetic masters, all good spirits and all humankind. Then we consider how to save those who are suffering. Having made such a contemplation, we should be reminded of our bodhi resolve and recognize that it is only by bringing forth a great resolve that we can hope to really rescue them.

This initial thought should spur us to bring on succeeding thoughts, so that the first thought expands to a second thought, then to a third thought, and thereafter to as many thoughts as can fill up a whole room, a space as large as one cubic *yojana*, the continent of Jambudvipa, and subsequently the other three continents. This contemplation should then increasingly expand to eventually include all the realms in the ten directions. Next, we visualize all beings in the east as our fathers, all living beings in the west as our mothers, all beings in the south as our elder brothers, all beings in the north as our younger brothers, all beings below as our sisters, all beings above as our teachers, and all beings in the intermediate directions as *shramanas* and *brahmans*. After these thoughts are established, we contemplate that we ourselves are experiencing their suffering, that we go to them and relieve them of their physical pain, and that we vow to eradicate their suffering. After they are free of immediate suffering, we proceed to speak the Dharma for them and praise the Buddhas, the Dharma, and the assembly of Bodhisattvas. By the time we finish our praises, these beings are joyful. Finally, seeing these living beings becoming joyful, we should rejoice as if their happiness is our own.

Today, we are here in this Bodhimanda due to our shared karma. We will never forsake our bodhi resolve due to hardships of taking living beings across. Let us now bring forth our utmost, heartfelt sincerity, bow in full prostration, be mindful as we recite aloud the following resolve: Henceforth until we attain Buddhahood, wherever we are born, may we who have participated in this assembly always be able to meet good and wise advisors who will inspire us to bring forth the resolve for unsurpassed bodhi. Even if we fall into the three evil destinies or encounter the eight difficulties[9], may we be constantly mindful of bringing forth our bodhi resolve and sustain it without cease.

We who are here in this Bodhimanda due to our shared karma should bring forth a courageous mind, a sincere mind, and a bodhi mind. Let us all now with utmost, heartfelt sincerity, bow in full prostration and take refuge with the Greatly Kind and Compassionate Ones who are like fathers to those of us in this world.

> Namo Maitreya Buddha
> Namo Shakyamuni Buddha
> Namo Courageous Giving Buddha
> Namo Purity Buddha
> Namo Pure Giving Buddha
> Namo *Swo Lyu Na* Buddha
> Namo Water-deva Buddha
> Namo Firm in Virtue Buddha
> Namo Chandana Merit and Virtue Buddha
> Namo Infinite Handfuls of Light Buddha
> Namo Bright Virtue Buddha

Namo Worry-free and Virtuous Buddha
Namo Narayana Buddha
Namo Flower of Merit and Virtue Buddha
Namo Steadfast, Courageous, and Vigorous Buddha
Namo Vajra Wisdom Bodhisattva
Namo Boundless Body Boddhisattva
Namo Guan Shi Yin Boddhisattva

Again, we take refuge with the Three Treasures of the ten directions to the ends of empty space. Before all the Three Treasures of the ten directions, we now bring forth our bodhi resolve. Henceforth until we attain Buddhahood, we vow to practice the Bodhisattva path without ever retreating. May we constantly be mindful to save all living beings, constantly be mindful to ensure their well-being, and constantly be mindful to protect and provide for them. If living beings do not become Buddhas before us, we vow that we will not attain Proper Enlightenment. We hope all Buddhas, great Bodhisattvas, sages and worthy ones in the ten directions bear witness and help us fully accomplish our vows and practices.

Today, we are here in this Bodhimanda due to our shared karma. We may have practiced various good deeds for many kalpas and attained the intermediary rewards of being reborn in the heavens or in the human realm. However, if we do not attain the ultimate fruition of transcending the mundane world, then when our blessings are exhausted, we eventually fall into evil destinies. Our bodies undergo decay and deterioration and are constantly oppressed by suffering and distress with no way of escape. It is only by making vast vows and bringing forth a great resolve that we can hope to be apart from all deterioration and afflictions and become adorned with hundreds of blessings.

Together we should wholeheartedly be mindful of all Buddhas and make a firm and solid resolve for bodhi. The merit and virtue of bringing forth the bodhi resolve is immeasurable, even Buddhas and Bodhisattvas can never finish speaking about it. Such power is

Inconceivable. How can we not single-mindedly set our thoughts on bodhi? The *Great Collection Sutra* states, "Although a room was dark for a hundred years, just a single lamp can dispel the darkness instantaneously." Therefore, we should apply effort and bring forth the bodhi resolve, even if it is just a single thought.

We kneel, place our palms together and single-mindedly contemplate the Three Treasures of the ten directions as we recite the following: Before all Buddhas of the ten directions, all venerated Dharma of the ten directions, all Bodhisattvas of the ten directions, and all sages and worthy ones of the ten directions, we with straightforward and proper mindfulness bring forth a sincere mind, a mind of vigor, a peacefully dwelling mind, a mind of joyful benevolence, a mind to rescue all beings, a mind that guards and protects all beings, a mind equal to that of all Buddhas and a resolve for bodhi. From now until we accomplish Buddhahood, we will not allow our mind to be attached to states of heavens or humans, hearers or Pratyekabuddhas. We will only bring forth the resolve for the Mahayana, the resolve for Wisdom of All Modes, and the resolve to accomplish *Anuttara-samyak-sambodhi*. May all Buddhas, great Bodhisattvas, and sages of the ten directions throughout empty space, based on their fundamental vows, bear witness to our resolve; may they also, based on their power of kindness and compassion, aid and gather us in, so that no matter where we are, we will always be steadfast and not retreat from the great resolve that we have established today. Even if we fall into the three evil destinies or encounter the eight difficulties, even if we are reborn in various types of bodies, undergoing various kinds of unbearable suffering in the three realms, we vow to never retreat from this great resolve that we have today. We would rather enter the *Avici* Hell and undergo various suffering in the great wheels of fire than to retreat from the great bodhi resolve that we have established today. This resolve and the vows we have made today are the same as that of all Buddhas.

Again we sincerely bow to the Three Treasures. We disciples from now until we attain Buddhahood, while in the midst of dualities will understand the emptiness of dharmas as we proceed to save all living beings in the ten directions. Let us now bring forth utmost, heartfelt sincerity, bow in full prostration and be mindful as we recite: We seek unsurpassed bodhi, not for our own sake, but for the sake of saving all living beings. From now until we realize Buddhahood, we vow to bear the responsibility to liberate all living beings and bring forth great kindness and compassion towards them. To the end of time, if living beings commit any offense that will cause them to fall into the three evil paths or undergo any distress or torment in the six destinies, we will not shun any suffering in order to personally rescue them, enabling them to dwell in peace and stability.

Namo Maitreya Buddha
Namo Shakyamuni Buddha
Namo Lotus-flower Light, Roaming in Spiritual Power Buddha
Namo Wealthy in Merit and Virtue Buddha
Namo Mindful of Virtue Buddha
Namo Well-renowned for Meirt and Virtue Buddha
Namo King Blazing Royal Crimson Banner Buddha
Namo Skillfully Traveling in Merit and Virtue Buddha
Namo Precious Flower Traveling Buddha
Namo King Precious Lotus Skillfully Dwelling Beneath a Sala Tree Buddha
Namo Victorious in Battle Buddha
Namo Skillfully Traveling Buddha
Namo Encompassing Adornments of Merit and Virtue Buddha
Namo Renouncing Hindrances of *Skandhas* Bodhisattva
Namo Tranquil Sense Faculties Bodhisattva
Namo Boundless Body Bodhisattva
Namo Guan Shi Yin Bodhisattva

May all Buddhas of the ten directions throughout empty space bear witness and, based on their power of great kindness and compassion, enable us to bring forth the resolve for bodhi, practice the Bodhisattva Path, fully accomplish whatever we set out to do, and liberate all living beings, wherever we may be.

Again, we sincerely bow in full prostration to the Three Treasures of the ten directions to seek and realize unsurpassed bodhi, not for our own sake, but for the sake of taking across all living beings of the ten directions. We resolve to help living beings enter the Buddhas' wisdom and to fully accomplish the Wisdom of All Modes. These are the living beings of the present and future who are dull or deluded, who are covered in darkness and unable to recognize the proper Dharma, who give rise to all kinds of deviant views, who may be cultivating the Way but have not yet comprehended the marks of Dharma. We vow to accomplish these tasks from now until the time we attain Buddhahood, by relying on the power of the Buddhas, power of the Dharma, power of the sages and worthy ones, and by employing all manner of expedient means. Let us all bring forth utmost, heartfelt sincerity, bow in full prostration, taking refuge with all Buddhas of the ten directions throughout the empty space.

Namo Maitreya Buddha
Namo Shakyamuni Buddha
Namo Universal Light Buddha
Namo Universal Understanding Buddha
Namo Universal Purity Buddha
Namo Tamalapattra and Chandana Fragrance Buddha
Namo Chandana Light Buddha
Namo Mani Banner Buddha
Namo Treasury of Happiness and Accumulation of Mani Jewels Buddha
Namo Supreme Great Vigor that All Worlds Delight to See Buddha
Namo Mani Banner and Lamps' Light Buddha
Namo Wisdom Torches' Shining Buddha
Namo Virtue's Radiance as Vast as the Sea Buddha
Namo Firm in Vajra, Shedding Golden Light Everywhere Buddha
Namo Great Strength, Vigor, and Courage Buddha

Namo Greatly Compassionate Light Buddha
Namo King of Kindness and Strength Buddha
Namo Treasury of Kindness Buddha
Namo Superior Wisdom Bodhisattva
Namo Never Leaving the World Bodhisattva
Namo Boundless Body Bodhisattva
Namo Guan Shi Yin Bodhisattva

We hope all Buddhas and great Bodhisattvas will help us with their power of great kindness and compassion, power of great wisdom, inconceivable power, immeasurable power of self-mastery, power of subduing the four demons, power of severing the five hindrances, power of eradicating all afflictions, immeasurable power of purifying karma and sense faculties, immeasurable power of developing contemplative wisdom, immeasurable power of developing non-outflow wisdom, immeasurable spiritual powers, immeasurable power of taking across living beings, immeasurable power of protecting living beings, immeasurable power of comforting living beings, immeasurable power of eradicating suffering, immeasurable power of liberating hell beings, immeasurable power of saving hungry ghosts, immeasurable power of rescuing animals, immeasurable power of gathering in and transforming asuras, immeasurable power of gathering in humans, immeasurable power of ending the outflows of all heavenly beings and ascetic masters, power of completely adorning the Ten Grounds, power of completely adorning the pure lands, power of completely adorning the Bodhimanda, power of the merit and virtue of completely adorning the fruition of Buddhahood, wisdom power of completely adorning the fruition of Buddhahood, power of completely adorning the Dharma body, power of completely adorning unsurpassed bodhi, power of completely adorning great Nirvana, the immeasurable and infinite power of merit and virtue, and the immeasurable and infinite power of wisdom.

May all Buddhas and great Bodhisattvas of the ten directions throughout empty space enable all living beings in the six paths and the four births, including all of us who have brought forth the bodhi resolve today, to perfect the power of merit and virtue, perfect the power of vows for bodhi, and perfect the power of practices for bodhi. May the Buddhas and great Bodhisattvas do this based on their immeasurable, inexhaustible, inconceivable powers and self-mastery, never forsaking their fundamental vows.

We now make the vow that all beings of the four births and the six paths of the ten directions throughout all times will attain purity through this Repentance Dharma, whether these beings are visible or invisible, friends or foes, neither friends nor foes, and with or without affinities. Wherever these beings may be born, may they all accomplish their vows, be steadfast and persevere without retreating from their resolve, and accomplish the Proper Enlightenment of the Tathagatas. This also includes living beings of inferior capacities who harbor deviant resolves or aspirations. May they also enter the sea of great vows, and quickly perfect their wisdom, merit and virtue. May they perfect the Bodhisattva practices of the Ten Grounds, accomplish the Wisdom of All Modes, be adorned with unsurpassed Bodhi, and attain ultimate liberation.

Section 5 Making Vows

Today, we are here in this Bodhimanda due to our shared karma. We have brought forth our bodhi resolve, and we feel limitless joy welling up. We recognize that in order to progress, we need to make great vows. With heartfelt sincerity, we now bow in full prostration and take refuge with the Greatly Kind and Compassionate Ones who are like fathers to those of us in this world.

Namo Maitreya Buddha
Namo Shakyamuni Buddha
Namo Victoriously Adorned in Chandana Cave Buddha
Namo Wholesome Worthy Leader Buddha

Namo Wholesome Mind Buddha
Namo King Vastly Adorned Buddha
Namo Golden Flower Buddha
Namo Jeweled Canopy Shining in Space King of Self-mastery
Power Buddha
Namo Light of Precious Flowers in Space Buddha
Namo King Adorned with Lapus Lazuli Buddha
Namo Form-body's Light Appearing Everywhere Buddha
Namo Unmoving Wisdom Light Buddha
Namo King Demon-horde-subduer Buddha
Namo Gifted and Brilliant Buddha
Namo Wisdom Victory Buddha
Namo Maitreya, Immortal Light Buddha
Namo Medicine King Bodhisattva
Namo Medicine Superior Bodhisattva
Namo Boundless Body Bodhisattva
Namo Guan Shi Yin Bodhisattva

May the inconceivable power of the Buddhas aid and protect us in accomplishing all our vows. Wherever we are born, we will never forget to strive for unsurpassed bodhi, the ultimate accomplishment of Proper and Equal Enlightenment. Henceforth, we vow that in life after life, at all times and places, we will always remember to bring forth and unceasingly maintain our bodhi resolve. Henceforth, we vow that in life after life, at all times and places, we will always be able to serve and make offerings to all the countless and boundless Buddhas, and that all our offerings will be complete and perfect. Henceforth, we vow that in life after life and at all times and places, we will always uphold and protect all Mahayana sutras and make complete and perfect offerings to the Dharma.

Henceforth, we vow that in life after life at all times and places, we will always encounter countless and boundless Bodhisattvas of the ten directions and make complete and perfect offerings to them. Henceforth, we vow that in life after life at all times and places, we will be able to encounter countless and boundless sages and worthy ones of the ten directions and make complete and perfect offerings to them. Henceforth, we vow that in life after life at all times and places, we will always be able to repay the kindness of our parents and make complete and perfect offerings to them. Henceforth, we vow that in life after life, at all times and places, we will always be able to encounter *upadayas* and *acharyas* and make complete and perfect offerings to them.

Henceforth, we vow that in life after life, at all times and places, we will be able to encounter great powerful heads of nations, and together we will help the Three Treasures flourish without cease. Henceforth, we vow that in life after life, at all times and places, we will be able to adorn all Buddhalands, so that even the names of the three evil paths or eight difficulties will not exist. Henceforth, we vow that in life after life, at all times and places, we will attain the four unobstructed eloquences and the six spiritual powers, and that they are always readily available to us, without our ever losing or forgetting them, so that we can teach and transform all living beings.

Let us all now with utmost, heartfelt sincerity, bow in full prostration and take refuge with the Greatly Kind and Compassionate Ones who are like fathers to those of us in this world.

Namo Maitreya Buddha
Namo Shakyamuni Buddha
Namo Light of Purity for the World Buddha
Namo King Well-stilled Moon Sound and Wonderful Venerable Wisdom Buddha
Namo Supreme and Venerable Dragon King Buddha
Namo Light of Sun and Moon Buddha
Namo Pearl-light of Sun and Moon Buddha
Namo Victorious Wisdom-banner King Buddha
Namo King Lion's Roar and Power of Self-mastery Buddha
Namo Supremely Wonderful Sounds Buddha
Namo Banner of Eternal Light Buddha

Namo Jeweled Banner Buddha
Namo Precious Brilliance Buddha
Namo Aksobhya Buddha
Namo Great Brilliance Buddha
Namo Infinite Sound Buddha
Namo Great Renown Buddha
Namo Attaining Great Peace and Tranquility Buddha
Namo Proper Voice Buddha
Namo Infinite Purity Buddha
Namo Moon Sound Buddha
Namo Infinite Renown Buddha
Namo Radiance of Sun and Moon Buddha
Namo Undefiled Light Buddha
Namo Pure Light Buddha
Namo Vajra Treasury Bodhisattva
Namo Treasury of Empty Space Bodhisattva
Namo Boundless Body Bodhisattva
Namo Guan Shi Yin Bodhisattva

Again, we take refuge with the Three Treasures of the ten directions to the ends of empty space. Based on the merit and virtue from bowing this Repentance and from making these vows, we vow that all beings of the four births and the six paths, henceforth until they attain Bodhi, will practice the Bodhisattva Path without ever becoming weary and will endlessly practice the giving of wealth and Dharma.

May they have the wisdom and expedient means to ensure that their efforts are never in vain. May they dispense Dharma medicine according to living beings' illness and potential, so that whatever these living beings see or hear can lead them to liberation.

We also hope that from now until we attain bodhi, we will practice the Bodhisattva Path free of any obstruction, and wherever we go, we always do the Buddha's work on a vast scale and establish Bodhimandas. May we attain mastery of mind and mastery of Dharmas, be able to enter each and every samadhi, open the door of dharani to reveal the Buddha's fruition, dwell on the Ground of the Dharma Cloud, shower sweet dew, and eradicate living beings' four demonic enmities, so that all will attain the wonderful fruition of the pure Dharma body.

May all the vows we make today be identical with those of all great Bodhisattvas in the ten directions. May all our vows also be identical with those great vows made by all Buddhas in the ten directions in their past cultivation. All these great vows are as vast as the Dharma nature and as ultimate as empty space. May we accomplish all that we wish for and perfectly fulfill our vows for bodhi. Likewise, we hope that all living beings fulfill their wishes and accomplish their vows.

May all Buddhas of the ten directions, all revered Dharmas, all Bodhisattvas, all sages and worthy ones, with their power of kindness and compassion, bear witness to our vows. May all heavenly beings, ascetic masters, good spirits, dragon spirits, with the power of their kindness and roots of goodness and their support of the Three Treasures, bear witness to our vows and enable us to have as-you-wish self-mastery in all of our practices and vows.

Section 6 Bringing Forth the Resolve to Dedicate Merit

Today, we are here in this Bodhimanda due to our shared karma. We have already brought forth our resolve for bodhi and have made great vows. Next we should bring forth the resolve to dedicate merit. Let us all now with utmost, heartfelt sincerity, bow in full prostration and take refuge with the Greatly Kind and Compassionate Ones who are like fathers to those of us in this world.

Namo Maitreya Buddha
Namo Shakyamuni Buddha
Namo Sunlight Buddha
Namo Infinite Jewel Buddha
Namo Most Honorable Lotus-flower Buddha

Namo Noble Physique Buddha
Namo Golden Light Buddha
Namo Brahma Self-mastery King Buddha
Namo Golden Brilliance Buddha
Namo Golden Sea Buddha
Namo Self-mastery Dragon King Buddha
Namo King of Trees Buddha
Namo King of Self-mastery with the Fragrance of All Flowers
Buddha
Namo Buddha Who Holds Firm a Staff with Courage and Vigor
and Renounces Battle
Namo Luxuriant Inner Pearl-light Buddha
Namo Infinite Fragrance and Brilliance Buddha
Namo Manjushri Bodhisattva
Namo Wonderful Voice Bodhisattva
Namo Boundless Body Bodhisattva
Namo Guan Shi Yin Bodhisattva

Again, we take refuge with the Three Treasures of the ten directions to the ends of empty space. May they, based on their power of
kindness and compassion, bear witness to our vows. We vow to dedicate all our wholesome deeds to living beings of the four births and
the six paths, be they deeds from the past, present, or future, and
whether they are many or few, great or small, enabling all beings to
bring forth the resolve for the Path. We do not aspire for the Two
Vehicles, nor for the Three Existences, but, we dedicate all merit so as
we proceed towards unsurpassed bodhi. We vow that all living beings
also dedicate the merit from their wholesome deeds, whether from
the past, present, or future, to the aspiration for unsurpassed bodhi,
rather than for the Two Vehicles, or for the Three Existences.

Today, we are here in this Bodhimanda due to our shared karma.
Together we have brought forth our resolve for bodhi, have made our
great vows, and have set our minds on dedication of merit. Our resolve
is as vast as the Dharma nature, and as ultimate as empty space. May

all Buddhas, Bodhisattvas, sages and worthy ones of the past, present, and future bear witness to this resolve. We again bring forth our ultimate sincerity and bow to the Three Treasures.

We have now completed bringing forth the bodhi mind and vows, and our hearts are overflowing with limitless joy. With utmost earnestness we again bow in full prostration on behalf of heads of nations, parents, teachers, elders, relatives throughout the kalpas, all retinues, good and bad advisors, heavenly beings, ascetic masters, the four world-protecting heavenly kings, spirits who bless the good and punish the evil, spirits who guard and protect those who uphold mantras, the dragon kings of the five directions, dragons and the rest of the eightfold division, and all other spirits, including all past, present and future karmic creditors and donors, beings of the four births and the six paths, and all living beings. May they all take refuge in you, the Greatly Kind and Compassionate Ones who are like fathers to those of us in this world.

Namo Maitreya Buddha
Namo Shakyamuni Buddha
Namo Lion Sound Buddha
Namo Great Strength, Vigor, Courage and Power Buddha
Namo Firm Dwelling Buddha of the Past
Namo King of Drum Sound Buddha
Namo Sun and Moon Flower Buddha
Namo Surpassing Multitude of Flowers Buddha
Namo Lamp Radiance for the World Buddha
Namo Abounds in Silence and Tranquility Buddha
Namo Precious Wheel Buddha
Namo Ever in Cessation Buddha
Namo Pure Enlightenment Buddha
Namo Limitless Precious Flower Radiance Buddha
Namo Sumeru Steps Buddha
Namo Precious Lotus Flower Buddha
Namo Collection of the Multitudes of Treasures Buddha
Namo Dharma Wheel and Universal Presence of Abundant Multitudes of Treasures Buddha

Namo Flourishing Tree King Buddha
Namo Surrounded by Pure Virtue, Distinguished and Honorable
Buddha
Namo Undefiled Light Buddha
Namo Sunlight Buddha

Again we bow to Sea-vast Virtue Tathagata of innumerable kalpas past, great teacher of Buddhas.

We also bow to boundless and countless Bodhisattvas throughout all of empty space who have realized the non-birth Dharma body.

We bow to boundless and countless Bodhisattvas throughout all of empty space who have attained the non-outflow Form body.

We bow to boundless and countless Bodhisattvas throughout all of empty space who have brought forth the bodhi resolve.

We bow to Ashvaghosa Bodhisattva, the great master who made the Proper Dharma flourish.

We bow to Nagarjuna Bodhisattva, the great master who made the Dharma flourish in the Dharma Image Age.

We bow to Boundless Body Bodhisattva who pervades the empty space of the ten directions.

We bow to Guan Shi Yin Bodhisattva who saves those suffering in the ten directions throughout empty space.

Praises and Prayers

The great sage, the World Honored One, is magnificent and towering.
With wonderful and penetrating wisdom, he is king among all sages.
He manifests pervasively in the six paths throughout the ten directions.
His head has a crown prominence, with an aura as brilliant as the sun;
His face, perfect as the full moon, is adorned with a wonderful golden hue;
His deportment, in movement or stillness, is upright and distinguished, always peaceful and serene.

His awe-inspiring virtue quakes the grea- thousand worlds, terrifying all demons.
His three insights thoroughly illuminate, causing the multitudes of evil to hide.
Seeing beings of evil disposition, he would surely save them;
Relieving beings of their suffering is his nourishment.
He sails the sea of birth and death, taking all beings across.

Thus we honor him as: the Thus Come One, Worthy of Offerings, of Proper and Universal Knowledge, Perfect in Understanding and Conduct, Skillful in Leaving the World through Liberation, Unsurpassed Knight, Taming Hero, Teacher of Gods and Humans, Buddha, World-Honored One[10] who takes across countless people, liberating them from the suffering of birth and death.

By the causes and conditions issuing from the merit and virtue generated in bringing forth the resolve, may the emperor, the crown prince, kings and their retinues, the president, vice president, civil and military officials from now until they accomplish bodhi:

- Renounce their lives for the sake of Dharma, as did Sadaprarudita Bodhisattva;
- Eradicate all offenses by practicing great compassion as did Empty Space Treasury Bodhisattva;
- Travel afar to listen to the Dharma as does Lapis Lazuli Light Bodhisattva, and
- Be skilled at comprehending difficult Dharma as does Undefiled Treasury Bodhisattva.

Furthermore, may all our parents and relatives from countless kalpas past, from now until they attain Buddhahood:

- Make their bodies expansive like empty space, as did Boundless Body Bodhisattva;
- Be replete with the ten merits and virtues, as did King of Noble Virtues Bodhisattva;

- Joyfully listen to the Dharma, as does Fearlessness Bodhisattva,
- And have courageous and vigorous spiritual powers, just as does Great Strength Bodhisattva.

May our teachers of Dharma, *acharyas*, our fellow cultivators and relatives, monastics of the three seniorities, and all wise advisors, henceforth until they accomplish Buddhahood:

- Be fearless, as is Lion King Bodhisattva;
- Teach and transform beings on a vast scale, as does Accumulation of Treasures Bodhisattva;
- Contemplate the cries of the world and rescue those suffering, just does Guan Yin Bodhisattva;
- Skillfully enquire and debate, as did Mahakashyapa.

May all of us, monastics and laity, faithful donors, good and bad advisors, and all retinues, from now until we attain Buddhahood:

- Resolve all dangers and difficulties, as does Rescuing Bodhisattva;
- Bear an adorned appearance, as did Manjushri Bodhisattva;
- Eradicate karmic obstructions, as did Renouncing Hindrances Bodhisattva;
- Provide the final offering to the Buddha, as did Venerable Cunda.

May all heavenly beings, ascetic masters, the four world-protecting heavenly kings, the intelligent and righteous spirits, celestial spirits, earth spirits, empty space spirits, spirits who guard and protect those who uphold mantras, spirits who bless the good and punish the evil, dragon kings of the five directions, dragons and the rest of the eight-fold division, visible or invisible spirits, all collectively together with their retinues, from now until they accomplish Buddhahood

- Protect all beings with great kindness, as does Ajita Bodhisattva;

- Vigorosly protect the Dharma, as does Never-Resting Bodhisattva;
- Certify from afar those who recite sutras, as does Samantabhadra Bodhisattva;
- Renounce and burn their bodies for the sake of Dharma, as did Medicine King Bodhisattva.

May all friends and foes, those neither friends nor foes, all beings of the four births and the six paths, and all living beings and their retinues, from now until they accomplish Buddhahood:

- Be free of the defilement of emotional love, as is Apart-from-Mind Maiden;
- Have wondrous eloquence, as does Queen Shrimala;
- Practice vigorosly, just as did Shakyamuni Buddha;
- Bring forth wholesome vows, as did Infinite Lifespan Buddha;
- Possess majestic and awe-inspiring powers, as do the heavenly kings;
- Be inconceivable, as was Vimalakirti.

May all merit and virtue be accomplished, and immeasurable Buddha-lands adorned. May the countless and boundless Buddhas, Bodhisattvas, sages and worthy ones of the ten directions throughout empty space, with their kindness and compassion gather us in, rescue and protect us. May they perfect their vows and with their solid faith, ever deepen their virtuous deeds. May they nuture all beings of the four births as if nurturing an only child. May they thus enable all living beings to:

- attain the four limitless minds and six paramitas;
- attain the ten kinds of proper concentrations in cultivating dhyana;
- be blessed by the three vows;
- see Buddhas appearing spontaneously in accord with their thoughts, just like Queen Shrimala;
- ultimately accomplish all vows and practices, and

- ascend to the stage of Proper Enlightenment equal to that of all Tathagatas.

Praise

As the bodhi resolve comes forth,
The light of wisdom the light of wisdom continues to reveal itself.
Every thought is accomplished and pervades the ten directions,
Realizing the ultimate and wordless.
Thought after thought pervades every direction, but the Ultimate is ineffable.
We bow in full prostration and
Dedicate all merit to those Supreme among the Multitudes.

Namo Ground of Transcending Defilement Bodhisattva Mahasattva

(three times)

Concluding the Repentance

His wondrous body, adorned with the myriad virtues,
While remaining in the Tushita Heaven, he descends to be reborn in the royal palace.
The Honored One of Kindness is replete with hallmarks and fine characteristics, borne of his hundreds of blessings.
Without leaving his seat under the Bodhi tree, he simultaneously ascends to the Trayastrimsa Heaven.
May the King of Enlightenment extend his great kindness and have sympathy for us.
May he rescue all drowning beings with his great compassion.
May he witness our sincerity with his perfect, discerning Dharma eye.

[Dharma Host]: On behalf of _____ [those who seek to repent], we practice this Repentance Dharma of Kindness and Compassion in the Bodhimanda. We have now successfully completed Roll Two, accomplishing its merit and virtue.

This great assembly of repentance, here in this bodhimanda, has commenced and concluded Roll Two, circumambulated, lit incense, offered flowers, and recited sutras and mantras. We now transfer the merit from participating throughout the two periods of time in Roll Two. The Buddha, Dharma, and Sangha within One Reality, together with heavenly beings, ascetic masters, earth and water spirits of the three realms are delighted, witnessing our sincerity. May they compassionately regard us as their only child and help us perfect our two adornments of blessing and wisdom.

On behalf of _____ [those who seek to repent], may the merit and virtue generated help all purify the three karmas and grow in the *two* adornments.

We bow and earnestly pray:

> May our *two* karmic obstructions[10], whether of phenomena or noumena, melt away;
> May we realize the *two* emptiness —of self and dharmas— and attain purity;
> May we never dwell in the *two* kinds of inverted minds[12], but be replete with the two adornments of samadhi and wisdom; and
> May we enter the non-dual Dharma-door, and realize true and ever-abiding wondrous principles.
> Furthermore, may all benefactors, friends and foes, and the rest of beings throughout the Dharma Realm share this benefit.
> May they all realize the *two* emptinesses of self and of dharmas, as well as the *two* kinds of patience[13] culminating in non-production.
> May they all attain the perfect clarity of the two wisdoms and complete the *two* practices[14],
> May they all glide across the sea of dharma with ease, in the boat of compassion.
> May they all constantly dwell in the bliss of *Sarvajna*[15].

[Dharma host]: Although we have repented according to the text, we fear that we have not been absolutely sincere. Thus I am taking the liberty to request that together, we continue to repent and reform.

Praise

The meritorious power of the Emperor of Liang Repentance Roll Two
Enables the deceased and the disciples to eradicate offenses of
divisive speech.
May all realize the Bodhisattva's Ground of Transcending Defilement.
As the Repentance is chanted our offenses are blown away like flower
petals in the wind.
Offenses repented, enmity resolved,
Wisdom and blessing increase as calamities are dispelled.
Liberated from suffering and reborn in the Trayastrimsha,
May we gather at the Dragon Flower's Three Assemblies
And receive a prediction personally from Maitreya Buddha.

Namo Dragon Flower Assembly of Bodhisattvas Mahasattvas
(three times)

Final Praise

Emperor of Liang Repentance Roll Two now concludes.
We dedicate its merit to the four benefactors and the three realms.
May all in this assembly enjoy increased longevity and blessings,
May the Dharma water cleanse our offenses.
May the deceased be reborn in the Western Pure Land.
May the Bodhisattvas of the Ground of Transcending Defilement
compassionately gather us in.

Namo Ascending the Path to the Clouds Bodhisattva Mahasattva
(three times)

End Notes

1. **Dual adornments:** blessings and wisdom.
2. *Turushka:* Indian incense.
3. *Pundarika:* the white lotus.
4. **Two karmas:** Also called two hindrances. a) obstacle of affliction, b) obstacle of worldly wisdom.
5. **Two emptinesses:** the non-existence of self and the non-existence of dharma.
6. **Two extreme deviant views**: annihilation and eternalism. These refer to two kinds of deviant views. One kind of thinking is that there is no continuity of life after death, and the other kind of thinking is that living beings will forever keep the same form of body life after life.
7. **Aksha:** The aksha fruit invariably forms as a cluster of three seeds. When this fruit ripens and falls, it remains together in a cluster instead of scattering, an analogy of the linkage between delusion, karma and suffering.
8. **Bodhi resolve** (bringing forth): generating the true intention of becoming enlightened, the initial and essential beginning step on the path to enlightenment.
9. **Eight difficulties**
   a) The difficulties of the hells,
   b) The difficulties of the hungry ghosts,
   c) The difficulties of animals,
   d) The difficulties of the remote border regions,
   e) The difficulties of the Heaven of Longevity,
   f) The difficulties of having many illnesses and disabilities although attaining a human body,
   g) The difficulties of being born in a family of deviant views,
   h) The difficulties of being born before or after a Buddha's time.
10. **Thus Come One . . . World Honored One:** list of ten titles of the Buddha

11. **Two karmic obstructions:** This refers to phenomenal hindrances and noumenal hindrances.
12. **Two kinds of inverted minds:** The two minds. a) The true mind. This refers to the mind of the Treasury of the Thus Come One. b) The false mind or the illusion mind.
13. **Two kinds of patience:** a) patience with the assaults of nature/dharma, such as heat, cold, the existence of nature. b) patience of human assaults, such as being insulted by people. Or the two patiences can refers to patience towards all under all circumstances, and the patience of non-birth.
14. **Two practices:** This refers to two practices of conduct which create blessing and wisdom.
15. *Sarvajna:* The complete and perfect wisdom of Buddhas.

ROLL THREE

Namo Buddhas and Bodhisattvas of the Dragon Flower Assembly
(*chant three times*)

Praise

Rows of dazzling lamps blaze on the jeweled platform,
Their bright light shines throughout realms numerous as sands,
Dark boulevards are bathed in full, unfiltered illumination.
Yama pays homage at the purple-golden platform.
Burning Lamp Buddha accomplishes the Way, venerated by humans
and gods.

Namo Universal Offering Bodhisattva, Mahasattva. (*bow three times*)

Listen respectfully

He perfected fruition after *three asamkhyeya kalpas*, and his
appearance in the world is as rare as an *udumbara* flower[1].
With *three* kinds of transformation bodies[2], he proclaims the
inconceivable teaching, vast like the sea.
Using *three* carts[3] to attract and guide, he rescues and ferries
across beings of the *three* realms.
With his *three* contemplations[4] clear and serene, he propagates
Dharma throughout the *three* thousand great thousand worlds[5].
Whether accordant or discordant with to those who receive
them, his teachings are all the Buddha's work,
Lifting his foot or putting it down, he creates a Bodhimanda
wherever he treads.
May the Greatly Enlightened One bear witness to our sincerity.

[Dharma Host]: On behalf of _____ [those who seek to repent], we practice this Repentance Dharma of Kindness and Compassion in the Bodhimanda. We have come to Roll *Three*. With all conditions fulfilled, we now enter the Repentance Platform.

Let us all now eagerly bow with earnest sincerity, contemplate the kind appearance of the Buddha, and praise his sacred name. We also offer delicacies and rare flowers seeking the Buddhas' compassion to lighten and eradicate the offenses of many lifetimes. We are earnestly mindful that from time without beginning until today, we have been confused by the *three* poisons[6], creating the causes of drifting in the *three* existences—rising, sinking and drowning. We have not awakened to the *three* emptinesses and have created the causes of suffering, thereby falling into the *three* evil paths[7]. We have given rise to the *three* delusions[8], which deepen the *three* karmas[9], resulting in increasing layers of wearisome dust obstructing us from the Buddha nature. We are unaware of and fail to cultivate samadhi, thus we have not been able to eradicate the *three* karmas.

In thought after thought, we continue to scheme and take advantage of conditions. We are like the silkworm that spins its own cacoon, or like a moth that flirts with fire only to get burned. We now realize that our body and mind are the cause for suffering, and believe that it is difficult to escape from the karma we create. So we clearly confess all our offenses to the Thus-Come One, by stating them and repenting. May the Buddha shine his light on us like the sun in the sky, illuminating the dark evil paths full of suffering; may he also assemble Sangha members who practice the *three* studies to bow to all the Greatly Enlightened Ones of the *three* thousand worlds. Our hearts are sincere, and the virtue of the Buddha is lofty. We now respectfully bow to the Greatly Compassionate One to invisibly bless and protect us.

> The host, master of kindness and compassion of three thousand worlds,
> Is also the great Dharma king of hundreds of millions of lands.
> May you open your lotus eyes and watch over us,
> And enable all beings to fulfill all wishes.

Commencement of the Repentance

We now begin the Repentance Dharma of Kindness and Compassion in the Bodhimanda. Together in this assembly, we single-mindedly return to and rely on all Buddhas of the three periods of time.

Namo Buddhas of the past, Vipashyin Buddha
Namo Shikhin Buddha
Namo Vishvabhu Buddha
Namo Krakucchanda Buddha
Namo Kanakamuni Buddha
Namo Kashyapa Buddha
Namo our Fundamental Teacher Shakyamuni Buddha
Namo Honored Future Buddha, Maitreya

Section 7 Revealing Retributions

Today, we are here in this Bodhimanda due to our shared karma. The text above has mentioned offenses and their consequences, which bring us trouble and woe. Because of trouble and woe, we have distanced ourselves from wholesome karma. Because of unwholesome karma, we fall into the three paths and suffer all types of evil destinies. Even when reborn as humans, we still undergo various types of suffering due to our corresponding past causes and conditions. We have been undergoing ceaseless rebirths, changing from one body to another. All Buddhas and great Bodhisattvas, with their spiritual power and heavenly eyes, can see all living beings in the three realms depleting their blessings and then, driven by their karma, falling into realms of suffering. They see living beings in the formless realm happily attached to samadhi. Yet before long their lives end and they fall into the desire realm[10]. When their blessings are exhausted, they consequently may be reborn as animals. Living beings in the heavens of the form realm can also fall from their pure abode into the desire realm, where even when they are in the defiled destinies, they continue to enjoy the pleasures of desire. When the blessings of the beings of the six desire heavens are exhausted, they may fall even as far as the hells and undergo boundless suffering.

The Buddhas and Bodhisattvas also see that because of the power of the ten good deeds, living beings gain human bodies. However, as humans they still suffer greatly, and when their lives end, most fall into different evil destinies. Living beings in the animal realm suffer manifold agony and woe. They are whipped, beaten with sticks, and forced to carry heavy loads over long distances. They are constantly distressed and oppressed, weary and exhausted. The necks of some are rubbed raw by with yokes, and their bodies branded with hot iron.

The Buddhas and Bodhisattvas see hungry ghosts constantly suffering from hunger and thirst that are as agonizing as burning flames which erupt at a kalpa's end. If they do not have the slightest bit of goodness, they will never be able to attain liberation. If they do have a few blessings, they may be reborn as humans, but with inferior features, many illnesses, and a short lifespan. That is how they will live their lives. Everyone should know that good and evil deeds can be likened to two ever-revolving wheels, and this cycle of cause and effect likened to an infinite interlocking chain. Wealth or poverty and high or lowly social status result from one's past deeds. Without a cause, there can be no retribution.

Therefore it is stated in the sutras, "If one is born honored and revered, into a position such as a king or elder, it is the result of supporting and venerating the Three Treasures in the past. If one is born with great wealth, it is the result of practicing giving in the past. Similarly, if one has a long lifespan, it is the result of upholding the precepts. If one is born with upright features, it is the result of practicing patience. If one is diligent in cultivation without ever becoming lax, it is the result of the practice of vigor. If one is born gifted and bright, with clear and far-reaching insight, it is the result of one's reward of wisdom.

If one has a clear, crisp and sonorous voice, it is the result of singing praises of the Three Treasures. If one is neat and clean and free of sickness, it is the result of practicing kindness.If one is big and tall, with fine features, it is the result of being humble and respectful. If one is small and short, it is the result of having looked down on others. If one is ugly, it is the result of being easily resentful and angry. If one is ignorant, it is the result of not seeking knowledge or learning.

If one is stupid and foolish, it is the result of being unwilling to teach others. If one is mute, it is the result of having slandered others. If one is servile and lowly, it is the result of not settling one's debts. If one is ugly and dark-skinned, it is the result of obstructing the Buddha's light. If one is born in a land where people are naked, it is the result of dressing indecently yet feeling superior to others. If one is born where people have big horse-hooved feet, it is the result of being egotistic and disrespectfully wearing improper and noisy footwear in front of Buddha images.

If one is born where people have holes in their chests, it is the result of regretting one's practice of giving or planting blessings. If one is born as a deer, it is the result of frightening others. If one is born as a dragon, it is the result of being fond of flirtatious conduct. If one has malignant sores, it is the result of flogging living beings. If one has a pleasing presence, it is the result of being amicable toward others. If one is constantly imprisoned, it is the result of caging beings in past lives.

Making divisive comments and criticizing a Dharma talk to confuse and disturb other listeners will result in one's birth as a dog with long ears. Listening to the Dharma with an unappreciative mind will result in one's birth as a long-eared donkey. Being stingy and greedy, refusing to share food with others will result in one's fall into the realm of hungry ghosts. Even when reborn as a human, one will continue to suffer hunger and poverty. Purposely giving others inedible food will result in one's birth as a pig or dung beetle.

Robbing others will result in one's birth as a goat to be skinned and eaten. Being fond of stealing will result in one's birth as a cow or horse, enslaved by humans. Being fond of lying and gossiping about others' evil deeds will result in one falling into the hells where molten copper is poured into one's mouth and one's tongue pulled out and plowed through by a cow. After retribution in the hells, one will be born as a myna bird with such an unbearably loathsome voice that people will curse it and wish it will die.

Being fond of intoxicants and becoming intoxicated will result in one falling into the Hell of Boiling Excrement or the *Niraya* Hell[11]. When this retribution is over, one will be born as an ape, and when this retribution ends, one will be born as an obstinate and ignorant human, despised by others.

Abusing others with excessive labor will result in one's birth as an elephant. Being wealthy and honored, but whipping and flogging people of inferior status, leaving them without recourse for justice, will result in one suffering the retribution of the hells for millions of years. When this retribution ends, one will be born as a buffalo with a pierced nose, pulling carts, plowing fields, and being beaten with big clubs. This will be the retribution for the misery one caused in the past.

If one is filthy, it is the result of being a pig in a past life. Similarly, if one is stingy, greedy, and unforgiving, it is the result of having been a dog. If one is ruthless, unreasonable and opinionated, it is the result of having been a goat. If one is frivolous, easily agitated, and lacks perseverance, it is the result of having been a monkey. If one's body has a fishy odor, it is the result of having been a turtle or fish. If one always is vicious, it is the result of having been a snake. If one lacks compassion, it is the result of having been a tiger or wolf.

Today, we are here in this Bodhimanda due to our shared karma. We should be mindful that we humans living in this world suffer a short life span and have many illnesses, the distress and pain of which are beyond description. All these result from our three karmas, which bring about the retribution of suffering in the three evil paths. These three evil paths come about from the three poisons of greed, hatred, and delusion. In addition, we are also ablaze with the three evils - speaking evil with our mouth, harboring evil thoughts in our mind, and doing evil deeds with our body.

Because of these aforementioned six, we are constantly afflicted, suffering unceasing agony. When this life ends, our soul leaves the world. We are alone and neither compassionate parents nor filial children are able to save us. All of a sudden, we appear at King Yama's palace, and regardless of our status, the guardians of hell tally the records of our good and evil deeds. At that time, we dare not conceal anything but readily confess everything. Due to these conditions, we are sent to various destinies, places of suffering or bliss, depending on our karma, undergoing these by ourselves alone. Thus, in darkness and obscurity, we become separated from our relatives for an infinitely long time, each taking his own path, not knowing if we will ever meet again.

Moreover, heavenly spirits record the good and bad deeds of everyone. They do not omit anything, not even a hair's breadth of any deed. Wholesome people do good deeds and obtain blessing and longevity. Unwholesome people do evil deeds, thus incurring endless suffering and a short life span. The cycle of rewards and retributions is thus. Further, they will fall into the realm of hungry ghosts, and after this retribution is resolved, they will be reborn as animals. The suffering that they undergo is endless and unbearable.

Today, we are here in this Bodhimanda due to our shared karma. We should all be aware of this and bring forth shame and remorse. The sutras state, "Those who do good reap wholesome rewards; those who do bad reap evil retributions." This is especially so in the world of the five turbidities where we should be careful not to do any evil. Doing good never fails to bring about rewards, whereas doing evil always brings about calamities.

This Repentance is not something to be casually practiced. The sutras state, "Do not slight small good deeds and consider that they bring no blessing. Accumulating drops of water can fill up a big tank." Without practicing and accumulating small good deeds, one will never become a sage. "Do not take lightly small evil deeds and consider that there is no offense. An accumulation of small evil deeds will eventually ruin us." Great assembly, we should recognize that all auspiciousness and calamities, blessings and misfortunes come from our mind alone. If no cause is created, there will be no subsequent reward or retribution. Our eyes do not see our offenses, no matter how big or heavy they are. This is what the Buddhas have stated, so how could we not believe it?

While still strong and healthy, we must exert all our effort to learn and practice wholesome deeds; otherwise when our time is up, we will regret and not be able to make amends. We are now becoming more aware of the karmic offenses and evil retributions described in the sutras. Since we realize our offenses, how could we not give up evil and practice good? If we fail to reflect within and apply effort, we can be sure that after we leave this very body, we will definitely fall into the hells. How can we assume that will happen?

We need each ask ourselves:

Could I be compelled by severe malice and intense hatred to do evil things? Could I get so angry with others that I hope they will die? Could I experience such jealousy of others that I would not be able to bear to see good things happen to them? Could I want to destroy someone so much that I would contrive to cause the person to become mired in all manner of misery? Could I want to beat someone so badly that I would devise all sorts of tortures for the person to undergo? Could I indulge in such raging anger and hatred that I would ignore any consideration of status and position? Could I become so focused on cursing others with foul language in a thunderous voice and eyes full of fire that I would lose all regard for their dignity?

Or we need to consider our behavior this way: When planting blessings, am I ineffectual in my wholesome resolve? Am I eager to begin with but then lose my enthusiasm? Do I start strong but then let my energy wane? Do I lose my determination and waver in my resolve until there's nothing left?

By reflecting thus we come to understand that when we engage in evil deeds, we are stubborn and strong; but when we engage in good deeds, we are weak and inadequate. With the scant goodness that we now have, how can we possibly be free from the retribution of our grave evil deeds?

The sutras state that through repentance all offenses can be eradicated. Thus when we repent, we should sincerely bow in full prostration, like a mountain collapsing, repenting with great diligence and discipline, to the point of renouncing our lives while we work to eradicate our offenses. Let us all be aware and reflect: How often have we applied utmost sincerity, reprimanded ourselves, and endured hardship while doing Repentances, even to the point of renouncing our lives?

We tire quickly after circumambulating for a short period; complain that we lack energy after only a few prostrations; seek to rest after only a short sit in meditation; do not like to subject our bodies to hard work and distress, and are only concerned about making sure we get sufficient rest and comfort. Once we stretch out our legs, we doze off and drift into a dead sleep. How often do we exhort ourselves to bow to the Buddhas, sweep the stupa grounds, wipe the floor, or do what is difficult to do? Moreover, the sutras clearly instruct that not a single bit of good can arise from laziness or laxity, not a single Dharma can arise from arrogance.

Though we have gained a human body in this lifetime, our mind opposes the Way. How do we know this? From morning to noon, from noon to dusk, from dusk to midnight, from midnight until dawn, in every single thought and in every moment, we are not mindful of the Three Treasures or the Four Noble Truths. We rarely have any thought of repaying the kindness of our parents, teachers and elders; rarely have any thought of practicing giving, upholding precepts, and being patient or vigorous; rarely have any thought of practicing Chan meditation or developing wisdom.

If we examine ourselves, we will realize that we do not have any accomplishments in dharmas of purity worthy of mention; instead, any way we look at it we will find our boundless afflictions and heavy karmic obstructions. Failing to carry out this kind of self-examination, we still consider that we have "great" merit and virtue. We may do some good, yet we are easily carried away by arrogance and pride, disregarding others as if they are non-existent, saying "I can do this; others are not able to. I practice well, others don't." It is truly shameful to be like this.

Now before the great assembly, we repent of all of our offenses. May the assembly also rejoice in our repentance and be free of obstructions in the future. May all in this assembly also be purified in body and mind. With the rewards and retributions of karma so well-stated in the previous text, how can we be so easily consoled and comforted with various excuses, and not seek to transcend the world? Great assembly! We should not think, "I have none of these offenses. Since I have none of such offenses, why do I have to repent?" If any one of us has this thought, we should rid ourselves of it immediately. Moreover, major problems can result from minor mistakes. From just a fleeting trace of dislike, the fire of anger or hatred flares up. Once habits become ingrained in our nature, they are very difficult to change. Thus, we should not allow our thoughts to wander wildly, or our minds to indulge in objects of desire. If we can be patient and keep our minds tame, then our afflictions can be eradicated. Neither laziness nor laxity will ever get one liberated.

Now, relying on the power of the Buddhas' kind and compassionate mindfulness and of all great Bodhisattvas' fundamental vows, we are quoting the *Sutra of the Buddha Speaking of Retributions for Offenses to Teach Beings in the Hells*. Each one of us should calm our minds and listen attentively, "Thus I have heard, at one time, the Buddha dwelt at Shravasti, in Mount Grdahrakuta, together with great Bodhisattvas, Hearers, their retinues, bhikshus, bhikshunis, upasakas[12], upasikas[13], heavenly beings, dragons, ghosts, and spirits. At that time Appearance of Faith Bodhisattva said to the Buddha, 'World-Honored One, whichever being of whatever class or category - hell-being, hungry ghost, animal, whether poor or wealthy, honorable or lowly - upon hearing the Buddha speak the Dharma, would feel like a child reuniting with its mother, like the sick treated by a doctor, like the naked obtaining clothing, like one in darkness finding a lamp.' This describes the measure of benefit that all beings derive from hearing the World-Honoed One speak Dharma.

"At that time the World-Honored One observed the time was right and knew that the Bodhisattvas were requesting Dharma with utmost sincerity. He then emitted a brilliant white light from between his eyebrows which illuminated limitless worlds in the ten directions. This caused the hells to cease functioning temporarily, and beings there received respite from their pain and suffering. At that time, guided by the light of the Buddha, all beings suffering the retributions from their offenses came to the Buddha. They circumambulated the Buddha seven times, bowed respectfully, and eagerly requested the Buddha to vastly proclaim the Way, enabling all beings to attain liberation."

Today, we are here in this Bodhimanda due to shared karma. We now sincerely make the same request to the Buddha, vowing that all living beings will also attain liberation. With utmost, heartfelt sincerity, we now bow in full prostration, requesting all Buddhas in the ten directions throughout empty space with their power of kindness and compassion to rescue those beings suffering from heavy afflictions, bringing them peace and happiness. Let us now bow in full prostration and take refuge in the Greatly Kind and Compassionate Ones who are like fathers to those of us in this world.

Namo Maitreya Buddha
Namo Shakyamuni Buddha
Namo Brahma Heaven Buddha
Namo Foremost in Turning the Never-regressing Wheel Buddha
Namo Great Flourishing Light King Buddha
Namo Honored Lineage of Dharma Buddha
Namo Lamp-light Radiance of Sun and Moon Buddha
Namo Sumeru Buddha
Namo Great Sumeru Buddha
Namo Surpassing Sumeru Buddha
Namo Analogous to Sumeru Buddha

Namo Fragrant Image Buddha
Namo Surrounded by Fragrance Buddha
Namo Pure Light Buddha
Namo Supreme in Dharma Buddha
Namo King of Mastery over Fragrance Buddha
Namo Great Accumulation Buddha
Namo Fragrant Radiance Buddha
Namo Fire Radiance Buddha
Namo Limitless Light Buddha
Namo Lion Lion Playfully Roaming Bodhisattva
Namo Lion Lion Swiftness and Vigor Bodhisattva
Namo Steadfast, Courageous, and Vigorous Bodhisattva
Namo Vajra Wisdom Bodhisattva
Namo Boundless Body Bodhisattva
Namo Guan Shi Yin Bodhisattva
Namo Buddha
Namo Dharma
Namo Sangha

Again, we take refuge with the Three Treasures of the ten directions to the ends of empty space. We sincerely pray that your great kindness and compassion will save all of us living beings from suffering and help us quickly gain liberation, enabling all to reform past offenses and cultivate future goodness. Henceforth:

- May we never fall into the three evil paths;
- May we purify our body, speech, and mind, and not dwell on the wrongdoings of others;
- May we rid ourselves of all karmic obstacles and do deeds that generate purity;
- May we never be moved or influenced by evil;
- May we constantly, with great courage and purity, practice the four great vows;
- May we plant myriads of virtue as our foundation and cultivate immeasurable practices;

- May we life after life, always be born in blessed places;
- May we be constantly mindful of the suffering in the three evil paths, bring forth the bodhi resolve and practice the Bodhisattva Path without rest;
- May we constantly embody the six paramitas and four great vows;
- May we gain mastery of the three clarities[14] and six spiritual powers[15], roam freely in the state of all Buddhas, be with all Bodhisattvas and together accomplish Proper Enlightenment.

Today, we are here in this Bodhimanda due to our shared karma. We should bring forth a mind of kindness and compassion coupled with trepidation, gather in our thoughts and then carefully and attentively listen. At that time, the World-Honored One emitted a brilliant light from between his brows, universally illuminating all living beings in the six paths. For the sake of all living beings, Appearance of Faith Bodhisattva, rose from his seat, came before the Buddha, placed his palms together and knelt, saying, "World-Honored One, there are beings in the hells tortured by hell guardians. Their bodies repeatedly cut, chopped and pounded from head to toe. As soon as they die from the torture, they are immediately revived by a ingenious wind[16] to undergo the same punishment. This retribution of intense suffering, the process of torture, dying, being revived for more torture, goes on unabated with no respite. What offenses have they committed to undergo such retribution?"

The Buddha replied, "These beings disbelieved in the Three Treasures, not knowing how to make offerings. They were unfilial and cruel to their parents, harboring vicious and heinous thoughts towards them. They slaughtered animals or executed people as their livelihood, harming and killing living beings. Because of these causes and conditions, they suffer such retributions."

"Furthermore, there are some other living beings whose bodies are stiff and numb without sensation and whose eyebrows and beards fall off. Covered with sores oozing pus, their bodies rot and stink.

Suffering thus from leprosy, they are abandoned by their families and relatives, living in the wilderness among animals with no one wishing to visit them. What offenses have they committed to undergo such retribution?"

The Buddha replied, "In their former lives, they did not have faith in the Three Treasures. They were not filial to their parents, destroyed stupas and monasteries, robbed or took advantage of the belongings of monastics, injured worthy ones and sages; harmed teachers and elders, all without ever reflecting on their own behavior. They turned their backs on their benefactors, disregarding their kindness and grace. They tarnished the family name by constantly engaging in impure conduct, sometimes even with family members or close relatives, without respecting family ties, and without any shame or remorse. Because of these causes and conditions, they suffer such retributions."

"Furthermore, there are living beings born deaf and dull in big bodies without feet, who must crawl on their stomach. They eat mud to survive; worms gnaw at their bodies, causing them endless suffering throughout the day and night. What offenses have they committed to receive such retribution?"

The Buddha replied, "In their former lives as people, they were obstinate, did not follow sound advice and were unfilial, disobedient and rebellious towards their parents. As landlords, village heads, supervisors, mayors, county magistrates, governors, ministers, law-enforcement officers or military commanders, instead of protecting and caring for the citizens, they abused their authority, encroached upon or robbed people's assets, thus impoverishing them and causing them to undergo hardship. Because of these causes and conditions, they suffer such retributions."

"Furthermore, there are living beings who are blind causing them to inadvertently bump into trees or fall into ditches and die. Even after they are reborn, they continue to suffer the same retribution of being blind. What offenses have they committed to receive such retribution?"

The Buddha replied, "In their past lives, they did not believe in the underlying principle of planting blessings and refraining from committing offenses, and they obstructed the light of the Buddha. Moreover, they stitched people's eyes, locked them in dark cages, or covered their heads with sacks to prevent them from seeing. Because of these causes and conditions, they suffer such retributions."

Today, we are here in this Bodhimanda due to our shared karma. We should be greatly fearful after hearing what is recorded in the sutras. We might have also committed the same offenses in the past. However, due to the covering of ignorance we do not remember them. Because the offenses we might have committed are countless and boundless, we will have to suffer the corresponding retributions in the future. Today, we join together to bring forth heartfelt sincerity and to bow in full prostration. Feeling shame and remorse, we repent of our faults and resolve to reform. We earnestly beseech: May all Buddhas bestow pity on us. May all our past offenses be eradicated through our repentance. May all of our future karma be pure. We look up to the Buddhas of the ten directions and bow in homage.

Namo Maitreya Buddha
Namo Shakyamuni Buddha
Namo Revealing Radiance Buddha
Namo Moon Lamp Light Buddha
Namo Light of Sun and Moon Buddha
Namo Radiance of Sun and Moon Buddha
Namo Fire Radiance Buddha
Namo Convergence of Sounds Buddha
Namo Most Awe-inspiring Deportment Buddha
Namo Honored Radiance Buddha
Namo Army of Lotus Flowers Buddha
Namo Lotus Flower Sounds Buddha
Namo Abundant Jewels Buddha
Namo Lion's Roar Buddha
Namo King of Lion Sound Buddha

Namo Vigor's Army Buddha
Namo Vajra Delightful Eagerness Buddha
Namo Transcending All Dhyanas, Ending All Doubts Buddha
Namo Vast Multitude of Followers Jewel Buddha
Namo Worry-free Buddha
Namo Grounds, Powers, Upholding, and Courage Buddha
Namo Most Delightful Eagerness Buddha
Namo Lion Deeds Bodhisattva
Namo Renouncing Hindrances of *Skandhas* Bodhisattva
Namo Tranquil Sense Faculties Bodhisattva
Namo Never Leaving the World Bodhisattva
Namo Boundless Body Bodhisattva
Namo Guan Shi Yin Bodhisattva
Namo Buddha
Namo Dharma
Namo Sangha

Again, we take refuge with the Three Treasures of the ten directions to the ends of empty space.

May you with your great kindness and compassion:

- Save, protect, support and gather in all living beings so that everyone can quickly attain liberation.
- Aid us in eradicating the karmas of the hells, ghosts, and animals, so that living beings will definitely not have to suffer evil retributions.
- Help living beings transcend the three evil paths and lead them to the Ground of Wisdom, enabling all to attain peace and ultimate happiness.

May you with your great radiance:

- Help us dispel the darkness of delusion.
- Expound each and every aspect of the wondrous and profound Dharma so that we can attain and perfect ultimate bodhi, Proper and Equal Enlightenment.

Today, we are here in this Bodhimanda due to our shared karma. We should again bring forth utmost sincerity and listen attentively to examples of retribution given in the sutras. In one instance, Appearance of Faith Bodhisattva asked the Buddha, "World-Honored One, there are living beings who are mute or who stutter or speak unclearly. What offenses did they commit to receive such retribution?"

The Buddha replied, "In their past lives, they slandered the Three Treasures, scorned and defamed the sagely Path, and gossiped about the good and bad or right and wrong of others. They deliberately made false accusations against the good, or were jealous and hateful of worthy ones. Because of these causes and conditions, they suffer such retributions."

The Bodhisattva continued to ask, "Furthermore, there are living beings with narrow throats and big stomachs, who cannot swallow any food. If they encountered food, it turns into pus and blood. What offenses were committed to cause such retribution?"

The Buddha replied, "In their past lives, they stole food from the Assembly or they furtively took a portion from a special meal offering to the Sangha and ate in hiding, as little as a few grains of sesame or rice. They were stingy about sharing their possessions yet greedy for the belongings of others. They constantly harbored evil thoughts or gave others poison which caused breathing difficulties. Thus, they suffer such retributions."

"There are also living beings who are constantly burned and roasted by hell-guardians. Molten iron is poured over their entire bodies, which are then pierced with nails. As soon as the nails penetrate, their whole body spontaneously catches fire, burns, blisters and festers. What were the offenses they committed?"

The Buddha replied, "In their past lives, they were acupuncturists who were unable to cure illnesses. They damaged bodies with needles, caused great pain, and swindled patients. Thus, they received such retributions."

"There are also living beings who are constantly in a cauldron. Ox-headed hell-guardians toss them into the cauldron with a pitchfork, boil and cook their bodies until they begin to disintegrate. Then the ingenious wind breathes life back into them and they are boiled again. What were the offenses they committed?"

The Buddha replied, 'In their past lives, they slaughtered innumerable living beings, immersing them in boiling liquid to remove their hair, feathers, or fur. Because of the evil karma they created, they received such retribution.' "

Today, we are here in this Bodhimanda due to our shared karma. We should feel great fear regarding what is stated in the sutras. We do not know if we have created such boundless evil karma in our past lives in various destinies that will cause us severe retribution in the future. We can also see for ourselves in this present life such suffering as stuttering, being mute, not being able to talk, or having a big stomach but a narrow throat, thereby being unable to swallow any food. Life is so uncertain. Though we may be comfortable today, there is no guarantee that we will be tomorrow. For when retribution comes, there is no escape. Thus each one of us should understand this point and bring forth the proper and straightforward mind without any stray thoughts. With heartfelt sincerity, we now bow in full prostration for the sake of all living beings in the four births and the six paths, on behalf of those beings who are suffering and those about to undergo suffering. Let us now take refuge with the Greatly Kind and Compassionate Ones who are like fathers to those of us in this world.

Namo Maitreya Buddha
Namo Shakyamuni Buddha
Namo King of Self-mastery Buddha
Namo Infinite Sound Buddha
Namo Radiance of Samadhi Buddha
Namo Precious Radiance Buddha
Namo Jeweled Canopy Shining in Space Buddha
Namo Wonderful Jewel Buddha
Namo Banner of Truth Buddha
Namo Banner of Purity Buddha

Namo Amitabha Buddha

Namo Unique and Supreme Buddha

Namo Convergence of Sounds Buddha

Namo Vajra Strides and Vigor Buddha

Namo King of Self-mastery, Spiritual Penetration Buddha

Namo Precious Fire Buddha

Namo Moon Banner of Purity, Renowned Radiance Buddha

Namo Wonderful Bliss Buddha

Namo Countless Banners and Flags Buddha

Namo Countless Flags Buddha

Namo Great Light Universally Shining Buddha

Namo Jeweled Banner Buddha

Namo Superior Wisdom Bodhisattva

Namo Never Leaving the World Bodhisattva

Namo Boundless Body Bodhisattva

Namo Guan Shi Yin Bodhisattva

Namo Buddha

Namo Dharma

Namo Sangha

Again, we take refuge with the Three Treasures of the ten directions to the ends of empty space. May all Buddhas and great Bodhisattvas, with your great kindness and compassion, save and protect all who are suffering. May you, with your spiritual powers, help eradicate the evil karma of all living beings, so that living beings will not fall again into destinies of suffering, but will gain lives of purity in realms that are pure, and be replete with inexhaustible merit and virtue. In life after life, may they be born in places where they will always encounter Buddhas, and together with all Bodhisattvas, attain Proper Enlightenment.

Today, we are here in this Bodhimanda due to our shared karma. We should again double our efforts and listen attentively. Appearance of Faith Bodhisattva asked the Buddha, "World-Honored One, there are living beings in the flaming city. With flames engulfing them, their minds ablaze, they dash towards the open gates of hell, which automatically close on them. They run hither and thither, trying to escape, but fail, and burn to death. What offenses did they commit?"

The Buddha replied, "In their past lives, they burned forests and wetlands, or drained ponds or lakes, or roasted and smoked poultry and their young. They caused living beings to die under such fiery conditions. Because of these causes and conditions, they suffer such retributions."

He further asked, "There are living beings dwelling in snow-covered mountains who are constantly whipped by cold winds causing their skins to crack and peel. Unable to die and unable to live, they suffer many forms of unbearably intense pain. What offenses did they commit to result in such retribution?"

The Buddha replied, "In their past lives, they robbed clothing from others for their own needs, even in the midst of winter, causing those they robbed to freeze to death. They skinned cows and goats, causing them unbearable agony. Because of these causes and conditions, they suffer such retributions."

He continued to ask, "There are living beings that are constantly trapped in the mountains of blades and trees of swords. Whatever they touch or hold will cause their limbs to be cut and their joints broken, such is the extreme bitterness and torment they suffer. What offenses did they commit to result in such retribution?"

The Buddha replied, "In their past lives, they were butchers or cooks, killing or cooking animals, beheading, chopping, cutting, skinning or deboning and dismembering them, hanging their parts for display and selling them by weight. They even hung live animals upside-down, inflicting unbearable pain on them. Because of such evil karma, they suffer such retribution."

Finally, he asked, "There are living beings whose five sense faculties are incomplete or defective. What offenses did they commit to result in such retribution?"

The Buddha replied, "In their past lives, assisted by hunting dogs and eagles, they shot and killed animals or birds, chopped off their heads, cut off their feet, broke off their wings, inflicting pain and suffering. Because of this evil karma, they suffer such retribution."

Today, we are here in this Bodhimanda due to our shared karma. We should feel great fear now knowing what is stated in the sutras. With heartfelt sincerity, we bow in full prostration on behalf of all living beings in the ten directions who are suffering or will undergo suffering. On their behalf, we take refuge with the Greatly Kind and Compassionate Ones who are like fathers to those of us in this world.

Namo Maitreya Buddha

Namo Shakyamuni Buddha

Namo Pure Light Buddha

Namo Supreme Jewel Buddha

Namo King of Tree Roots and Flowers Buddha

Namo Vipashyin Adornments Buddha

Namo Guiding and Teaching Bodhisattvas Buddha[17]

Namo Freeing His Beholders of Fear Buddha

Namo Perfection of One Vehicle Buddha

Namo King of Abundant and Sublime Inner Virtue Buddha

Namo Vanquishing and Dispelling with Sturdy Vajra Buddha

Namo Precious Fire Buddha

Namo Jeweled Moon's Radiance Buddha

Namo Most Worthy Buddha

Namo Precious Lotus Traveling Buddha

Namo Lone Traveler Slashing Demons' Net Buddha

Namo Strength of Lion's Roar Buddha

Namo Compassionate and Vigorous Buddha

Namo Precious Golden Radiance Buddha

Namo Limitless Honor and Abundance Buddha

Namo King of Boundless Honor Transcending Defilement Buddha

Namo Foremost in Virtue Buddha

Namo Medicine King Bodhisattva

Namo Medicine Superior Bodhisattva

Namo Boundless Body Bodhisattva

Namo Guan Shi Yin Bodhisattva

Again, we take refuge with the Three Treasures of the ten directions to the ends of empty space. May all of you out of great kindness and compassion rescue all living beings of the ten directions. May those currently suffering be instantly liberated and may those destined to suffer in future be free of that retribution. Ultimately, may no one ever fall into the evil destinies again. We pray that, from now until we attain Buddhahood, that all three karmic hindrances be eradicated, and all five fears[18] be dispelled, that we may become fully enhanced by with wisdom, merit and virtue, gather in all living beings, together make complete dedication towards unsurpassed bodhi, and realize Proper and Equal Enlightenment.

Today, we who are here in this Bodhimanda due to our shared karma, should again respectfully and attentively listen. Appearance of Faith Bodhisattva asked the Buddha, "World-Honored One, there are living beings with locked joints, spastic limbs, hunched backs, disjointed waists and hips or those suffering various other deformities such as mutilated hands or crippled feet that render them unable to walk. What offenses did they commit that resulted in such retribution?"

The Buddha replied, "In their past lives as humans, they were cruel and mean. Along paths or trails, they created traps lined with sharpened stakes, pits to entrap living beings, or they shot them with arrows. Because of this evil karma, they suffer such retribution."

"There are living beings who are seized and held in captivity by prison guards. They are chained and shackled and have no way of escaping their distress. What offenses did they commit that resulted in such retribution?"

The Buddha replied, "In their past lives, they netted beings, caged and penned livestock. When they were government officials or figures of authority, they adversely possessed people's properties out of greed, and made false accusations against good people or imprisoned them, leaving them no means to seek justice. Because of this evil karma, they suffer such retribution."

"There are living beings that are psychotic, delusional, idiotic, lunatic, or unable to tell right from wrong. What offenses did they commit that resulted in such retribution?"

The Buddha replied, "In their past lives, they were fond of taking intoxicants and consequently committed the thirty-six offenses or mistakes. So they were reborn as idiots, like drunkards unable to differentiate who is who, including their social status. Because of this evil karma, they suffer such retributions."

"There are living beings who have a tiny body but huge scrotum. They constantly must bear this burden and consequently tire easily because they have to assume a crouched position to move or walk. Thus, they have great difficulty in walking, sitting, standing, or reclining. What offenses did they commit that resulted in such retribution?"

The Buddha replied, "In their past lives, earning a livelihood through trading or sales, they made exaggerated claims on their own products and denigrated those of others. They secretly altered the trading scales to deceive and shortchange their customers. Because of this evil karma, they suffer such retributions."

Today, we who are here in this Bodhimanda due to our shared karma are fearful of what the Buddhas have said. With utmost, heartfelt sincerity, we now bow in full prostration and take refuge with the Greatly Kind and Compassionate Ones who are like fathers to those of us in this world, on behalf of all beings who are suffering or may suffer in the future, including the beings in the six paths. We further take refuge on behalf of our parents, teachers, elders, faithful donors, good and bad advisors, and the rest of the beings in the ten directions.

Namo Maitreya Buddha
Namo Shakyamuni Buddha
Namo Infinite Vigor and Thriving Abundance Buddha
Namo Supreme Wordless Buddha
Namo Abundant Freedom from Ignorance Buddha
Namo Abundant Moon Brilliance Buddha
Namo Abundant Light of Non-difference Buddha

Namo Non-emptiness Radiance Buddha
Namo Countless Banners of Utmost Purity Buddha
Namo King Delightfully Dwelling in Truth Buddha
Namo Abundance in Accomplishing All Buddhalands Buddha
Namo Abundance in Purity, Wisdom, and Virtue Buddha
Namo Wheel and Banner of Purity Buddha
Namo Supreme Abundance of Lapis Lazuli Light Buddha
Namo Precious Virtue Traveling Buddha
Namo Jewel-like Abode of the Virtue of Utmost Purity Buddha
Namo Jewel of Crossing-Over, Radiant Stupa Buddha
Namo Foremost Abundant Gold, Boundless Shame and Remorse
Buddha
Namo Manjushri Bodhisattva
Namo Samantabhadra Bodhisattva
Namo Boundless Body Bodhisattva
Namo Guan Shi Yin Bodhisattva

Again, we take refuge with the Three Treasures of the ten directions to the ends of empty space. Today, we rely on the power of Buddhas, the power of Dharma, the power of Bodhisattvas, and on behalf of all living beings, we bow in full prostration. May the Buddhas and Bodhisattvas show us sympathy as we repent. May living beings who are currently suffering be liberated by the power of great kindness and compassion of the Buddhas and Bodhisattvas. May beings, who are not suffering, from now until attaining Buddhahood, never again fall in the evil paths, be free from the suffering of the eight difficulties, be born among the eight places of blessings, attain the roots of goodness, accomplish equanimity, be replete with wisdom, purity, and self-mastery, and attain Proper Enlightenment just like all Tathagatas have done.

Today, we who are here in this Bodhimanda due to our shared karma should increase our efforts in listening attentively. Appearance of Faith Bodhisattva again asked the Buddha, "World-Honored One, there are living beings with extremely ugly features, such as pitch-black bodies, green ears, protruding cheek bones, blistered faces, flattened noses, red-yellow eyes, missing teeth, or foul breath. They are squat and grossly obese, with pot bellies and narrow waists, twisted and deformed hands and feet, hunched backs and ribs that stick out; they need frequent changes of clothing and consume a lot of food. Their bodies are either bloated or withered, oozing with pus and blood, coated with scabies and ulcers. Their bodies are plagued by a multitude of problems. They are ignored when they try to befriend others, and they are blamed for the offenses committed by others. Misfortunes often befall them. They never see the Buddhas, never hear the Dharma, never recognize Bodhisattvas or worthy ones. They go from one form of suffering to another, unceasingly. What were the offenses they committed?"

The Buddha replied, "In their past lives as children, they were not filial to their parents. As officials, they were not loyal to their king or emperor. As leaders or superiors, they did not take care of their followers or subordinates. As followers or subordinates, they were not respectful to their leaders or superiors. As friends, they were not trustworthy. As members of their communities, their actions were not righteous. As officials in royal courts, they did not adhere to the codes of conduct for government officials. As magistrates, they were not just and fair. These people's minds were confused, inverted, and lacked restraint. They committed regicide, or killed officials, and looked down on honored elders. They invaded other countries and robbed their citizens. They laid siege to cities, ruined forts, and plundered. Their evil karma was manifold. They praised themselves and belittled others, bullied and insulted the elders or orphans, falsely accused the worthies and virtuous ones, and bullied and deceived the lowly. Because of all such offenses committed, they receive these evil retributions.

At that time, upon hearing what the World-Honored One said, all those who suffered such retributions wept tears like rain and wailed so loud that the earth trembled. They pleaded with the Buddha, "We hope the World-Honored One dwells forever in the world and speaks Dharma to teach and transform us, so that we can be liberated."

The Buddha replied, "If I remain long in this world, those with scant blessings will not plant good roots, thinking that if I remain in the world forever, they need not be mindful of impermanence, and thus will commit boundless unwholesome acts. Later, they will regret, but it will be too late to make amends. Good men! It is just like an infant whose mother is always by his side he will take her for granted. If the mother goes away, then the child will miss and long for her. When the mother returns, then the child will be wholeheartedly happy. Good men! It is also the same for me. Knowing that beings' mind are not resolved on eternal Buddhahood, I therefore enter Nirvana."

At that time, the World-Honored One spoke this verse for those offenders:

> Ever-flowing water will not pool;
> Raging fire does not blaze long;
> The sun rises but soon sets;
> The moon waxes and wanes;
> Much more temperal are riches and honor.
> Those who possess them will find them impermanent.
> Be mindful of this and be ever vigorous.
> Reverently bow to the unsurpassed Honored Ones.

After the World-Honored One spoke this verse, all those laden with offenses sorrowfully asked, "World-Honored One, what wholesome deeds can living beings do to leave suffering far behind?"

The Buddha replied, "Good men! One should be filial and diligently take care of one's parents; respect and serve spiritual teachers, mentors and elders; take refuge with and serve the Three Treasures; diligently practice giving; uphold the precepts; practice patience and vigor; and cultivate samadhi, wisdom, kindness, compassion, joy, and equanimity. Regard all equally, be they friends or foes; do not deceive or take advantage of orphans or elders, nor despise the poor or lowly.

Instead, be as instinctively protective of others as you are concerned about yourself and do not give rise to thoughts of hatred. If you can practice in this way, then you are already repaying the kindness of the Buddhas and will forever leave the three evil paths and no longer undergo manifold suffering.

After the Buddha spoke this Sutra, the Bodhisattvas Mahasattvas immediately attained *Anuttara-samyak-sambodhi*. Hearers and Those Enlightened to Conditions immediately attained the six spiritual powers and the three clarities and became replete with the eight liberations. Other members of the assembly all attained the pure Dharma-eye. If living beings hear this Sutra, they will not fall into the three evil paths or eight places of difficulties, and if they are in the hells, the hells will cease to function, and they will receive respite from their pain and suffering.

Appearance of Faith Bodhisattva asked the Buddha, "World-Honored One, what should the name of this sutra be? How should Bodhisattvas Mahasattvas uphold this sutra?" The Buddha replied, "Good Man! It should be called *The Sutra of Karmic Offenses, Retributions, and Teaching and Transforming Hell Beings.* You should all revere and uphold this sutra, and widely spread it, thus creating boundless merit and virtue." At that time, when the great assembly heard this Dharma, they were single-mindedly joyful, accepted it, and respectfully practiced accordingly.

Today, we who are here in this Bodhimanda due to our shared karma, having heard what the Buddha said, should feel great fear. We should all now bring forth a mind of fear, a mind of kindness and compassion, and with the help of the Buddhas' power, practice the Bodhisattva Path. Mindful of the suffering in the hells, we bring forth the bodhi mind. Today, for all beings who are suffering in the hells, all beings who are suffering in the realm of hungry ghosts, all beings who are suffering in the realm of animals, including all other living beings suffering in the six paths, we bow wholeheartedly and repent for the sake of them all, wishing that all may be liberated. If we do not diligently practice changing calamities into blessings, we will then have a share of the offenses that leads to each and every hell.

Together we are mindful that our parents, teachers, elders, relatives, and retinues will suffer retributions in the future. Further, we ourselves too are now undergoing and will have to undergo such suffering. We bow in full prostration with heartfelt sincerity and diligence, willingly enduring pain and hardship. With a single thought may we evoke a response from the Buddhas of the ten directions, and with a single bow may we eradicate endless suffering. By the power of the Buddhas, the power of the Dharma, and the power of the sages and worthy ones, may living beings in the six paths who have been suffering attain liberation. By the power of the Buddhas, the power of the Dharma, and the power of the sages and worthy ones, may living beings who are due to undergo suffering avoid that suffering and attain liberation. From this day forth, may living beings definitely not fall into any evil path. May they have their three karmic obstacles eradicated and be reborn according to their wishes. May their five fears be extinguished so they may be liberated and at ease. May they diligently cultivate the Way without rest, be adorned by wonderful practices, surpass the Ground of the Dharma Cloud, enter the vajra mind[19] and accomplish Proper and Equal Enlightenment.

Today, we who are here in this Bodhimanda due to our shared karma, should again focus our minds and listen attentively. Contemplate well the following from the *Miscellaneous Store Sutra*. A ghost spoke to the Venerable Mahamaudgalyayana, saying, "My two shoulders have eyes and my chest has a mouth and a nose, yet I don't have a head. What offenses did I commit that resulted in such retribution?"

Venerable Mahamaudgalyayana replied, "In your past life, you often worked as an executioner. When executing people, your heart would well forth with joy as you tied their heads with ropes. Because of such causes and conditions, you receive this punishment, but this is only an intermediary retribution[20]; the eventual retribution will be in the hells."

Another ghost spoke to the Venerable Mahamaudgalyayana saying, "My body is like a lump of flesh without hands, feet, eyes, nose, and the like, and it is constantly pecked by birds or gnawed by worms, causing unbearable pain. What offenses did I commit that resulted in such retribution?"

Venerable Mahamaudgalyayana replied, "In your past life, you administered poison to cause abortions or miscarriages, killing fetuses. Because of such causes and conditions, you receive this punishment. But this is only your intermediary retribution; the eventual retribution will be in the hells."

Another ghost spoke to the Venerable Mahamaudgalyayana, saying, "My stomach is huge but my throat is as narrow as a needle. Throughout the years, I have been unable to eat any food. What offenses did I commit that resulted in such retribution?"

Venerable Mahamaudgalyayana replied, "In your past life, you were the chief of a community. You abused your position and wealth, indulged in alcohol and behaved without restraint, bullied and deceived people, robbing them of their food and leaving them in hunger and difficulty. Because of such causes and conditions, you receive this punishment. But this is only your intermediary retribution; the eventual retribution will be in the hells."

Another ghost spoke to Venerable Mahamaudgalyayana, saying, "I was born with two hot iron wheels under my armpits which burn my whole body. What offenses did I commit that resulted in such retribution?"

Venerable Mahamaudgalyayana replied, "In your past life, when you made pastries for the great assembly, you stole two, and hid them under your armpits. Because of such causes and conditions, you receive this punishment. But this is only your intermediary retribution; the eventual retribution will be in the hells."

Another ghost spoke to Venerable Mahamaudgalyayana, saying, "I always have my head shrouded, as I am greatly fearful that someone will come to kill me. What offenses did I commit that resulted in such retribution?"

Venerable Mahamaudgalyayana replied, "In your past life, you committed sexual misconduct and feared others would see you. You were afraid your spouse would catch, bind, hit, or kill you, so you were constantly in a state of fear. Because of these causes and conditions, you receive this punishment. But this is only your intermediary retribution; the eventual retribution will be in the hells."

Today, we are here in this Bodhimanda due to our shared karma. We should all feel fear after reading this sutra passage. From time without beginning until now, we have committed boundless offenses such as these because we lacked kindness and compassion. Consequently, we bullied and oppressed the weak, harmed living beings, and even robbed others of their property. We were confused and lost, slandered the good and worthy, and committed all kinds of offenses. With such offenses, we will definitely suffer the retributions of the evil paths.

With utmost, heartfelt sincerity, we now bow in full prostration and beseech the Buddhas for sympathy. We repent on behalf of all beings in the six paths, who already have undergone suffering, or who are due to undergo suffering. We also bow and repent on behalf of our parents, teachers, elders, and all relatives. Finally, we bow and repent for ourselves. May all the offenses that have been committed be eradicated, and may we commit no further offenses. Now we again take refuge with the Greatly Kind and Compassionate Ones who are like fathers to those of us in this world.

Namo Maitreya Buddha
Namo Shakyamuni Buddha
Namo Lotus Flower Honor and Abundance Buddha
Namo Pure Jewel Flourishing and Abundance Buddha
Namo Lightning Lamp Banner King Buddha
Namo Dharma Emptiness Lamp Buddha
Namo Accomplishing Multitudes of Virtue Buddha
Namo Virtuous Flag and Banner King Buddha

Namo Replete with Delicately Crafted and Colored Jewel
Buddha
Namo Severing Doubt, Uprooting Desire, and Dispelling Dark-
ness Buddha
Namo Fearless, No Hairs-standing-on-end Buddha
Namo Lion Buddha
Namo Far-reaching Renown Buddha
Namo Named-after-Dharma Buddha
Namo Reverently in Accord with Dharma Buddha
Namo Dharma Banner Buddha
Namo Sumeru Lamp Radiance Buddha
Namo Precious Treasury Adornment Buddha
Namo Chandana Mani-light Buddha
Namo Golden Sea Self-mastery King Buddha
Namo Greatly Compassionate Radiance King Buddha
Namo Supreme Utpala Lotus Buddha
Namo Lotus Stamen Adornment King Buddha
Namo Solid Vajra Self-mastery King Buddha
Namo Supreme Moon King Buddha
Namo King of Sunlight and Moonlight Buddha
Namo Great Strength Bodhisattva
Namo Ever-vigorous Bodhisattva
Namo Never Resting Bodhisattva
Namo Treasury of Empty Space Bodhisattva
Namo Boundless Body Bodhisattva
Namo Guan Shi Yin Bodhisattva

Again, we take refuge with the Three Treasures of the ten directions to the ends of empty space. May you, with your great kindness
and compassion, protect and rescue all beings in the six paths, now
suffering, or due to undergo suffering, enabling them to quickly attain
liberation. May you with your spiritual power eradicate all evil paths
and hell-bound karma, so that all living being, from now until attaining Buddhahood, will never fall into evil destinies. May all living

beings renounce their current retribution bodies and attain vajra bodies. May the four limitless minds[41] and the six paramitas always manifest before them. May they attain as-you-wish self mastery of the four eloquences and six spiritual powers. May they be courageously vigorous, not resting until they perfect cultivation of the Ten Grounds. May they then return to take across and liberate all living beings.

Praise

Learning of our mistakes and offenses,
We know retributions follow like shadows,
And unceasing create the cycles of rebirth.
Willingly we reveal our good and evil.
Shrouded in the soundless and hazy darkness,
May the Buddha's light illumine us.

Namo Bodhisattvas Mahasattvas of the Ground of Emitting Light

(three times)

Concluding the Repentance

The Buddha's hallmarks are lofty and radiant like a purple-golden mountain.
The Dharma sea is clear, tranquil, and bright like the silver moon in the sky.
Bodhisattvas, sages and worthy ones, receive offerings of gods and humans.
Pratyekabuddhas and Arthats speak Dharma in this and other worlds,
Like bright beacons for three thousand seas of worlds,
Like brilliant moons illuminating ten billion paths of darkness.
The profundity of their merit is beyond fathom;
The depth of their virtue is beyond measure.
They preside over the three realms,

Doing the Buddha's work throughout the three times.

[Dharma Host]: On behalf of _____ [those who seek to repent], we practice this Repentance Dharma of Kindness and Compassion in the Bodhimanda. We have now successfully completed Roll Three, accomplishing its merit and virtue.
We cultivate dhyana, entering and exiting the *three* times,
And with one mind constantly return to and rely on the *Three Treasures*.
We burn Five True Incenses[22] and scatter fresh flowers of the *three* spring months,
We offer dishes of wondrous delicacies and cups of fragrant teas.
Large bells and hand bells chime in harmony,
Issuing forth Brahma melodies, sonorous and wondrous.
Chanting and reciting, our meditative thoughts are clear and serene.
With sincere hearts we make all these offerings, and now complete this dedication of merit.

Amitabha Buddha in the Land of Ultimate Bliss, our Teaching Host Shakyamuni Buddha, Guan Yin Bodhisattva, Earth Store Bodhisattva, Arhats, Hearers, Worthy Eminent Ones in the heavens above and earth below, as well as those in the *three* realms:
May all of you rejoice in our efforts and bear witness to this superior merit;
May vigor sustain you and ward off weariness as you continually regard us with compassion;
May you render your protection over the multitudes of beings.
With these causes and conditions of infinite merit, we pray on behalf of _____ [those who seek to repent]:
May all sever the roots of the *three* poisons, and escape the net of the *three* realms.

We bow and earnestly pray:
May all be cleansed of the *three karmas* and accomplish the *three* doors of liberation, attain the sudden enlightenment of the *three-fold* emptiness and clearly understand the *three* non-outflow studies;
May all be forever free of the retributions of the *three* evil paths and be born into the family of the *Three* Treasures;
May all realize the sudden enlightenment of the threefold emptiness with regard to body and mind;
May all be liberated from the *three* hindrances.
May all perfect the fruition within *three* asamkhyeya kalpas;
May all accomplish the merit of the *threefold* enlightenment;
May all practitioners of the *three* vehicles become sages and worthy ones, and
May all of the *three* existences share this benefit and happiness.
[Dharma host]: We may have performed the Repentance but fear we have not been sincere enough. Thus I am taking the liberty to request that together, we continue to repent and reform.

Praise

The meritorious power of the Emperor of Liang Repentance Roll Three
Enables the deceased and the disciples to eradicate three-poison offenses
May all realize the Bodhisattva's Ground of Emitting Light
As the Repentance is chanted our offenses are blown away like flower petals in the wind.
Enmity resolved, offenses eradicated,
Wisdom and blessing increase as calamities are dispelled.
Liberated from suffering and reborn in the Trayastrimsha,
May we gather at the Dragon Flower's Three Assemblies
And receive a prediction personally from Maitreya Buddha.

Namo Dragon Flower Assembly of Bodhisattvas Mahasattvas

(three times)

Final Praise

Emperor of Liang Repentance Roll Three now concludes.
We dedicate its merit to the four benefactors and the three realms.
May all in this assembly enjoy increased longevity and blessings,
May the Dharma water cleanse our offenses.
May the deceased be reborn in the Western Pure Land.
May the Bodhisattvas of the Ground of Emitting Light compassion-
ately gather us in.

Namo Ascending the Path to the Clouds Bodhisattva Mahasattva

(three times)

End Notes

1. **Udumbara flowers:** *Udumbara* flowers refer to the Buddha's teaching and sutras. The *udumbara* flowers blossom from the legendary *udumbara* tree which, according to legend, blooms only once every 3,000 years. They are exceptionally rare and symbolize the rarity of a Buddha's appearance in the world.
2. **Three kinds of transformation bodies:** the dharma body, the retribution body, and the response body. The dharma body refers to the true wondrous nature. The retribution body refers to the manifestation body that Buddha uses to communicate in this ordinary world. The response body refers to the transformation bodies that the Buddha uses to accord with the needs of all living beings and manifests in various bodies accordingly.
3. **Three carts:** This refers to three kinds of teachings. a) The goat cart refers to the teaching for sound hearers. b) The deer cart refers to the teaching for Bodhisattvas. c) The ox cart refers to the teaching of ultimate Buddhahood.
4. **Three contemplations:** contemplation of all as void, contemplation of all as unreal, and contemplation of all as non-void

and not unreal, which is the Buddha's state of emptiness. Alternatively, it may be said as contemplation of emptiness, contemplation of falseness, and the contemplation of non-emptiness and non-falseness.

5. **Three thousand great thousand worlds:** It is the combination of three kinds of thousand world systems. One thousand worlds come together to form a small world system. One thousand small world systems come together to form a medium world system. One thousand medium worlds come together to form a great world system. Since there are three numbers of a thousand, so it is called the three thousand world system.

6. **Three poisons:** greed, hatred, and stupidity.

7. **Three evil paths:** the hell realm, the hungry ghost realm, and the animal realm.

8. **Three delusions:** view delusion, thought delusion, and delusions as many as dust and sand, which refers to the final delusion of a Bodhisattva.

9. **Three karmas:** Karma that is created from body, mouth, and mind. Or good karma, bad karma, and the karma that is neither good nor bad.

10. **Desire realm:** The lowest realm among the three realms of existence, in which beings are characterized by their thirst for sensual pleasures.

11. *Niraya* **Hell:** transliteration of the Sanskrit, meaning joyless hell.

12. **Upasakas:** laymen who follow and are devoted to the teachings of Buddhism.

13. **Upasikas:** laywomen who follow and are devoted to the teachings of Buddhism.

14. **Three clarities:** clarity of the heavenly eye, clarity of past lives, and clarity of exhaustion of outflows. Clarity means understanding or wisdom.

15. **Six spiritual powers or six penetrations:** penetration of the heavenly eye, penetration of the heavenly ear, the penetration

of past lives, penetration of other's thought, penetration of the extinction of outflows, penetration of the complete spirit.

16. **Ingenious wind:** It is said that after one falls into hell, one suffers greatly and dies. There is a kind of wind that revives the offender in hell so that he receives the same suffering over and over again.

17. **Guiding and Teaching Bodhisattvas Buddha:** Could also be interpreted as Buddha who in a past life was a Bodhisattva who guided and taught.

18. **Five fears:**
    a) Fear of not being able to survive (after having donated everything)
    b) Fear of having a bad reputation
    c) Fear of death
    d) Fear of falling into the evil paths
    e) Fear of facing the great assembly

19. **Vajra mind:** A term for the state of the final stage of the Bodhisattva's Ten Grounds, also known as the adamantine absorption, the diamond-mind, or adamantine mind. The hardness and sharpness of vajra as metaphor for the wisdom of the Bodhisattva, which penetrates everything and is incorruptible.

20. **Intermediary retribution:** Literally: flower retribution, as the flower is the intermediary stage before the fruit, the final retribution.

21. **Four limitless minds:** mind of unlimited kindness, mind of unlimited compassion, mind of unlimited joy, and mind of unlimited renunciation.

22. **Five true incenses:** precept incense, samadhi incense, wisdom incense, liberation incense, liberation of knowledge of view incense.

ROLL FOUR

Namo Buddhas and Bodhisattvas of the Dragon Flower Assembly
(*bow three times*)

Praise

> *Caoxi's water carries the lineage eastward.*
> *Guanyin's sweet dew eradicates all calamities;*
> *It anoints the crown, purifying all defilements,*
> *Moistening withered plants wherever the willow sprinkles.*
> *The throat is nourished by the sweet dew,*
> *Ever-refreshing is the flavor of this nectar.*

Namo Universal Offering Bodhisattva Mahasattva (*three times*)

Listen respectfully

His wondrous embodying of the perfect and bright *four* wisdoms[1]
Makes him as majestic as the clear moon among the stars.
With his unobstructed and profound *four* eloquences[2] he has proclaimed;
Through many kalpas the superb teachings in Emptiness.
The *four* minds[3] are applied amidst the *four* evil paths[4],
The *four* marks[5] are transcended within the *four* births[6].
We have great faith in the expansiveness of the Buddha's kindness, and gaze upwards in admiration of the ever-increasing loftiness of the sages' virtue. May the Greatly Enlightened One bear witness to our sincerity.

[Dharma Host]: On behalf of _____ [those who seek to repent], we practice this Repentance Dharma of Kindness and Compassion in the Bodhimanda. We have come to Roll Four. With all conditions fulfilled, we now enter the Repentance Platform.

The entire assembly of the *four* siddhantas[7] in accord with the *four* deportments, body upright and mind focused, prostrate with utmost sincerity. We offer vases of spring flowers from the three islands, burn *six* measures of exquisite incense forming a cloud canopy, and light the lamp ablaze with the flames of wisdom. We make these sincere offerings emulating Cunda[8]. We bow in reverence and circumambulate; we extol and praise; we confess with earnestness, and repent with great diligence.

We are earnestly mindful that from many kalpas past until the present, we have been deluded by this body composed of *four* elements, revolving in the retributions of *four* births. Entertaining the four marks with our inverted minds, we violate the *four* major precepts and deportment. We drift from delusion to delusion; we plunge from one suffering into another. We are blown adrift by the 'winds' of of circumstances, both favorable and unfavorable, until we become submerged, drowning in the ocean of emotional love. Our ignorance is so heavy and deep; our afflictions are as sticky as glue and paint. By relying on the proclamation of the Great Dharma and the delineation of the Truths, we believe that we can attain great liberation. Our hearts become filled with joy that penetrates to our very bones and marrow; our every cell tingles with delight. In the presence of the assembly of the greatly virtuous ones, we now focus our minds to commence the repentance. May you, out of your great kindness, invisibly bless and protect us.

> With his thirty-two hallmarks, dignified, wondrous and subtle,
> Attained through three asamkheya kalpas' cultivation,
> His countenance is like the full moon, his eyes like lotuses.
> He is admired and revered in the world and the heavens.

Commencement of the Repentance

We now begin the Repentance Dharma of Kindness and Compassion in the Bodhimanda. Together in this assembly, we single-mindedly return to and rely on all Buddhas of the three periods of time.

Namo Buddhas of the past, Vipashyin Buddha
Namo Shikhin Buddha
Namo Vishvabhu Buddha
Namo Krakucchanda Buddha
Namo Kanakamuni Buddha
Namo Kashyapa Buddha
Namo our Fundamental Teacher Shakyamuni Buddha
Namo Honored Future Buddha, Maitreya

Section 7 Continuing to Reveal Retributions

Today, we are here in this Bodhimanda due to our shared karma. Let us bring forth utmost sincerity and listen attentively. The Buddha once dwelt in Rajagrha, at Karanda's bamboo grove. At that time, Venerable Mahamaudgalyayana came out of samadhi, and as he walked along the Ganges River bank, he saw many hungry ghosts suffering because of various offenses. At that time, each hungry ghost came to Venerable Mahamaudgalyayana and respectfully asked about the causes and conditions of their individual past lives.

One ghost said, "I have had to endure constant hunger and thirst throughout this lifetime and have had to eat excrement from the toilet. A ghost with great strength from the toilet lashes out at me with his whip in order to prevent me from entering. What offense have I committed to receive such retribution?"

Venerable Mahamaudgalyayana replied, "In the past, when you were an abbot in a monastery, a guest monk came to your monastery and asked for food. Because of stinginess, you refused to share with him. When the guest monk left, you divided all the food with the resident Sangha members. The consequence of the improper method in which you handled the food of the eternally dwelling has led to your current retribution. But this is just an intermediary retribution. Your major retribution will be in the hells."

Another ghost asked Venerable Mahamaudgalyayana, "Ever since birth, I have been shouldering a big copper jar filled with molten copper. I scoop it out and pour it over my head, causing me unbearable pain. What offense have I committed to receive such retribution?"

Venerable Mahamaudgalyayana replied, "You were the cantor in charge of the affairs of the monastery. However, you hid a bottle of ghee and did not share it with the assembly at the proper time. Only after all the guest monks had left did you take it out to share with the resident Sangha members. That ghee was the property of the Sangha of the ten directions, so every monastic should have gotten an equal share. Because you lacked principle and were stingy in handling the affairs of the great assembly, you receive such retribution. But this is only an intermediary retribution; the major retribution will be in the hells."

Another ghost asked Venerable Mahamaudgalyayana, "Ever since birth, I have been swallowing hot iron pellets. What offense have I committed to receive such retribution?"

Venerable Mahamaudgalyayana replied, "When you were a novice in your past life, one of your chores was to prepare drinks from rock sugar. The rock sugar looked so large and solid, that you were tempted to steal some. You cracked a small portion and ate one mouthful before it was served to the assembly. Because of such a cause and its conditions, you receive this punishment. But this is only your intermediary retribution; the major retribution will be in the hells."

Today, we are here in this Bodhimanda due to our shared karma. Because of what Venerable Mahamaudgalyayana had seen, we should be greatly fearful. We might have all committed similar offenses in the past, but because of ignorance, we have forgotten about them. If we had committed any of the immeasurable offenses, we will definitely have to suffer retributions like these. Therefore, let us all today, feeling shame and remorse, bring forth the mind of utmost sincerity and bow in full prostration to repent, beseeching for such offenses to be eradicated.

Also, we universally repent for the sake of all hungry ghosts of the ten directions throughout empty space, for the sake of our parents and teachers, for the sake of our ordination certifying masters and fellow monastics of the three seniorities, for the sake of good and bad advisors, including also all immeasurable living beings of the four births and the six paths of the ten directions. Through this repentance, may all these past offenses be eradicated; may no one dare commit such offenses in the future. We look up to the Buddhas of the ten directions and bow in homage.

Namo Maitreya Buddha
Namo Shakyamuni Buddha
Namo Krakucchanda Buddha
Namo Kanakamuni Buddha
Namo Kashyapa Buddha
Namo Lion Buddha
Namo Bright Light Buddha
Namo Mani Buddha
Namo Wonderful Flower Buddha
Namo Flower Family Buddha
Namo Dwelling in Goodness Buddha
Namo Guiding Master Buddha
Namo Great Arms Buddha
Namo Great Strength Buddha
Namo Constellation King Buddha
Namo Concocting Medicine Buddha
Namo Name and Mark Buddha
Namo Great Brilliance Buddha
Namo Blazing Shoulders Buddha
Namo Illumination Buddha
Namo Sun Treasury Buddha

Namo Moon Family Buddha
Namo Multitudes of Flames Buddha
Namo Wholesome Brightness Buddha
Namo Worry-free Buddha
Namo Lion Playfully Roaming Bodhisattva
Namo Lion Swiftness and Vigor Bodhisattva
Namo Boundless Body Bodhisattva
Namo Guan Shi Yin Bodhisattva
Namo Buddha
Namo Dharma
Namo Sangha

Again, we take refuge with the Three Treasures of the ten directions to the ends of space. May you with your great kindness and compassion save all beings now suffering in the realm of hungry ghosts throughout the ten directions. May you also save all living beings throughout the ten directions who are now in the realms of hells, animals, and humans and free them from countless suffering, so that they can be liberated. May their three karmic obstacles [9] and five fears be eradicated. May they gain the eight liberations [10] to purify their mind and make the four great vows [11] to rescue all beings. May they then be able to reverently receive the wonderful Dharma directly from the Buddha and end all outflows without removing themselves from whatever situation they are in. Thereafter, may they widely travel to all Buddhalands in spontaneous response to the thoughts of beings. May they quickly perfect their vows and practices and accomplish Proper Enlightenment.

Today, we who are here in this Bodhimanda due to our shared karma should again bring forth utmost sincerity and listen attentively. The Buddha once stayed in the city of Rajagrha. In the southeastern part of that city was a pond with an extremely foul stench, filled with excrement and urine. A huge creature without limbs, several meters long, lived in that pond and crawled around within it. Thousands of people came to see it. After seeing this,

Venerable Ananda reported it to the Buddha, who then brought the assembly to the pond. Members of the assembly anticipated that the Buddha would explain the causes and conditions of the creature.

The Buddha said, "After the Nirvana of Vipashyin Buddha, there was a monastery with stupas dedicated to this Buddha. One day five hundred bhikshus passed by this monastery. The abbot there joyfully invited them to stay and whole-heartedly made generous offerings of food without withholding any. Shortly thereafter, five hundred merchants, who had been treasure-hunting in the sea, also came by the monastery. Seeing the five hundred bhikshus diligently practicing the Way, they were inspired, and happily had a discussion, considering this a rare opportunity to plant blessings. They decided that each of them should make an offering, and each gave a mani-pearl, totaling five hundred mani-pearls in all. They entrusted these pearls to the abbot as an offering to the five hundred bhikshus However, the abbot had the unwholesome thought of keeping the pearls for himself instead of distributing them among the bhikshus.

When the assembly of the five hundred bhikshus asked the abbot, "Those merchants donated the pearls to us. Can you distribute them to us?"

The abbot replied, "These pearls were given to me. If you insist that I give them to you, I will only give you excrement instead. You'd better leave now or I shall cut off your hands and feet and throw them into the cesspool."

Upon hearing the abbot's words, the monks could only feel pity for his ignorance, and all left quietly. Because of such an offense, the abbot received the retribution of being a worm. Later, he will fall into the hells and undergo a multitude of suffering."

When the Buddha was in the city of Rajagrha, there was a being with a huge tongue that was blazing and pierced with nails, suffering tremendously throughout the day and night. Venerable Mahamaudgalyayana asked about the causes and conditions of such retribution.

The Buddha replied, "In this being's past life, as the abbot of a monastery, he cursed and chased away both guest and resident bhikshus, and refused to give them food or their fair share of the donors' offerings. Because of these causes and conditions, this being suffers such retributions."

There was another being with a huge body and a burning cauldron on top his head which continuously overflowed with molten copper, burning and scalding his body. He ceaselessly ran about in desperate search of respite. Venerable Mahamaudgalyayana asked about the causes and conditions of such retribution.

The Buddha replied, "This living being used to manage the affairs of a monastery. He did not share the donors' offering of oil with the guest monks, but waited for them to leave before sharing it with the resident monks. Because of these causes and conditions, this being suffers such retributions."

Another living being constantly suffered from burning iron pellets that entered his body from the top and exited from the bottom. He ran about in desperate search of respite from the unbearable pain. Venerable Mahamaudgalyayana asked about the causes and conditions of such painful retribution.

The Buddha replied, "In his past life, he was a novice who stole seven pieces of fruit from the garden of his monastery. After his death, he fell into the hells and suffered immeasurable pain. Because there were still karmic debts left to settle, he now suffers this retribution."

There was another big fish with hundreds of different kinds of heads on his body that got caught in a fisherman's net. Upon seeing this, the World-Honored One entered the kindness samadhi to call to the fish which instantly responded.

The World-Honored One asked the fish, "Where is your mother now?" The fish replied, "My mother is a worm in the toilet."

The Buddha then said to the bhikshus, "This fish was a Tripitaka master when Kashyapa Buddha dwelt in the world. Because of violating the precept against harsh speech, he received the retribution of being born with many heads on his body. As for his mother who received from him the offerings meant for the monastics, she is now undergoing the retribution of being a worm in the toilet."

The Buddha said, "The living beings who received the aforementioned retributions, committed the offenses of harsh speech, coarse speech, and divisive speech, stirring up discord and contention between parties, so they fell into the hells after their death. The hell guardians burn their tongues with red-hot iron tools, hooked and cut off their tongues with fiery triple-bladed iron hooks, and plowed through their tongues. Moreover, the guards used red hot iron pestles to pierce their throats. Passing through millions of kalpas to resolve their karmic debts in the hells, they are then reborn in the animal realm."

The Buddha continued, "If one speaks ill of one's rulers, parents, elders, and teachers, one commits even more serious offenses than the ones mentioned above."

Today, we are here in this Bodhimanda due to our shared karma. Hearing what the Buddha has said, we should be greatly fearful. We can now, without any doubt, clearly see the two paths of good and evil and understand their corresponding rewards of blessings and retributions for offenses. We should therefore make every effort and diligently practice the repentance.

As we together read and chant these sutra passages in the repentance text, we all clearly learn about these retributions. If we do not apply effort, and even worse, if we begin to be lax and retreat, how can we possibly benefit from our present repentance? It is just like a needy person who is hungry fantasizing about enjoying the hundreds of gourmet flavors; these thoughts do not help lessen his afflictions of hunger at all. So we should know that if we wish to seek the supremely wonderful Dharma and to take beings across, we cannot merely think about it. Since we already have the aspiration, we should strive to diligently put it into practice.

Let us all bring forth firm resolve and heartfelt earnestness, bow in full prostration and repent on behalf of all beings in the paths of hells, hungry ghosts, animals, and humans. We also bow and repent on behalf of our parents, good and bad advisors, relatives, and ourselves. May this repentance eradicate all our past offenses and prevent us from committing such offenses in the future. We look up to and bow to you, the Greatly Kind and Compassionate Ones who are like fathers to those of us in this world.

Namo Maitreya Buddha
Namo Shakyamuni Buddha
Namo Tisya Buddha
Namo Dazzling Brilliance Buddha
Namo Holding Garlands Buddha
Namo Brilliance of Merit and Virtue Buddha
Namo Explaining Principles Buddha
Namo Dazzling Lamps Buddha
Namo Flourishing and Prosperous Buddha
Namo Medicine Master Buddha
Namo Skillful Nurturing Buddha
Namo White Curl Buddha
Namo Steadfast Buddha
Namo Blessings and Awe-inspiring Virtue Buddha
Namo Indestructible Buddha
Namo Hallmarks of Virtue Buddha
Namo Rahu Buddha
Namo Master of the Multitudes Buddha
Namo Brahma Sound Buddha
Namo Solid Boundary Buddha
Namo Untowering Buddha
Namo Brilliant Practice Buddha
Namo Great Mountain Buddha
Namo Vajra Buddha
Namo Leading the Multitudes Buddha
Namo Fearless Buddha
Namo Precious Jewels Buddha
Namo Lion Banner Bodhisattva
Namo Lion Deed Bodhisattva
Namo Boundless Body Bodhisattva
Namo Guan Shi Yin Bodhisattva

Again, we take refuge with the Three Treasures of the ten directions to the ends of empty space. May you, with your power of kindness and compassion, power of great wisdom, power of inconceivable strength, and power of self-mastery, take across all living beings and eradicate all suffering in the six paths. May all living beings cut off the karmic offenses of the three evil paths, so they will no longer commit any of the five rebellious acts or the ten evil deeds. From this day forth, we will relinquish rebirths characterized by retributions full of suffering, and be reborn in the pure land. We will relinquish our life characterized by retributions full of suffering and gain a wisdom life. We will relinquish this body characterized by retributions full of suffering and gain a vajra body. We will relinquish the agony of the evil paths and gain the bliss of Nirvana. We will be mindful of the suffering of the evil paths and bring forth the bodhi resolve. We will always be mindful of the four limitless minds[12] and practice the six paramitas[13]. We shall attain the four eloquences and the six spiritual powers[14] to fulfill as-you-wish self-mastery. We will cultivate courageously and vigorously without rest until we perfect the Ten Grounds and are able to take all living beings across.

Section 8 Exiting the Hells

Today, we are here in this Bodhimanda due to our shared karma. We should know that although there are myriad dharma categories with various functions, they do not go beyond the two categories of good and evil, contrasting like light and darkness. So if we discuss goodness, there are the superior rewards of heavenly beings and humans; and if we discuss evil, there are the three evil paths with their dire retributions. Even though the manifestations of good and evil deeds in the world are always clear and never false, still the deluded and ignorant often harbor suspicion and deviant theories. They argue that rewards of humans and heavenly beings are mere fabrications and retributions of hells are non-truths.

They fail to verify their present retributions through inference of past causes; nor do they try to discover their past causes by examining their present retributions. Since they do not understand clearly cause and effect, they insist on their own mundane views, talking about emptiness, existence, and also writing essays or articles about them. Thus they turn their backs on supreme goodness and never feel that their views may be wrong. Even when they are taught the proper teachings, they become ever more stubborn in holding on to their own views. With the swiftness of an arrow shot from a bow, such people will plunge into the evil paths and throw themselves into the hells; neither their compassionate parents nor their filial children can save them. Thus, they cannot help but head directly towards the fiery cauldrons of the hells, where they are broiled till their bodies and minds are shattered, and their spirits endure horrendous suffering. By then, it will be too late to repent!

Today, we are here in this Bodhimanda due to our shared karma. We should understand that good and evil coexist like echoes and shadows, capitalizing on each other. It is all just a matter of time; rewards and retributions await each being in different destinies. We hope that the assembly will have faith and clear understanding in this and not give rise to doubt.

What are the hells? The sutras state, "Hells are in a dark space between two great Iron Ring Mountains of the Three Thousand Great Thousand Worlds. The dimensions of the hells are each sixteen million miles[15] and within the hell-city there are eighty-four thousand sections. The city is covered with an iron-net above, and its ground is made of iron. The whole city is ablaze, with flames surging upwards and flaring downwards, making it red hot inside and out.

"The hells have different names, such as Crushing and Squeezing, Pitch Darkness, Forest of Swords, Wheels of Blades, Forest of Thorns, Iron Traps, Iron Nets, Iron Caverns, Iron Pellets, Sharp Stone, Charcoal Pits, Burning Forests, Tigers and Wolves, Howling and Screaming, Cauldron of Seething Broth, Stove of Glowing Coals, Tree of Swords, Mountain of Blades, Fiery Mills, Flaming Cities, Copper Pillars, Iron Beds, Fire Carts, Fiery Wheels, Swallowing Molten Copper, Spurting

Fire, Extreme Blazing Heat, Extreme Freezing Cold, Pulling Tongues, Nailing the Body, Plowing, Chopping and Cutting, Military Weaponry, Slaughter and Dismembering, River of Ash, Boiling Excrement, Freezing Ice, Mired in Mud, Ignorance and Delusion, Wailing, Deaf-Blind-Mute, Iron Hook, and Iron Mouth. Furthermore, there are many other hells, big and small, as well as the *Avici* Hell."

The Buddha told Ananda, "How did *Avici* get its name? 'A' means no; '*vici*' means discriminating. 'A' means no; '*vici*' means rescue. So *Avici* means without discriminating and without rescue. Also 'A' means uninterrupted or intermittent; '*vici*' means unmoving. 'A' means extremely hot; '*vici*' means extremely afflicted. 'A' means no pausing; '*vici*' means no stopping. So *Avici* Hell means without pausing or stopping. 'A' means great flame; '*vici*' means severely hot. So *Avici* Hell means the hell where severe heat pierces one's heart."

The Buddha told Ananda, "Each dimension of the *Avici* Hell measures three hundred and twenty thousand miles. Within that hell, there are seven layers of iron walls and seven layers of iron netting. In its vertical dimension, there are eighteen layers of sub-hells, each of which is surrounded by seven layers of forests of blades and forests of swords. Within each of the eighteen layers of sub-hells, there are eighty-four thousand cells. There is a copper dog at each of the four corners of the *Avici* Hell. Their bodies measure sixteen thousand miles long; their eyes are like lightning bolts; their fangs are like trees of swords and their molar teeth are like mountains of blades; their tongues are like iron thorns. Blazing fire rages forth from each strand of their hair, and the smoke gives off the foulest stench in the world.

"There are eighteen hell-guardians whose heads are like those of rakshasas, and whose mouths are like those of yakshas. Each has sixty-four eyes blasting out iron pellets, shaped like ten-mile carts. Their hooked teeth protrude one hundred and sixty miles. Flames shoot out from the tips of their teeth, burning the iron carts before them and turning each of the rims of their wheels into ten million fiery blades such as sharp knives, swords, and halberds that shoot forth from within the flames.

"All these fires burn the *Avici* Hell, making it as red-hot as molten copper. On the head of each hell-guardian are eight ox heads, and each ox head has eighteen horns. Each horn emits a fire ball which turns into eighteen fiery rims of a wheel. Each rim turns into a great wheel of blades, as big as a carriage wheel; each wheel of blades is close to the next and rolls in continuous succession, pervading the *Avici* Hell.

"When the copper dogs open their mouths, they stick out their tongues, which are like iron-spiked tongues and which reach the ground. As soon as their tongue is stuck out, countless more iron spike tongues manifest, pervading the entire *Avici* Hell. Within the seven layers of walls are seven iron flagpoles. Flames flare forth from the top of the flagpoles, like a boiling spring. Molten iron gushes everywhere, pervading the *Avici* Hell.

"The *Avici* Hell has four gates. At each threshold are eighteen boiling cauldrons brimming over with molten copper, flowing from the gates and flooding the *Avici* Hell. In each of the cells, there are eighty-four thousand huge iron pythons pervading the entire *Avici* Hell. They spew forth fire and poison and roar with thunder-like sounds. Huge iron pellets also rain down over the entire *Avici* Hell. There are eighty millions of billions of types of bitterness in this hell, within which each and every kind of extreme bitter torment converges. There are also fifty billion worms, each with eighty-four thousand mouths, from which fire rains down over the entire *Avici* Hell. When such worms descend, the entire hell is filled with a great fire illuminating three million three hundred sixty thousand square miles. This red-hot fire shoots up from the *Avici* Hell to the great ocean above, which covers Mount Patala, causing huge drops of ocean water, as big as carriage axles, to rain down in the form of sharp iron spikes all over the *Avici* Hell."

The Buddha told Ananda, "A living being who harms or kills his parents or insults and maliciously berates his six relatives will see such manifestations of the hells when he is dying: Copper dogs with open mouths, from which appear eighteen golden transformation carts topped with glistening canopies of fire. The flames of fire then turn into beautiful maidens. Upon seeing these maidens from afar, the offender feels elated and thinks, 'I want to be with them! I want to be with them!' Meanwhile, he suffers disintegration as a wind cuts his body like slicing blades. Chilled to the bone, he cannot help but scream desperately, 'I need fire! I want to sit in the cart among those maidens, even if it means I will be burned to a crisp.' With this single thought his life ends. Instantaneously, he is already seated in the golden cart, gazing admiringly at the maidens, only to see them wield iron axes and cut up his body. At the same time, fire surges up from underneath his body like a turning wheel of fire, and in an instant, quick as a mighty warrior's thrust, he falls into the *Avici* Hell. His body plummets, like a spiraling flame; his spirit descends all the way down, passing from the upper levels to the lowest level, where his body fills the entire space. At this time, the copper dogs bark and howl, crunch his bones and eat his marrow. The rakshasa hell-guardians wield huge iron pitchforks, forking the offender's head and lifting him up. Fire spews forth, burns his body and engulfs the entire hell. From an iron net, knives rain down, piercing the offender's pores.

King Yama appears in his transformation body and reads aloud his sentence, 'You idiot! You hell being! You were unfilial to your parents, arrogant, deviant, and lacked virtue! You are now reborn in the *Avici* Hell. You did not know to repay kindness and lacked a sense of shame and remorse. Now you are suffering. Do you enjoy it?' After saying this, King Yama instantly disappears.

At that time the hell-guardians drive the offender from the lowest level of the hell to the uppermost level of the hell, the offender being squeezed through eighty-four thousand levels until he reaches the iron net boundary. Through all these, within a single day and night, he undergoes each and every kind of suffering of the hells, and his lifespan there is one great kalpa. One day there equals sixty small kalpas in Jambudvipa.

One who commits any of the five rebellious acts and is devoid of shame and remorse will, at the end of his life, have his body cut and sliced by the eighteen kinds of wind-knives, which are as fast and furious as a fiery iron cart racing through.

Oppressed by such suffocating heat, the offender says, "Wouldn't it be wonderful to be playing under the cool shade of a big tree with beautiful flowers?"

With this thought, right before the offender's eyes, a forest of eighty-four thousand swords in the *Avici* Hell suddenly turns into an orderly-array of jeweled trees, each full of fruit and flowers. Under each tree, each intensely scorching flame turns into a lotus flower. Seeing this, the offender thinks that his wish has come true. As soon as he has this thought, with the speed of a raging tempest, he finds himself seated on one of the lotuses. Instantly, worms with iron mouths pop out of the lotus flower and drill into offender's bone and marrow, boring through his heart and brain. Because of this, he climbs onto the trees but all the swords slice his flesh and bone. A rain of myriads of knives showers down from above, and eighteen different kinds of punishments, such as fire carts and stoves of glowing coals simultaneously converge upon him. When this happens, the offender falls to the ground of the lowest level of the hell, and his body pervades the whole lowest level of the hell like a blossoming flower. At the same time, the flaming fire blazes from the lowest all the way through to the uppermost level of the hell, where his body also pervades the entire space. Oppressed by the heat, he desperately opens his eyes wide and sticks out his tongue. Because of his offenses, millions of billions of tons of molten copper and hundreds of thousands of wheels of blades rain down, entering his head and exiting his feet. His other multitudes of tormenting agony are hundreds of thousands of millions of times greater than those mentioned above. Those who commit all the five rebellious acts have to suffer a total of five kalpas in the hells.

Furthermore, there are living beings who break the precepts, fail to use donors' offerings properly, slander the Dharma, and give rise to deviant views. Ignorant of cause and effect, they cut off others' study of Prajna, slander, damage or ruin Buddhism, steal the property of a monastery, indulge in defiled thoughts and engage in acts of impurity. They have no sense of shame, bring disgrace upon their parents and relatives, and commit all other types of evil deeds. The retributions for these beings would be: At end of their lives, as they experience disintegration with wind cutting their bodies like slicing blades, they become restless, ill at ease in any position and feel like they are being flogged or clubbed. Lost and confused, they become crazy and delusional. They see the young and old, male and female, and everything, including their homes, all mired in a stinking swamp of urine and excrement, which ooze from their houses.

At this time, the offender asks, 'Why am I here? There are no beautiful cities, mountains, and trees for me to enjoy! Instead, I am mired in such filth.' After saying that, he is forked into the *Avici* Hell by the rakshasa hell-guradian with a great iron pitchfork, where the forests of blades transform into jeweled trees and cool ponds. The flames turn into lotus flowers with golden leaves. The iron-mouthed worms turn into wild ducks and geese and the woeful cries in the hells sound like hymns and songs. Upon hearing this, the offender thinks this is such a wonderful place to stroll around. Instantly with this thought, he finds himself sitting on the fiery lotus and the iron-mouthed worms gnaw his body, starting from the pores. Hundreds of thousands of iron wheels descend and saw through him him from top to bottom. Iron forks, numerous as sand grains in the Ganges River, gouge out his eyes. The copper dogs of the hell turn into hundreds of millions of iron dogs, each rushing to tear apart his body and devour his heart. Instantly, his body turns into iron flowers pervading all the eighteen levels of hell; each flower has eighty-four thousand leaves; on the tip of each leaf are his body and limbs. While at that level, he perceives that the hell is not big and his body is not small and pervades the entire hell.

The offenders have to undergo such retribution in this hell for eighty-four thousand great kalpas. When this *Avici* Hell perishes, he further undergoes similar retributions in the eighteen levels of the *Avici* Hell in the east. There are also *Avici* Hells in the south, west and north, each of which has eighteen levels. Those offenders who committed offenses, such as slandering the Mahayana sutras, committing the five rebellious acts, berating the sages and worthy ones, thus severing roots of goodness, will find their bodies pervading the entire *Avici* Hell, their limbs also pervading throughout all the eighteen levels. The *Avici* Hell serves to burn these hell-bound beings.

As the kalpa comes to its end, the eastern gate opens. Outside the gate, clear springs with flowing water, flowers, fruits, and trees manifest. When the offenders see this scene from the lower level of the hell, the fire in their eyes ceases temporarily. They then crawl on their belly from the lower levels, squeezing through to the upper level, where their hands grab a wheel of blades and at that time, hot iron pellets rain down from empty space, causing the offenders to dash to the eastern gate. At the threshold of that gate, the rakshasa hell guardians pierce their eyes with iron pitchforks while copper dogs bite and tear their hearts, and the offenders faint and die. They immediately revive and see the southern gate open with an identical scene. They then undergo the same retribution as that at the eastern gate. The same process is repeated at the western and northern gates. The whole process spans a period of a half kalpa.

After suffering in the *Avici* Hell, the offenders will be reborn in the Hell of Freezing Ice. Subsequently, the offenders will be born in a pitch-dark place, remaining there for eighty million years without being able to see. During that period, they will be reborn as a huge snake-like creature, slithering about, blind and ignorant of what is going on. Hundreds of thousands of wolves and foxes seize them, drag them, and devour them. After that retribution, the offenders will be again reborn in the animal realm as a bird or beast for the next fifty million years. When this retribution is over, they will be reborn in the human realm, deaf, blind, mute, covered with sores, impoverished, and low in social status, beset by all manner of misfortune and sickness. After being in such abysmal conditions for five hundred lifetimes, they will be reborn in the hungry ghost realm, where the fortunate ones will encounter great Bodhisattvas and other good advisors.

The great Bodhisattvas admonish them, saying, 'In your past lives, you committed immeasurable offenses, such as disbelieving or slandering the Three Treasures, so you fell into the *Avici* Hell to undergo indescribable suffering. You should now bring forth the resolve of kindness and compassion!'

Upon hearing these words, the hungry ghosts together recite, 'Homage to Buddha.' By the power of the Buddhas' kindness, their lives immediately end, and they are born in the Heaven of Four Heavenly Kings. After rebirth in the heavens, they repent remorsefully, self-reprimand and bring forth the bodhi resolve. Thus, Buddhas, who never give up on these beings, illuminate and gather them in, regarding them like the Buddha regarded his only son Rahula, teaching them to avoid falling into the hells, caring for these beings as if caring for their own eyes.

The Buddha told the great king, "You should know that the Buddha's mind is the mind that is constantly illuminating all living beings and saving all the suffering and helpless. The Buddha's mind constantly reaches out to extremely evil beings, hoping that the power of the Buddha's mind will be a positive influence on these beings, and that they will be able to bring to bring forth the bodhi resolve, irrespective of the number of kalpas needed."

Today, we are here in this Bodhimanda due to our shared karma. Having heard all the suffering mentioned by the Buddha, we should concentrate our minds and not be slack. If we still do not diligently practice the Bodhisattva Path, then we will still have our share of offenses that will bring retributions in each and every hell. On behalf of all beings who are now undergoing, and those who are destined to undergo such suffering in the *Avici* Hell, including all the inexhaustible number of beings who are now or will in the future undergo suffering in all the hells throughout the ten directions to the ends of the worlds, we, with utmost heartfelt sincerity, bow in full prostration and take refuge with the Greatly Kind and Compassionate Ones who are like fathers to those of us in this world.

Namo Maitreya Buddha

Namo Shakyamuni Buddha

Namo the seven Buddhas of the past

Namo the ten Buddhas of the ten directions

Namo the thirty-five Buddhas

Namo the fifty-three Buddhas

Namo the one hundred and seventy Buddhas

Namo the thousand Buddhas of the Adornment Kalpa

Namo the thousand Buddhas of the Worthy Kalpa

Namo the thousand Buddhas of the Stars and Constellations Kalpa

Namo Bodhisattvas Mahasattvas of the ten directions

Namo the twelve Bodhisattvas

Namo Earth Store Bodhisattva

Namo Boundless Body Bodhisattva

Namo Guan Shi Yin Bodhisattva

Furthermore, we pay homage to the countless Buddha images of the ten directions to the ends of empty space: the gold and sandalwood images made by King Udayana, the bronze images made by King Asoka, the stone images from Suzhou[16], and the jade images in the kingdom of Simhaladvipa[17]. We also pay homage to all the Buddha images in all countries, made of gold, silver, lapis lazuli, coral, amber, moonstones, carnelian, pearl, precious mani-jewel, and jambunada gold of superior purple color. (*one bow*)

Furthermore, we pay homage to all the Tathagatas' stupas in ten directions, housing the Buddhas' relics such as hair, molar teeth, front teeth, nails, crown bones, other shariras of the body, and all their personal implements such as kasaya[18] robes, bowls, spoons, bath bottles, and tin staffs. (*one bow*)

Furthermore, we pay homage to the stupas erected where the Buddha was born, accomplished the Way, turned the Dharma-wheel, entered Nirvana, as well as Many-Jeweled Buddha's stupa, the eighty-four thousand stupas established by King Asoka, all stupas in the heavens and in this world, and all the precious stupas in the dragons' palaces. (*one bow*)

Again, we take refuge with all the Buddhas of the ten directions to the ends of empty space, with all the honored Dharma of the ten directions to the ends of empty space, and with the Sangha of all sages and worthy ones of the ten directions to the ends of empty space. May the Three Treasures, with the power of kindness and compassion, the power of comforting living beings, the infinite powers of self-mastery and spiritual penetrations, gather in all of us today in this Bodhimanda who are repenting on behalf of beings who are suffering in the great *Avici* Hell and all the other ineffably many hell-beings throughout the ten directions, as well as all parents, teachers, and all other relatives and kin.

We now repent and pray that the Three Treasures use the water of great kindness and compassion to eradicate the suffering of beings in the *Avici* and other hells, so that their offenses be cleansed and their purity restored. May this water also cleanse the offenses of all living beings repenting together in this Bodhimanda, as well as the offenses of their parents, teachers, and all relatives. May all regain purity. May this water further cleanse the offenses of all living beings in the six paths, enabling all to become ultimately pure and attain Buddhahood.

We pray that from now until we attain Buddhahood:

> May the suffering in *Avici* Hell be eradicated completely;
> May the ineffably ineffable suffering in the other hells of the ten directions throughout empty space be cut off as well;
> May beings never again enter the three evil paths, never again fall into the hells;
> May living beings never again commit the offenses of the ten evil deeds and the five rebellious acts, which will cause them to

undergo suffering. May all such offenses be completely eradicated;

May they completely eliminate rebirth in the hells and be reborn in the Pure Land;

May they abandon life in the hells and gain the life of wisdom;

May they discard their hell-retribution bodies and gain vajra bodies;

May they leave behind the suffering of the hells and gain the bliss of Nirvana;

May they be mindful of the suffering in the hells and bring forth the resolve for bodhi;

May the four limitless minds and the six paramitas will always be clear to them;

May the four eloquences and six spiritual powers be employed by them with ease;

May they always perfect their wisdom while tirelessly cultivating the Bodhisattva Path with courage and vigor;

May they further perfect the practices of the Ten Grounds, gain entry into the vajra mind, realize Proper and Equal Enlightenment, and return to take across all beings throughout the ten directions.

Today, we are here in this Bodhimanda due to our shared karma. It is hard to describe all the types of suffering in all the other hells. The names and cruelties in those hells are innumerable, and we can only gain a comprehensive understanding of them by learning about them in the sutras. The sutras state, "Because of a single evil thought King Yama had in the past, he is reaping the retribution of being the lord of the hells." He himself also undergoes unspeakable suffering. In the past, when King Yama was the King of Bimbisara, he battled the king of Vedashi and was defeated. Because of this he made the vow that in his future life he would be the ruler of the hells and punish his enemies from the battlefield. At that time his eighteen ministers, as well as millions of soldiers, also made the same vow of revenge. The former King of Bimbisara now is King Yama. His eighteen ministers are now rulers of the eighteen hells. The millions of soldiers are now the ox-headed guardians, and together, all come under the authority of the northern King of Vaisravana.

The *Sutra of Dirghagama* states, "King Yama lives in a palace more than six thousand yojanas[19] in size, located at Vajra Mountain in the southern part of Jambudvipa." Also the *Sutra of Hell* states, "King Yama lives in a hell-city palace measuring over thirty thousand miles, which is made entirely of iron and copper. Throughout the day and night, a cauldron full of molten copper appears. A huge hell-guardian lays the king down on a hot iron bed, forces open his mouth with an iron hook, then pours molten copper into his mouth, completely burning and scorching him from the throat down. His ministers also undergo the same retribution in hell.

The names of the eighteen rulers of the hells are:

1. Kayana, ruling the *Niraya* Hells,
2. Quzun, ruling the Hell of Mountain of Blades,
3. Boiling Jivana, ruling the Hell of Boiling Sand,
4. Boiling Kubja, ruling the Hell of Boiling Excrement,
5. Kaloka, ruling the Hell of Black Ear,
6. Gaishe, ruling the Hell of Fire Carts,
7. Hot Broth, ruling the Hell of Seething Broth,
8. Iron Katu, ruling the Hell of Iron Beds,
9. Evil Birth, ruling the Hell of Crushing Mountain,
10. Moaning and Groaning, ruling the Hell of Freezing Ice,
11. Vika, ruling the Hell of Flaying-skin,
12. Shaking Head, ruling the Hell of Animals,
13. Tiva, ruling the Hell of Military Weaponry,
14. Jidhar, ruling the Hell of Iron Mill,
15. Pleasing the Head, ruling the Hell of River of Ash,
16. Piercing Bones, ruling the Hell of Iron Scroll,
17. Name and Body, ruling the Hell of Maggots, and
18. Contemplating the Body, ruling the Hell of Molten Copper.

Each of these hells has countless subsidiary hells, each with its own ruler.

The ox-headed guardians in the hells are fierce and cruel, without any compassion, concerned only that beings undergoing retribution do not suffer sufficiently and that the tortures are not sufficiently cruel.

Someone asked the hell-guardians, "These beings are so pitiful and suffer so much, yet you are still so cruel and vicious. Why don't you have any compassion towards them?"

The hell-guardians replied, "These offenders are suffering so much because they were not filial to their parents; slandered the Buddha, the Dharma, and all sages and worthy ones; reviled or insulted their relatives; and despised and slighted their teachers and elders. They also defamed others, framed them, and committed harsh and divisive speech. They flattered and were jealous. They forcibly separated people's relatives and loved ones from each other. They were hateful, irascible, and murderous. They were greedy and deceived others, earning their livelihood and achieving their ends through deviant means. They harbored deviant views, were lax, lazy, self-indulgent, and caused resentment and animosity everywhere. Hence, these beings are here now to receive their retribution. When they have resolved their debts in hell and are about to leave, I always exhort them not to create any further offenses that would cause them to undergo such unbearable suffering again. However, these offenders were not truly remorseful nor repentant, so soon after their release, they came back here. They continue to revolve and undergo suffering because they haven't learned from the pain they undergo.

"Having to continually confront them and torture them kalpa after kalpa really exhausts and drains me. Therefore, I do not show the least bit of kindness to them, instead I deliberately intensify the means of torture hoping they become aware that they create the source of this suffering, develop a sense of shame and remorse, and do not return. However, I find that these beings willingly suffer instead of trying to avoid these extreme retributions. They definitely do not want to do good, to tend towards Nirvana. Since they are so ignorant, not knowing how to avoid suffering and seek bliss, I must increase and intensify their suffering many times more than that in the human world. Thus, given their situation, why should they deserve my compassion and empathy?"

Today, we are here in this Bodhimanda due to our shared karma. We understand that what the guardian has said is not mere fabrication by using the analogy of criminals in prisons in our world. If one were repeatedly imprisoned, his relatives would lose patience in trying to bail him out and save him, and they would no longer feel sorrow or empathy for him. So we can understand how the hell-guardians feel, seeing the same offenders repeatedly coming and leaving and suffering greatly for long periods. Having been relieved of suffering, we should cultivate the mind and change our bad habits. If we do not repent and reform, then we will forever sink in an endless wheel of suffering, undergoing one agony after another, without any respite.

Therefore, all animosity of the three periods of time is based on the mutually interrelated cycle of cause and effect. The respective cycles of good and evil never stop, not even for a single moment! Retributions are clearly evident. Those who commit evil will suffer greatly in the hells to the exhaustion of kalpas. After their retribution in the hells end, they will be reborn in the animal realm, and after this retribution ends, they will be born in the realm of hungry ghosts. They will endure such boundless pain and suffering over countless births and deaths.

Knowing this, how can we not bring forth a sense of urgency to practice the Bodhisattva Path? Today, let us all with utmost and heartfelt sincerity, bow in full prostration, beseech the Buddha for compassion and repent on behalf of all throughout the ten directions: the rulers, ministers, ox-headed guardians and their retinues in the hells; spirits of hungry ghosts and their respective retinues, together with all beings in the realm of hungry ghosts; animal spirits and their respective retinues, together with all beings in the animal realm, including all other countless beings. May we all rectify our bad habits and reform. May the offenses we have committed be eradicated and may we never again dare commit further offenses. May all Buddhas in the ten directions use your inconceivable spiritual power of self-mastery to save, protect, pity us and gather us in. May all living beings be immediately liberated. We now take refuge with the Greatly Kind and Compassionate Ones who are like fathers to those of us in this world.

Namo Maitreya Buddha
Namo Shakyamuni Buddha
Namo Magnificent Sun Buddha
Namo Army Power Buddha
Namo Flower Light Buddha
Namo Humane and Benevolent Buddha
Namo Great Awe-inspiring Virtue Buddha
Namo Brahma King Buddha
Namo Boundless Brilliance Buddha
Namo Dragon Virtue Buddha
Namo Firm Stride Buddha
Namo Never Seen in Vain Buddha
Namo Vigor in Virtue Buddha
Namo Skilled in Protecting Buddha
Namo Joyous Buddha
Namo Non-retreating Buddha
Namo Lion Hallmark Buddha
Namo Supreme Knowledge Buddha
Namo Dharma Clan Buddha
Namo Joyful King Buddha
Namo Wonderful Maneuvering Buddha
Namo Gladly Working Buddha
Namo Arm of Virtue Buddha
Namo Fragrant Elephant Buddha
Namo Contemplative Observation Buddha
Namo Cloud Sound Buddha
Namo Skillfully Contemplating Buddha

Namo Lion Banner Bodhisattva
Namo Lion Deeds Bodhisattva
Namo Earth Treasury Bodhisattva
Namo Boundless Body Bodhisattva
Namo Guan Shi Yin Bodhisattva

Again, we take refuge with the Three Treasures of the ten directions to the ends of empty space. May you with your spiritual power of self-mastery, save beings in the hell realm: the rulers, ministers, ox-headed guardians and all beings who are undergoing suffering, including those in the eighteen-leveled hells, the subsidiary hells, and all other hells.

- May all these beings be liberated henceforth and the causes of offenses and effects of suffering be eradicated. From this day forth, may they forever cut off the karma the of hells, and never again fall into the three evil paths.
- May they never again be born in the hells and instead be reborn in the pure land.
- May they abandon the destiny of the hells and gain the life of wisdom.
- May they discard their hell retribution bodies and gain vajra bodies.
- May they be uprooted from the suffering of the hells and attain the bliss of Nirvana.
- May they be mindful of the suffering in the hells and bring forth the resolve for bodhi.
- May they always dwell in the four limitless minds and the six paramitas.
- May they have complete mastery of the four eloquences and the six spiritual powers.
- May they always be courageous and vigorous, without resting or pause.

- May they further proceed to perfect all the practices of the Ten Grounds, come back to take across all living beings in the ten directions, attain the vajra mind, and accomplish Proper and Equal Enlightenment.

Praise

Causes and conditions, with their effects and retributions, are obvious Laws.
The iron city pervades the three thousand great thousand worlds;
The suffering within is relentless and endless.
Prostrating to the Golden Immortal[20],
One immediately transcends all tormenting agonies.

Namo Ground of Blazing Wisdom Bodhisattva Mahasattva

(three times)

Concluding the Repentance

In the heavens above and below, the Buddha is most honored.
Among the transcendental and mundane, this Dharma reigns supreme.
Its sprinkling of sweet dew nourishes worlds many as dust motes;
Its bodhi fragrance permeates throughout the world.
The Buddha's crown radiates fine white jade-like brilliance,
And his body of wondrous adornment glows with a golden hue.
With utmost sincerity we mundane beings pray,
In response, you appear before us immediately.
May you with your vast kindness take pity on us and gather us in.

[Dharma Host]: On behalf of _____ [those who seek to repent], we practice this Repentance Dharma of Kindness and Compassion in the Bodhimanda. We have now successfully completed Roll Four, accomplishing its merit and virtue. Now, let us again subdue our thoughts and with utmost sincerity bring forth the mind of compassion.

Before us, wisps of auspicious smoke rise from the agarwood incense; the candle flame takes the *udumbara* form; wondrous offerings from the celestial kitchen are presented; a vast array of delicacies full of flavorful dhyana-bliss is served; the chiming bells resonate with heavenly music, and the brahma chants harmonize with wondrous melodies.

May all the goodness amassed universally benefit all sentient beings and may this merit be further dedicated to:

- Shakyamuni Buddha, the Awakened One surpassing Heaven, the Full Moon, the Competent One of Humaneness.
- The Dharma, the *Half-word and Full-word* Teachings[21] of the truths;
- The Sangha, those who are still in the learning stage and those who are beyond learning;
- Heavenly beings, spirits, ghosts and others in the world or in the underworld throughout heaven and earth, the wise sentient beings --who are either on land or in the water;
- Deities guarding monuments dedicated to government officials;

May all of them bear witness to our allegiance to the Buddha, which is an allegiance like a sunflower that always follows the sun. May all of them also bestow their kindness and protection on all. With the merit and virtue accrued from bowing, on behalf of _____ [those who seek to repent], we repent and eradicate the *four* offenses[22] and enter the proper samadhi of the *four* types of emptiness.

We bow and earnestly pray:

May the fundamental causes of the *four* births melt like snow when hot water is poured over it.

May the defiled affliction-obstacles of the *four* dwellings disappear like frost in the sun.

143

May we transcend the *four* currents[23] and leave the torrential river of emotional love, quickly accomplish the *four* virtues[24] and tend toward to the great path of the Land of Ultimate Bliss. May we abide in the *four* peaceful and joyful conducts[25] and affirm our *four* great vows. May we together with parents of our many lives past gain the gateway to liberation.

May we together with our friends and foes of many lives past certify to the fruition of bodhi.

[Dharma host]: We have now repented according to the text, but fear that the karma accumulated from past lives is hard to eradicate. Thus I am taking the liberty to request that together, we continue to repent and reform.

Praise

The meritorious power of the Emperor of Liang Repentance Roll Four
Enables the deceased and the disciples to eradicate the four grave offenses
May all realize the Bodhisattva's Ground of Blazing Wisdom.
As the Repentance is chanted our offenses are blown away like flower petals in the wind.
Offenses repented, enmity resolved,
Wisdom and blessing increase as calamities are dispelled.
Liberated from suffering and reborn in the Trayastrimsha,
May we gather at the Dragon Flower's Three Assemblies
And receive a prediction personally from Maitreya Buddha.

Namo Dragon Flower Assembly of Bodhisattvas Mahasattvas
(three times)

Final Praise

Emperor of Liang Repentance Roll Four now concludes.
We dedicate its merit to the four benefactors and the three realms.
May all in this assembly enjoy increased longevity and blessing,

May the Dharma water cleanse our offenses.
May the deceased be reborn in the Western Pure Land.
May the Bodhisattvas of the Ground of Blazing Wisdom compassion-
ately gather us in.

Namo Ascending the Path to the Clouds Bodhisattva Mahasattva
(three times)

End Notes

1. **Four wisdoms**: the great perfect mirror wisdom, the wisdom of equality, the wisdom of wonderful contemplation, the wisdom that accomplishes what is done.
2. **Four eloquences**: unobstructed eloquence of Dharma, unobstructed eloquence of principle, unobstructed eloquence in phrasing, unobstructed eloquence of delight in speech.
3. **Four minds**: This is the same as the four limitless minds of kindness, compassion, joy, and renunciation.
4. **Four evil paths**: Asura realm, animal realm, hungry ghost ream, hells.
5. **Four marks**: mark of self, mark of living beings, mark of others, mark of life span.
6. **Four births**: egg-born, womb-born, moisture-born, transformation-born.
7. **Four siddhanta**: ordinary methods of giving, individual treatment, diagnosing and treating moral diseases, primary truth.
8. **Cunda**: the last disciple who made offerings to Shakyamuni Buddha before he entered Nirvana.
9. **Three karmic obstacles**: obstacle of the retribution-cycle of birth and death, obstacle of karma-delusion, obstacle of affliction - greed, hatred, stupidity.
10. **Eight liberations**:
    The liberation in which inside there is form; outward form is contemplated.

The liberation in which inside there is no form; outward form is contemplated.
The pure body of liberation certifies to the perfect dwelling.
The liberation of emptiness without limit.
The liberation of consciousness without limit.
The liberation of nothing whatsoever.
The liberation of neither perception nor non-perception.
The liberation of the samadhi of the extinction of feeling and thought.

11. **Four great vows**:
Living beings are limitless; I vow to cross them over.
Afflictions are inexhaustible; I vow to cut them off.
Dharma-doors are immeasurable; I vow to learn them all.
The Buddha-path is unsurpassed; I vow to realize it.

12. **Four limitless minds:** kindness, compassion, renunciation, joy.

13. **Six paramitas** giving, holding precepts, patience, vigor, dhyana samadhi, Prajna wisdom.

14. **Six spiritual powers**: the penetration of the heavenly eye, the penetration of the heavenly ear, the penetration of past lives, the penetration of others' thoughts, the penetration of the complete spirit, the penetration of the extinction of outflows.

15. **mile** – the actual term used was *li*, which is a Chinese mile equal to one third of an English mile.

16. **Stone images from Suzhou:** Wujung is the city of Suzhou in Jiangsu Province, China. The Kai Yuan Monastery in Suzhou has two stone images of Kashya Buddha and Vipashyin Buddha. There is a saying that before the Tang Dynasty, they were floating on the sea by themselves. But when fishermen tried to move them, the images were unmovable. So people drew lots and came to the conclusion that the images should be placed in Suzhou. This is why the two stone images are now in Kai Yuan Monastery.

17. **Simhaladvipa:** refers to the present Sri Lanka.

18. **Kasaya:** A rectangular ceremonial sash worn over the left shoulder by Buddhist monks in East Asia and is symbolic of the robes originally worn by Buddhist monks in India. The Chinese *jiasha* is a transliteration of the Sanskrit kaṣāya or 'ochre.'
19. **Yojanas:** unit of distance.
20. **Golden Immortal:** which means the greatly enlightened one, the Buddha.
21. **Half-word Teaching:** initial teaching, the Small Vehicle Teaching, the Hinayana teaching, as compared to the Great Vehicle Teaching which is called the Whole-word Teaching.
    The Agama Period's Teaching is that of the Half-word. The Prajna and Dharma Flower-Nirvana Periods' Teachings are Whole-word Teachings. The Sudden Teaching and the Perfect Teaching are both Whole-word Teachings. The Final Teaching is partly Half-word Teaching and partly Whole-word Teaching, or is a "Revelation of the Whole to the Half."
22. **Four offenses:** the four major offenses of killing, stealing, sexual misconduct, and lying. These four offenses are also known as four fundamental afflictions or offenses.
23. **Four currents:** the illusion of view, the illusion of desire, the illusion of existence, the illusion of ignorance.
24. **Four virtues:** permanence, joy, true-self, and purity.
25. **Four peaceful and joyful conducts:** Attaining the joyful contentment by proper deeds of body, proper words of the mouth, proper thoughts in the mind, and the proper vows.

ROLL FIVE

Namo Buddhas and Bodhisattvas of the Dragon Flower Assembly
(*bow three times*)

Praise

All sweet and delicious fruits of the Jeta Grove,
Melons, persimmons, pears, lychees and longans,
Together with the peerless amalaka fruit,
Presented on the lotus dias,
Are served as perfect offerings,
Personally by a Brahman ascetic master.

Namo Universal Offerings Bodhisattva Mahasattva (*three times*)

Listen respectfully

The compassionate Honored One, with his pure *five* eyes[1],
manifests resplendent wondrous hallmarks;
As teacher of the ocean-vast *five*-vehicle Dharma, he proclaims
esoteric Prajna with a resonant and clear voice.
Sages and Worthy Ones of the fifty-*five* Stages perfect the
fruition of bodhi in each and every thought.
Great Knights with the *five* roots and *five* powers readily tap
into each and every state as causes and conditions for
liberation.
Returning to and relying on them increase our blessings;
Devotion to and mindfulness of them eradicate our offenses.
Tranquil and unmoving, they respond to our requests.
May they shine their light of kindness on us and bear witness
to our practice.

[Dharma Host]: On behalf of _____ [those who seek to repent], we practice this Repentance Dharma of Kindness and Compassion in the Bodhimanda. We have come to Roll Five. With all conditions fulfilled, we now enter the Repentance Platform.

We meticulously prepare lamps, candles, fruit, teas, and all other wondrous rare and special items and reverently offer them to all Buddhas, sages and worthy ones. We respectfully chant their exalted names, bow to them, take refuge with them, and confess all our wrongs and sincerely submit ourselves before them.

We are earnestly mindful that, since distant kalpas past until today, we have all been deluded by the arising and ceasing of the *five skandhas*, tossed about in the turbulence of the *five* turbidities, entangled in the *five* desires, and obscured by the *five* defilements. We have are not immune from committing the *five* rebellious acts and continue to give rise to thoughts of self and others, love and hatred. We have not understood the *five* dharmas and continue to allow our own emotions and afflictions, as well as those of others, to increase and intensify. Since cause and effect never err, karmic retributions are hard to avoid. Now, with a resolution of utmost sincerity, all of us in this Dharma assembly open the door to liberation, take refuge with the sagely teachings and purify ourselves of offenses in the sea of bodhi. These are our resolves, and the Buddhas will surely pity us. We bow and request that you, out of your great kindness, invisibly bless and protect us.

> The Buddha's body is as pure as lapis lazuli,
> His face is like the radiant full moon.
> The Buddha is able to rescue beings suffering in the world.
> His mind is ever-compassionate everywhere.

Commencement of the Repentance

We now begin the Repentance Dharma of Kindness and Compassion in the Bodhimanda. Together in this assembly, we single-mindedly return to and rely on all Buddhas of the three periods of time.

Namo Buddhas of the past, Vipashyin Buddha
Namo Shikhin Buddha
Namo Vishvabhu Buddha
Namo Krakucchanda Buddha
Namo Kanakamuni Buddha
Namo Kashyapa Buddha
Namo our Fundamental Teacher Shakyamuni Buddha
Namo Honored Future Buddha, Maitreya

Section 9 - Dispelling Enmity and Resolving Animosity

Today, we are here in this Bodhimanda due to our shared karma. We should know that all living beings are saddled with animosity. How do we know this? If there is no animosity, then the evil paths will not exist. Up until now, beings continue to be embroiled in the suffering of the three evil paths. Hence we know that living beings have been mired in endless animosity. The sutras state, "All living beings have the Buddha nature and are capable of becoming Buddhas" but living beings have become inverted. They indulge in and become attached to the mundane world, fail to understand the essentials for transcending the world, create causes for suffering, allow the root of animosity to grow, and thus turn on the wheel of the three existences and the six paths and endlessly revolve in the cycle of birth and death. Why does this happen?

Due to a single thought of confusion, from time without beginning, with deluded consciousness, we living beings perpetuate existence, life after life. We are covered by ignorance, drown in the waters of emotional love, and fertilize the root of the three poisons and four inverted views. From the root of the three poisons, ten afflictions sprout forth. Based on attachment to the view of self, the five wrong views are produced. Based on the five wrong views, sixty-two views are produced. Through our body, speech, and mind, we commit the ten evil deeds:

- Our body commits killing, stealing, and sexual misconduct;
- Our mouth is involved with false speech, frivolous speech, divisive speech, and harsh speech;
- Our mind engages in greed, hatred, and ignorance.

We commit the ten evil deeds ourselves, tell others to commit them, praise the ten evil dharmas, and praise those who commit them. Thus through body, speech, and mind, we commit forty kinds of evil. Moreover, following our six emotions[2], we are attached to the six sense objects[3], resulting in the wearisome dust of the eighty-four thousand afflictions. Within a single thought, we give rise to sixty-two kinds of views. Within a single thought, we commit forty kinds of evil deeds. Within a single thought, we generate eighty-four thousand wearisome afflictions. How many more offenses do we commit in a day, a month, a year, or have we committed from countless kalpas past? All such offenses are limitless and boundless, and every being seeks to avenge wrongs, resulting in a never ending cycle of animosity.

We living beings are enmeshed in delusion, our wisdom is shrouded by ignorance, and our true mind covered by afflictions. Yet we remain unaware. Our minds are inverted; we do not believe in the teachings of the sutras; we do not rely on and follow the teachings of the Buddha; we do not realize the need to resolve animosity, and we do not seek for liberation. As a result, we are propelled into the evil paths in the same way a moth flies into fire. Throughout endless kalpas, we undergo endless suffering like passing through a long, dark night. Even if our evil karmic retribution ends and we regain a human body, we still fail to reform. For the sake of all living beings who harbor animosity, all sages bring forth their great kindness and compassion. Thus we should also all bring forth the bodhi resolve and practice the Bodhisattva Path.

Bodhisattvas Mahasattvas look upon rescuing living beings from suffering as their sustenance and helping beings resolve animosity as their major practice. Bodhisattvas never give up on living beings and endure hardship as the foundation of their practice. Let us now emulate them in the same manner. We shall bring forth a courageous mind, a kind and compassionate mind, and a mind equivalent to that of the Tathagata. Now relying on the power of all Buddhas, we hoist the banner of the Bodhimanda, strike the Dharma drum, sprinkle sweet dew, and draw the bow of wisdom and arrow of determination. May all knots of animosity be resolved for all beings of the four births and the six paths, aggrieved parties throughout the three periods of time, our parents, teachers, elders, and the six relatives. May all past animosity be resolved and may there definitely be no future animosity.

May all Buddhas and Bodhisattvas, with their power of kindness and compassion, the power of their fundamental vows, the power of spiritual penetrations aid and protect, discipline and harmonize, and gather in all beings, thus enabling measureless foes of the three periods of time, from now until they attain bodhi, to resolve knots of existing animosity and allow no further animosity to arise. May all suffering be totally eradicated. Let us all bring forth firm resolve and heartfelt earnestness, bow in full prostration and repent on behalf of all beings in the four births and the six paths, those throughout the three periods of time who are foes, our parents, teachers, elders and all relatives. We take refuge with the Greatly Kind and Compassionate Ones who are like fathers to those of us in this world.

> Namo Maitreya Buddha
> Namo Shakyamuni Buddha
> Namo Wholesome Mind Buddha
> Namo Apart from Defilement Buddha
> Namo Moon Hallmark Buddha
> Namo Great Fame Buddha
> Namo Pearl Prominence Buddha
> Namo Awe-inspiring Courage Buddha
> Namo Lion Stride Buddha
> Namo Tree of Virtue Buddha
> Namo Happily Freeing Buddha
> Namo Amassing Wisdom Buddha

Namo Peacefully Abiding Buddha
Namo With Intention Buddha
Namo Angata Buddha
Namo Limitless Mind Buddha
Namo Wondrous Form Buddha
Namo Much Wisdom Buddha
Namo Radiance Buddha
Namo Firm in Precepts Buddha
Namo Auspicious Buddha
Namo Precious Hallmark Buddha
Namo Lotus Flower Buddha
Namo Narayana Buddha
Namo Peace and Bliss Buddha
Namo Accumulating Wisdom Buddha
Namo Revered Virtue Buddha
Namo Steadfast, Courageous, and Vigorous Bodhisattva
Namo Vajra Wisdom Bodhisattva
Namo Boundless Body Bodhisattva
Namo Guan Shi Yin Bodhisattva

Again, we take refuge with the Three Treasures of the ten directions to the ends of empty space. Among all those who are foes throughout the three periods of time, may all in the six paths who have suffered the retribution from animosity be liberated by the power of the Buddha, the power of the Dharma, and the power of sages and worthy ones. By these powers too, may all beings who are suffering or are due to suffer animosity never fall into the evil paths, never harbor enmity or ill-will towards each other, and never inflict torture or pain upon each other.

May beings practice giving without discriminating between friends or foes; may all of their offenses be eradicated; may all animosity be resolved; may all be united in harmony, like a blend of milk and water. May they enjoy happiness resembling that experienced on the First Ground; may they enjoy infinite longevity with eternal bliss in body and mind. May they be reborn in the heavens or pure lands as they wish, where food and clothes appear at will. May all sounds of animosity, contention, arguments, and fighting never again arise. May their bodies composed of the four elements be unaffected by change, and the five sense faculties undefiled by sense objects. May the multitudes of goodness spring forth and rush to converge upon them, and may all evil spontaneously vie to vaporize. May they bring forth the Mahayana resolve, practice the Bodhisattva Path, be replete with the four limitless minds and the six paramitas, end the cycle of birth and death, and, together accomplish Proper Enlightenment.

Today, we are here in this Bodhimanda due to our shared karma. What are the roots of animosity and the source of suffering? The eye craves forms; the ear, sounds; the nose, fragrances; the tongue, flavors; the body, fine sensations. The five sense faculties are always bound by the five sense objects. That is why beings pass through kalpas of long dark nights, unable to attain liberation.

Moreover, the six kinds of kinship and relatives are our root source of animosity throughout the three periods of time. All animosity arises due to kinship. Without kin, there would be no animosity. To stay away from kin is to stay away from animosity. Why is that? If two people live in different places, far apart from each other, animosity and resentment would not arise between them. Animosity and resentment arise because of closeness. Through the roots of the three poisons, we mutually afflict each other; afflicted, we usually become resentful and hateful.

It is because kin and relatives have expectations of each other. Parents place demands and expectations on their children; children have expectations of their parents; so also between brothers and sisters, as well as among the rest of immediate and distant kin. The more they expect from each other, the more likely hatred will arise. Then, when their expectations are not met even over trivial matters, this causes blame and anger. If wealth and treasures are involved, relatives vie for them. When they are poor, nobody cares about them. Once they gain some wealth, they are not satisfied; the more they gain, the more inadequate they feel. Even if their every wish is fulfilled, they are still not satisfied. When just one incident does not go their way, their hatred and disappointment are aggravated. As a result, ill-will develops, discord sets in; feuds arise and calamities follow, continuing on life after life without end. We can infer from this that our foes and enemies of the three periods are none other than our own immediate and distant kin. Thus we should understand that our own kin are our worst enemies.

How can each and every one of us not diligently and earnestly repent and reform? From the time we first had consciousness until now, all our parents and relatives of all lifetimes from kalpas past, and others in the six paths of the hells, animals, hungry ghosts, asuras, humans, heavenly beings and ascetic masters, have harbored knots of animosity, both light and severe. We now bring forth a mind of kindness and compassion, a mind free of discrimination between friends or foes, and a resolve and vow like that of the Buddhas. On behalf of all these parents, relatives and beings, with utmost sincerity, we now bow in full prostration and take refuge with the Greatly Kind and Compassionate Ones who are like fathers to those of us in this world.

Namo Maitreya Buddha
Namo Shakyamuni Buddha
Namo Brahma Virtue Buddha
Namo Accumulation of Treasure Buddha
Namo Blossoming in Heaven Buddha
Namo Skillful in Contemplation Buddha
Namo Mastery in Dharma Buddha
Namo Renowned Intention Buddha
Namo Delight in Proclaiming and Gathering Buddha
Namo Vajra Hallmark Buddha
Namo Striving to Benefit Buddha
Namo Roaming in Spiritual Penetrations Buddha
Namo Apart from Darkness Buddha
Namo Multitudes of Heaven Buddha

Namo Meru Hallmarks Buddha
Namo Manifold Radiance Buddha
Namo Jewel Treasury Buddha
Namo Supreme and Lofty Conduct Buddha
Namo Tisya Buddha
Namo Pearl Horn Buddha
Namo Praising Virtue Buddha
Namo Brilliance of Sun and Moon Buddha
Namo Brilliance of Sun Buddha
Namo Stars and Constellations Buddha
Namo Lion Hallmark Buddha
Namo King *Wei Lan* Buddha
Namo Treasury of Blessings Buddha
Namo Renouncing Hindrances of *Skandhas* Bodhisattva
Namo Tranquil Sense Faculties Bodhisattva
Namo Boundless Body Bodhisattva
Namo Guan Shi Yin Bodhisattva

Again, we take refuge with the Three Treasures of the ten directions to the ends of empty space. By the power of the Buddhas, Dharma, Bodhisattvas of the Great Grounds and all other sages and worthy ones may our parents and relatives in the six paths who harbor animosity gather together now at this Bodhimanda. Let us together repent of past offenses and resolve all knots of animosity. If these beings cannot be physically present, may the power of the Three Treasures draw them in so that they can be spiritually present. May these beings all bring forth a compassionate heart and receive our repentance so that all animosity can be resolved.

Now let all of us here in this Bodhimanda be mindful and recite: From the time we first had consciousness until now, we have together been rooted in the three poisons, and we have committed the ten evils toward our parents of past lives, and our kin of many kalpas, including aunts, uncles, all other blood relatives and in-laws. Because of ignorance, we lacked awareness, lacked faith, lacked cultivation, and thus gave tied up various knots of animosity. Further we became enemies with our parents and relatives and other beings in the six paths. All such offenses are boundless and measureless. Today we repent of all these offenses and pray that they will be eradicated. Moreover, from time without beginning until now, due to the roots of the three poisons of greed, hatred, and delusion, we have committed many kinds of offenses. All such offenses and evils are measureless and boundless. Full of shame and remorse, we repent and plead that all offenses be eliminated.

Moreover, from time without beginning until now, we have created the karma of animosity over issues of land, property, or money, even resulting in killing our relatives. Such offenses of killing cannot be fully described, and the animosity can never cease. Filled with shame and remorse we confess and repent. We pray that our parents and the rest of the six relatives, including all their kin, will compassionately accept our repentance, relinquish all of their animosity, and never hold any vengeful thought.

The same applies to the offenses of stealing, sexual misconduct, lying, the ten evil deeds and the five rebellious acts. There is no offense that we have not committed. With our false and inverted thoughts, we schemed and took advantage of situations and thus committed all kinds of offenses. All such offenses are measureless and boundless, committed, from the time we first had consciousness until now, against our six relatives, whether they were our parents, brothers, sisters, aunts, or uncles.

These offenses - their causes and the severity of their retributions, the magnitude of animosity and the number of kalpas over which we have to suffer the animosity, - are only completely known by Buddhas and Bodhisattvas of various Grounds, throughout the ten directions.

Only Buddhas and Bodhisattvas can fully see and know the characteristics of all such offenses – the type and magnitude of the animosity, the number of kalpas one will suffer the animosity, and when in future one will be confronted by his foes.

Today, tearful and feeling greatly shameful, we reproach ourselves. We resolve to rectify all our past faults and do what is right in the future, not daring to commit these offenses again. We only hope all our past and present parents, kin, and relatives will accept our repentance with a gentle and supple mind, a harmonious mind, a mind that delights in doing all good, a mind that delights in giving, a joyful mind, a protective mind, and a mind equal to that of the Tathagatas. May they relinquish all their animosity, and be free of any discrimination between friends or foes.

Moreover, may our parents and relatives in the six paths who harbor animosity towards us, relinquish such animosity. May other beings in the six paths do the same! May all knots of animosity that exist in the three periods of time be eradicated immediately. From now until we attain Buddhahood, may all of us forever be free from the three evil paths and the suffering of the four births. May we always be in harmony, like a blend of milk and water. May we be as free of any obstruction as empty space. May we forever become kin in Dharma and members of the compassionate family. May everyone of us cultivate, accomplish limitless wisdom and be replete with all merit and virtue. May we be courageous and vigorous, without ceasing or resting; may we practice the Bodhisattva Path, without ever becoming weary. May our minds be equal to that of Buddhas, and may we make the same vows as those made by the Buddhas. May we attain the Buddha's threefold esoteric modes, be replete with the fivefold bodies and ultimately realize unsurpassed bodhi, accomplishing Proper and Equal Enlightenment.

Today, we are here in this Bodhimanda due to our shared karma. We have resolved the animosity towards our parents. Next we should resolve the animosity towards our teachers. Before perfecting our Dharma body and becoming a Buddha, even a Bodhisattva at the position of patience with non-production of dharmas is still bound by the ever-changing Three Marks[4]. Even Buddhas need to use skillful means, such as using harsh words to teach evil-natured living beings to awaken to the Way. With their brilliant virtues in teaching and transforming, they still need to use such methods; how much the more would our mundane and ordinary teachers, who may not have yet perfected their understanding or have yet reached maximum purity and quiescence need to use such methods.

With our mixture of good and evil and lack of understanding and discernment, how could we possibly avoid making mistakes with our three karmas. Upon hearing this, we should repent and be grateful for the kindness of our teachers. Instead of being terrified by harsh words, being prone to doubt, or harboring evil thoughts, we should be grateful for the kindness of our teachers, deeply repent and reprimand ourselves.

It is mentioned in the sutras that although one may have left the householder's life, one has not attained liberation. Thus, monastics should take care not to say casually, "I am free of all evil-doing." Nor should it be assumed that to be a householder is to lack goodness.

That being said, in the sutras the Buddha told the great assembly, "You should contemplate the kindness of your teachers. Although our parents gave us life and taught us, they are not able to help us escape the three evil destinies."

Our spiritual teachers, with their great compassion, can draw in the young and beginners in Dharma, teaching and guiding them to leave the householder's life, receive the Complete Precepts, and thus plant the seed of Arhatship and its future fruition. They teach us how to escape the suffering of birth and death and to attain the bliss of Nirvana. It is our teachers' kindness that enables us to transcend the world. How can we possibly repay this kindness? Even if we practice the Way throughout our life, we are just benefiting ourselves rather than repaying our teachers' kindness.

The Buddha said, "Of all good friends in the world, none is greater than our spiritual teachers."

Today, we are here in this Bodhimanda due to our shared karma. It is just as the Buddha has stated, "Our teachers have showered us with so much kindness, but we have not even had a single thought of repaying their kindness nor believed or accepted their teachings."

Worse still, we have even been rude and slanderous, making ground-less remarks and gossiping about our teachers, thus causing the decline of the Buddhadharma. With such offenses, how can we not fall into the three evil destinies?

No one will suffer this retribution on our behalf. When we reach the end of our lives, all joy vanishes to be replaced by pain and suffer-ing. Our soul will be miserable and afflicted, and our mind muddled. Our six sense faculties fade and become dull; our five organs deterio-rate and fail to function; we want to walk, but our legs refuse to move; we want to sit, but our bodies cannot remain upright; we want to lis-ten to the Dharma, but our ears cannot hear; we want to see the auspicious states, but our eyes cannot see. When that time comes, we will realize how difficult it is to get the opportunity to practice this current Repentance, because we will soon have to face the innumera-ble suffering of the hells to undergo the retributions for our past actions.

Thus the sutras state, "If people are deluded, arrogant, refuse to believe in dire retributions, and slander and are jealous of their teach-ers, they become great demons in the Dharma, planting seeds for falling into the hells. Such people tie knots of animosity and will have to face limitless retributions."

This is like the case of Bhikshu Flower Light who was well-versed in speaking the Dharma. He had a disciple who was very arrogant and refused to accept any of his teachings, saying, "My Venerable Master only knows how to extol the teaching of emptiness; he lacks wisdom. I don't wish to see him anymore in my future lives."

This disciple distorted the proper Dharma to be improper, and regarded improper dharmas as proper. Although he upheld the pre-cepts without violating them, because of his erroneous view and perspective, after his death, he fell into the Avici Hell as quickly as an arrow is shot and had to suffer greatly for eight billion kalpas.

Today, we are here in this Bodhimanda due to our shared karma. We should give rise to great fear after hearing what has been said in the sutras. Just because of a single criticism of his teacher, this bhikshu fell into the *Avici* Hell for eight billion kalpas. How much the more severe might the retributions be for those who, after renouncing the householder's life, proceeded to commit countless offenses towards their teachers? When this life as a monastic is over, they will definitely undergo similar retributions. Why is that? It is because our teachers of Dharma or *acharyas*[5] constantly teach and guide us, but not only do we fail to accord or comply with their teaching, we also always go against them. Perhaps those who become monastic disciples grow discontent with how their teachers provide for them. Perhaps our teachers were angry with us, or we disciples with the teachers. Thus throughout the three periods of time, we have given rise to boundless anger towards our teachers, resulting in incalculable offenses.

It is mentioned in the sutras that a single thought of hatred can result in boundless animosity. This animosity occurs not only among relatives but also among teachers and disciples and among fellow practitioners of the three seniorities living together. We fail to firmly believe that leaving the householder's life is the way to transcend the mundane. We do not know that patience is the practice leading to peace and bliss. We do not know that equanimity is the path to bodhi. We do not know that to cut off false thinking is to make a world-transcending resolve. Teachers and disciples dwelling together have not eliminated karmic fetters, which can lead them to disagree with and oppose each other, thereby thereby stirring up much contention and strife and causing disharmony that continues for life after life.

Also, monastics who study under the same teacher or practicing together, become angry or harbor malice when they see others excel, gain praise or promotion. We fail to reflect on our own past lack of cultivation of wisdom and on our own lack of the roots of goodness. We are unable to accept that others have greater virtue and blessings. With our mind plagued with outflows, we are quick to discriminate between our superiors and subordinates. Constantly giving rise to contention, we rarely dwell in harmony. We fail to yield or benefit others or to be willing to be put at a disadvantage. Instead, we may even react with hatred and resentment. Not only do we not reflect on our own errors and mistakes, but we also gossip about the faults of others. We may slanders others with our three poisons. We do not have loyalty and faith; we lack a mind of respect and reverence. When have we reflected that we may have violated various aspects of the Buddha's precepts? How many times have raised our voices, berating, swearing or cursing others?

We lack faith in and refuse to accept our teachers' instructions. We harbor hatred towards monastics of the three seniorities. Because of hatred, we further gossip about right and wrong. Animosity is prevalent in the evil paths and much of it can be traced to the times when we were teacher-students or fellow monastics of the three seniorities, practicing and living together. Just a single thought of hate can evolve into such limitless animosity. Therefore, the sutras say: "One slight thought of hatred or jealousy in this life can intensify, multiply, and turn into severe animosity in future lives." How much more severe is our evil karma over our entire life.

Today, we are here in this Bodhimanda due to our shared karma. We do not know when and in which realm we created knots of animosity with our teachers or with our fellow practitioners of the three seniorities. Such animosity, endless and formless, endures for ages and kalpas. When it is our turn to undergo this suffering, we will find it impossible to bear. That is why Bodhisattvas Mahasattvas renounce the mindset of friends or foes and do do not further entertain any such thoughts. They bring forth the mind of kindness and compassion to gather in all living beings equally. Together today, we who have brought forth the bodhi resolve and made the vow for bodhi, should practice Bodhisattva conduct, such as the four limitless minds, the six paramitas, the four great vows, and the four dharmas of attraction.

Henceforth, we should practice all these deeds, in the same way that all Buddhas and Bodhisattvas practice. May we regard all friends or foes impartially, thus freeing ourselves and them of such obstacles. From now until we attain bodhi, we vow to save and protect all living beings and enable all living beings to ultimately accomplish Buddhahood.

For any of us who have been monastics, from the time we first had consciousness until now, throughout the many lives that we may have renounced the householder's life, we created animosity with our teachers of Dharma and *acharyas,* the ordination certifying masters, and fellow monastics of the three seniorities. Further, we have also created animosity with living beings who have or do not have affinities with us, including others and their relatives in the four births and six paths of the ten directions and three periods of time. This animosity may be light or heavy, already encountered, now being encounter or yet to be encountered, and these beings may have been enemies or foes in the past, present or future. On behalf of all of them we bow together in full prostration with a mind of utmost sincerity. We now repent and reform all such animosity and beseech that this animosity be totally eradicated. Henceforth, may we regard with kindness and compassion, all beings in the six paths who harbor animosity and regard them without the distinction of friends or foes.

On behalf of all our foes throughout the three periods of time, we sincerely seek to repent. May we relinquish all animosity and never again harbor any evil thoughts or malice towards each other. May all living beings in the six paths also relinquish all animosity and become joyful. May all knots of animosity be resolved, and may we never again become resentful or hateful. May all be respectful and appreciative of one another. May our minds be identical with that of all Buddhas, and may we make the same vows made by all Buddhas. With utmost sincerity, we take refuge with the Greatly Kind and Compassionate Ones who are like fathers to those of us in this world.

Namo Maitreya Buddha
Namo Shakyamuni Buddha
Namo Discerning Extreme Views Buddha
Namo Radiance of Lightning Buddha
Namo Gold Mountain Buddha
Namo Lion-virtue Buddha
Namo Supreme Mark Buddha

Namo Bright Praise Buddha
Namo Firm Vigor Buddha
Namo Praised for Being Complete Buddha
Namo Fearless Lion Buddha
Namo Accordance with Heaven Buddha
Namo Great Lamp Buddha
Namo Understanding the World Buddha
Namo Wondrous Sound Buddha
Namo Upholding Superior Merit and Virtue Buddha
Namo Apart from Darkness Buddha
Namo Jeweled Praise Buddha
Namo Lion-cheek Buddha
Namo Eradicating Faults Buddha
Namo Upholding Sweet Dew Buddha
Namo Moon of Humanity Buddha
Namo Delightfully Seen Buddha
Namo Adornment Buddha
Namo Pearl's Radiance Buddha
Namo Mountain Peak Buddha
Namo Name and Mark Buddha
Namo Accumulation of Dharma Buddha
Namo Superior Wisdom Bodhisattva
Namo Never Leaving the World Bodhisattva
Namo Boundless Body Bodhisattva
Namo Guan Shi Yin Bodhisattva

Again, we take refuge with the Three Treasures of the ten directions to the ends of empty space. By the power of the Buddha, the power of the Dharma, the power of the great Bodhisattvas, and the power of sages and worthy ones may all the immeasurable animosity from the three periods of time be completely resolved, whether or not it has to do with us directly. May all beings throughout empty space and the dharma realm also repent together in the same manner to resolve all their animosity. May all beings relinquish all animosity and not discriminate between friends or foes. May we always be in harmony, like a blend of milk and water. May we enjoy happiness just like that experienced on the First Ground. May we be as free of any obstruction as empty space is. From now until we attain bodhi, may we forever be kin in Dharma, aligned and united in purpose and always be a member of the kind and compassionate retinues of Bodhisattvas.

Now, may the merit and virtue of bowing this Repentance create the causes and conditions for untying all knots of animosity and for enabling the karmic offenses and obstacles of all teachers of Dharma, acharyas, ordination certifying masters, fellow monastics of the three seniorities, their relatives, including all beings of the four births and the six paths, throughout the three periods of time, to be completely eradicated. Now, may the animosity of all beings throughout the ten directions and three periods of time be resolved. May all beings include those we have encountered and those we have not, those in the heavenly realm, and those in the realms of ascetic masters, asuras, the hells, hungry ghosts, animals, humans as well as those who are our relatives.

From now until we attain bodhi, may all our karmic offenses and obstacles be completely eradicated, and may we also be ultimately liberated from all animosity. May we be free from the fetters of habitual afflictions and attain eternal purity. May we forever leave the four destinies and have self-mastery over all future births. May our every thought flow with the Dharma and our mind be constantly at ease. May we be replete with the adornments of the six paramitas, ultimately perfect the practices and vows of the Ten Grounds, attain the Buddha's ten powers[6] and unobstructed spiritual prowess. May we soon accomplish anuttara-samyak-sambodhi, the Proper and Equal Enlightenment.

Today, we are here in this Bodhimanda due to our shared karma. The previous texts have explained the overall concepts and methods for resolving all animosity of the three periods of time. Next, let us focus on self-purification. Each of us needs to watch over and discipline our minds. Up till now, why have we not gained liberation? We not only have missed the opportunity to personally receive a prediction from a Buddha, but we also have been unable to hear the singular sound of the Buddhas' teaching. Because our karmic offenses are so grave and our animosity so ingrained, we fail to see previous Buddhas, Bodhisattvas, sages and worthy ones, and we also risk failing to see them in the future. We are also fearful that we may not be able to hear the twelve-division Dharma, except for the echoes of the Teaching, and so are at risk that our minds may be forever obstructed by ignorance. Thus we are unable to free ourselves from animosity and the evil paths. When we reach the end of our lives, we will find ourselves embroiled in the sea of suffering, repeatedly revolving in the three paths of woe, undergoing each and every dire retribution in the evil destinies. When will we be able to regain a human body? Thinking and contemplating thus, we truly feel heart-wrenching sadness and deep agony.

Those of us who are or have been monastics have been gathered in and transformed by the virtuous breeze of the Mahayana. We have renounced the householder's life, severed the ties with our beloved ones, bade farewell to our parents, forsaken the mundane world of vanity, and freed ourselves of mundane conditions. How can we not cherish our time and seek to become established in cultivation? If we are not firm in our resolve, patiently enduring suffering and toil, swallowing our sorrow and woes, then when we suddenly become gravely ill, the intermediate *skandhas* state will manifest before us. Then we will see hell guardians, such as rakshasas, ox-headed guardians, each with strange or ghastly appearances who arrive instantaneously. As wind-knives slice our body, we become terrified and confused, unaware of our moaning or wailing relatives. At that moment, how could it be possible to muster even a single thought of wholesome resolve, not to mention to bow this Repentance that we have today? At that time, what awaits us are the three evil destinies with their limitless suffering.

Each and everyone one of us in this assembly today should apply great effort and cherish every minute. If we allow ourselves to seek comfort and do as we please, we will delay progress in cultivation. If we can patiently endure all suffering, we will accelerate the bringing forth of our courageous mind.

So the sutras say, "Compassion is the Bodhimanda because it enables one to endure suffering; bringing forth the resolve and cultivation is the Bodhimanda, because it enables one to achieve the mission."

Becoming adorned by myriads of goodness comes about through diligent effort. Is it possible to cross over the vast ocean without a boat? To merely wish to cultivate without actually doing it, when aspirations and actions do not tally, will not result in any fruition. This is akin to a starving person just imagining all kinds of delicacies. It does not help resolve his hunger; he will still remain hungry! Thus we should understand that if we really want to attain supreme and wondrous fruition, our aspirations and actions must always match. We should cherish our time, bring forth the enhanced resolve, and with deep shame and great remorse, repent in order to eradicate our offenses and resolve all animosity.

Otherwise, we will continue to dwell in darkness and will never see the dawn of day. And then, when we see others gain liberation, we will be even more regretful, but it will be too late. Let us all now with utmost, heartfelt sincerity, bow in full prostration and take refuge with the Greatly Kind and Compassionate Ones who are like fathers to those of us in this world.

Namo Maitreya Buddha
Namo Shakyamuni Buddha
Namo Defining Principles Buddha
Namo Vow to Give Buddha
Namo Precious Assembly Buddha
Namo Leader of Multitudes Buddha
Namo Traveling Stride Buddha
Namo Peace and Tranquity Buddha
Namo Differentiating Dharma Buddha
Namo Superior and Honored Buddha

Namo Extremely Lofty Virtue Buddha
Namo Superior Sound of the Lion Buddha
Namo Delightful and Playful Buddha
Namo Dragon Brilliance Buddha
Namo Flower Mountain Buddha
Namo Dragon Delight Buddha
Namo King of Mastery over Fragrance Buddha
Namo Great Fame Buddha
Namo Heavenly Power Buddha
Namo Virtue Banner Buddha
Namo Foremost among Dragons Buddha
Namo Mind for Practicing Goodness Buddha
Namo Adornment of Causes Buddha
Namo Supreme Wisdom Buddha
Namo Countless Moons Buddha
Namo Words of Truth Buddha
Namo Brilliance of Sun Buddha
Namo Medicine Superior Bodhisattva
Namo Supreme Medicine Bodhisattva
Namo Boundless Body Bodhisattva
Namo Guan Shi Yin Bodhisattva

Again, we take refuge with the Three Treasures of the ten directions to the ends of empty space. We have accumulated karmic obstacles that are deeper than the great earth. We are shrouded by ignorance, unawakened from the endless night. We are constantly led by the three poisons, creating the causes of animosity. Consequently, we are lost and drown in the realm of the three existences, never escaping. Today, relying on the power of the great compassion and kindness of all Buddhas and Bodhisattvas, we begin to awaken and understand. Feeling shame and remorse, we sincerely confess and repent, seeking the Buddhas and Bodhisattvas to compassionately gather us in.

With their power of great wisdom, inconceivable power, power of infinite self-mastery, power of subduing the four demons, power of extinguishing all afflictions, power of resolving all animosity, power of taking across all living beings, power of bringing peace and comfort to all living beings, power of liberating beings from the hells, power of helping and taking across hungry ghosts, power of rescuing animals, power of gathering in and transforming asuras, power of gathering in humans, power of ending the outflows of heavenly beings and ascetic masters, power of boundless and measureless merit and virtue, and power of endless and measureless wisdom, may they enable all living beings with animosity in the four births and the six paths to come to this Bodhimanda to accept our repentance.

May we discard all animosity and free ourselves from thoughts of friends or foes. May all of us be liberated from the karma of animosity and forever leave behind the eight difficulties and the suffering in the four destinies. May we always encounter Buddhas, hear the Dharma and be enlightened to the Way. May we bring forth the bodhi resolve to walk the transcendental path, practice profoundly the four limitless minds and six paramitas. May we perfect all practices and vows and eventually reach the Tenth Ground. May we realize the vajra mind and accomplish Proper Enlightenment.

Today, we are here in this Bodhimanda due to our shared karma. If we are to seek the cause of all animosity, we realize that it and everything else originate from the three karmas. That is why often we see practitioners of the Way having to bear with various retributions of suffering. Since we are aware that this is the source of all suffering, we should bring forth a courageous mind to overcome and eliminate it. The key to eradicate suffering is solely through repentance. Therefore, the sutras extol the two kinds of wholesome people - first are those who do not commit any evil, and second are those who are able to repent and reform. Now we in the great assembly who seek to repent and reform, should purify our mind and be solemn in demeanour. Within, we should feel shame and remorse, and outwardly, we should have deep compassionate regard for all.

If we can bring forth two kinds of minds, we can eradicate all offenses. What are these two kinds of minds? One is shame, and the second is remorse. Facing sages, we are ashamed; facing humans, we are remorseful. With shame we will be able to repent and eradicate all animosity; with remorse, we will be able to teach and enable others to untie all knots of animosity. Shame can spur a person to offer various kinds of good deeds, while remorse enables one to rejoice in others' good deeds. Shame is the internal feeling of self-humiliation, while remorse is the outward expression of confessing one's wrongdoing. By applying this Dharma of shame and remorse, cultivators can attain unobstructed happiness.

Today, giving rise to great shame and remorse, we sincerely carry out this great repentance before all living beings of the four births and the six paths. Why? Because the sutras state that all living beings have close affinities with us. They may have been our past parents, teachers, or siblings, including all other relations. Having fallen into the net of ignorance, we are mutually unaware. We are unable to recognize each other and frequently casue each other to be afflicted. Consequently, we create unlimited and endless animosity. All of us in this great assembly are now awakened to this. With great sincerity and earnestness, our one single thought will surely evoke a response from the Buddhas of the ten directions, and our one bow can eradicate endless animosity. Let us all now with utmost, heartfelt sincerity, bow in full prostration and take refuge with the Greatly Kind and Compassionate Ones who are like fathers to those of us in this world.

Namo Maitreya Buddha
Namo Shakyamuni Buddha
Namo Mind in Samadhi Buddha
Namo Limitless Appearance Buddha
Namo Bright Illumination Buddha
Namo Precious Hallmark Buddha
Namo Severing Doubt Buddha
Namo Skilled in Clarity Buddha

Namo Firm Strides Buddha
Namo Enlightened Buddha
Namo Flower Hallmarks Buddha
Namo King Lord of Mountain Buddha
Namo Great Awe-inspiring Virtue Buddha
Namo Pervasive View Buddha
Namo Limitless Names Buddha
Namo Jeweled Heaven Buddha
Namo Dwelling in Principles Buddha
Namo Contentment Buddha
Namo Superb Praise Buddha
Namo Worry-free Buddha
Namo Undefiled Buddha
Namo Brahma Heaven Buddha
Namo Radiant Flower Buddha
Namo Different Bodies Buddha
Namo Illuminating the Dharma Buddha
Namo Exhaustive Views Buddha
Namo Virtuous Purification Buddha
Namo Manjushri Bodhisattva
Namo Samantabhadra Bodhisattva
Namo Boundless Body Bodhisattva
Namo Guan Shi Yin Bodhisattva

Again, we take refuge with the Three Treasures of the ten directions to the ends of empty space. May the Three Treasures aid and gather us in so that we can eradicate our offenses and return to purity through this repentance. From now until we attain bodhi, may all of us now repenting be liberated from all animosity. May all our suffering be eradicated. May we be forever pure, free from habits and fetters of afflictions. May we forever leave the four destinies and have self-mastery over all future births. We will personally attend to the Buddhas and receive predictions from them. We will readily practice the six paramitas and the four limitless minds. We will possess the four eloquences and gain the ten powers of the Buddhas. Our bodies will be adorned with hallmarks and fine features, and we will possess unobstructed spiritual powers. We will realize the vajra mind and accomplish Proper and Equal Enlightenment.

Praise

> *Coming and going in the four births,*
> *We revolve in the six paths,*
> *Because of continuous delusion and animosity.*
> *Relying on the Buddha's empathy,*
> *May our animosity be resolved,*
> *And all fallen ones be free and at ease.*

Namo Ground of Difficult to Surpass Bodhisattva Mahasattva

(three times)

Concluding the Repentance

> His wonderful hallmarks tower magnificently, like the mid-day sun shining brilliantly in the sky.
> His compassion is like a sweeping breeze, awakening the earth with spring thunder.
> He sprinkles sweet dew on defiled minds and showers ghee-like nourishment unto beings numerous as Ganges sands;
> He responds to every wish and fulfills every vow.
> The Tathagata unfurls the radiance of the Five Eyes, mingling its light with the Buddha's work throughout the Five Periods[7].

[Dharma Host]: On behalf of _____ [those who seek to repent], we practice this Repentance Dharma of Kindness and Compassion in the Bodhimanda. We have now successfully completed Roll Five, bowing the Repentance based on all the aforementioned texts and accomplishing its merit and virtue.

Lofty Sanghans of *five* virtues[8] gather, worshipping before the wondrous-hallmark Buddhas abiding at *five* celestial locations. The *fivefold* true incense is lit, and the wisdom torch of the *five* directions[9] kindled. The verse of praise resonates in unison, as flowers of the *five* colors[10] adorn elegantly. With the delicacies we have humbly prepared as offerings, we bow faithfully to the Buddhas, just as the sunflower tends towards the sun. We dedicate the supreme merit from our contemplation and recitation to the Buddha's bodhi and to all beings throughout the dharma realm.

The rare merit attained is hereby dedicated to _____[those who seek to repent] so that they can repent what they have yet to repent and gather the supreme causes they have yet to gather.

We bow and earnestly pray:

May the clouds of the *five* skandas[11] naturally disperse, and the *five* signs of decay[12] not appear; the *five* roots and *five* powers[13] be perfected, the *five* coverings[14] and *five* obstructions[15] melt away; the *five* flowers blossom[16] – awakening of our minds – and the *five* major pure precepts[17] be upheld. May our present family and relatives obtain all of the *five* blessings, our ancestors accomplish the *five* studies[18], and beings in the lowly paths cease revolving on the wheel of samsara and together realize bodhi. May all animosity among foes be resolved, and may foes together be reborn in wholesome paths.

[Dharma host]: With such a short and brief practice of repentance, it is hard to completely wipe out all subtle karmic retributions. For each of the previous wishes or prayers, we can only rely on the Sangha to conduct such Repentance repeatedly.

Praise

The meritorious power of the Emperor of Liang Repentance Roll Five
Enables the deceased and the disciples to eradicate offenses of the
five rebellious acts.

May all realize the Bodhisattva's Ground of Difficult to Surpass.
As the Repentance is chanted our offenses are blown away like flower petals in the wind.
Offenses repented, enmity resolved,
Wisdom and blessing increase as calamities are dispelled.
Liberated from suffering and reborn in the Trayastrimsha,
May we gather at the Dragon Flower's Three Assemblies
And receive a prediction personally from Maitreya Buddha.

Namo Dragon Flower Assembly of Bodhisattvas Mahasattvas
(three times)

Final praise

Emperor of Liang Repentance Roll Five now concludes.
We dedicate its merit to the four benefactors and the three realms.
May all in this assembly enjoy increased longevity and blessings,
May the Dharma water cleanse our offenses.
May the deceased be reborn in the Western Pure Land.
May the Bodhisattvas of the Ground of Difficult to Surpass compassionately gather us in.

Namo Ascending the Path to the Clouds Bodhisattva Mahasattva
(three times)

End Notes

1. **Five Eyes:** The heavenly eye, the flesh eye, the Dharma eye, the wisdom eye, and the Buddha eye.
2. **Six emotions:** the emotions that are produced from the six organs.
3. **Six sense objects (six dusts):** The objects that match with the six sense organs, which are sight, sound, smell, taste, object of touch, and dharma.

4. **Three Marks:** three marks of production, extinction, and change. Or the three forms of nirvana (liberation), non-nirvana, and absence of both (extinction).

5. *Acharya:* spiritual teacher

6. **Ten powers:**
   a) the wisdom power of knowing points of enlightenment and non-enlightenment,
   b) the wisdom power of knowing the karmic retribution of the three periods of time,
   c) the wisdom power of knowing all the dhyanas, liberations, and samadhis,
   d) the wisdom power of knowing the superiority or baseness of the roots of all living beings,
   e) the wisdom power of knowing the various understandings,
   f) the wisdom power of knowing the various realms,
   g) the wisdom power of knowing where all paths lead,
   h) the wisdom power of knowledge of the unobstructed heavenly eye,
   i) the wisdom power, without outflows, of knowing former lives,
   j) the wisdom power of eternally severing all habitual energies.

7. **Five periods:** Buddha's teaching is divided into five periods and eight kinds of teachings. The five periods are the period of Avatamsaka, agama, vaipulya, prajna, and nirvana.

8. **Five virtues:** warmth, good-heartedness, respect, thrift, yielding.

9. **Five directions:** east, west, south, north, and center.

10. **Five colors:** blue, yellow, red, white, black.

11. **Five skanda:** form skanda, feeling skanda, cognition skanda, formation skanda, and consciousness skanda. Skanda means gathering.

12. **Five signs of decay:** there are two kinds of decaying, the five major signs of decaying and the five minor signs of decaying.

When the five signs of decaying appear in heavenly beings, it indicates those living beings will face the end of their life in the heaven. The five major signs of decaying are:

a) Flowers on the head wither: the ever-fresh flower head dresses of the gods begin to wilt.

b) Uncontrolled defilement: the permanently clean clothes of the gods become soiled.

c) Sweating armpits: the gods never sweat, but a sign of their decay is that they perspire under their arms.

d) Unpleasant odor: the normally fragrant bodies of the gods begin to stink when the signs of decay appear.

e) Uneasiness: the gods normally sit still and composed, as if in samadhi. When the signs of decay appear, they begin to fidget.

13. **Five roots** and **five powers:** The five roots are faith, vigor, mindfulness, samadhi or concentration, and wisdom. The five powers are the power that come from the five roots, the power of faith, the power of vigor, the power of mindfulness, the power of samadhi, and the power of wisdom.

14. **Five coverings:** mental and moral hindrances, which are desire or greed, anger, drowsiness or torpor, excitability, and doubt.

15. **Five obstructions:** hindrances of the passion-nature, of karma caused in previous lives, of the affairs of life, of no friendly or competent perceptions, and partial knowledge.

16. **Five flower blossoms (five minds):** the first impression, attention, decision, effort, and the production from other causes.

17. **Five pure precepts:** refraining from killing, stealing, sexual misconduct, lying, and taking intoxicants.

18. **Five studies:** in ancient India, there were five kinds of studies, also known as five understandings of knowledge.

a) sabda: the study of sound, this refers to the study of language, such as grammar and composition;

b) silpakarmasthana: the arts;
c) cikitsa: medical study which refers to all studies in medical field;
d) hetu: this refers to the present logic studies
e) adhyatma: inner study, refers to all studies of religion or philosophy.

ROLL SIX

Namo Buddhas and Bodhisattvas of the Dragon Flower Assembly
(*bow three times*)

Praise

Spring comes, flowers bud;
The hundred grasses turn vibrantly green.
The tea shoots release fragrant vapors
As snow flakes shimmer in the jade tea cups.
The story of Master Zhaozhou comes to life,
Dispelling the sleep demon to its sunset.

Namo Universal Offering Bodhisattva Mahasattva (*three times*)

Listen respectfully

The king of enlightenment Shakyamuni Buddha manifests *six* years of ascetic practice and accomplishes the Way. He subdues the demons in the *six* desire heavens and radiates his spiritual light. He is adorned with retinues of Bodhisattvas who all practice the *six* paramitas. He is surrounded by throngs of Hearers who realize the fruition of the *six* spiritual powers. He bestows predictions, and heaven and earth in the *six* directions quake and tremble. He speaks Dharma, and flowers shower profusely throughout the *six* periods. His wondrous virtues are inconceivable and his radiance of kindness shines on all.

[Dharma Host]: On behalf of _____ [those who seek to repent], we practice this Kindness and Compassion Repentance Dharma in the Bodhimanda and have now come to Roll Six. With all conditions fulfilled, we now enter the Repentance Platform.

Exquisite fragrance effuses forth from *six zhu* of incense;
The lamp's radiance penetrates the *six* heavens;
Six flowers hover throughout space in the *six* directions;
Offered are the *six* flavors[1] to Buddha images in the *six* heavens.

We bow with utmost sincerity, and diligently repent of our faults. We are earnestly mindful of the retributions we now suffer, resulting from causes planted in kalpas past. We follow and drift along with our *six* sense faculties and indulge ourselves. Our *six* consciousnesses seek and grasp for conditions of advantage and benefit. We are greedy for the *six* sense objects and their illusory states, thus creating the revolving wheel of the *six* destinies. We disregard the cultivation of the *six*fold mindfulness[2] and have not perfected the pure practices of the *six* paramitas.

Birth after birth, we receive the endless suffering of retributions, and life after life we fail to put an end to conditions of delusion. Now, our hearts are laden with shame and remorse, while our minds are filled with utmost sincerity. By imperial decree, the greatly virtuous Sanghans of the *six* harmonies have composed this Repentance text leading to the *six* paramitas. Throughout the *six* periods we earnestly repent to resolve the offenses of birth in the *six* destinies. Looking up to you with reverence, King of Enlightenment, we pray that you will invisibly bless and protect us.

> To the greatly kind, compassionate ones who rescue living beings,
> The ones of great joyous giving who rescue conscious beings,
> The ones adorned with the light of hallmarks and fine characteristics,
> The Assembly return their lives in worship with utmost sincerity.

Commencement of the Repentance

We now begin the Repentance Dharma of Kindness and Compassion in the Bodhimanda. Together in this assembly, we single-mindedly return to and rely on all Buddhas of the three periods of time.
Namo Buddhas of the past, Vipashyin Buddha

Namo Shikhin Buddha
Namo Vishvabhu Buddha
Namo Krakucchanda Buddha
Namo Kanakamuni Buddha
Namo Kashyapa Buddha
Namo our Fundamental Teacher Shakyamuni Buddha
Namo Honored Future Buddha, Maitreya

Section 9 Resolving Animosity (continued)

Today, we are here in this Bodhimanda due to our shared karma. We first repent of our evil karma of the body before all living beings of the four births and the six paths. The sutras state, "Suffering arises because we have a body. Without the body, suffering ceases." Thus we know that our body is the root of all suffering. The severe retribution of the three evil paths comes about from the presence of a body. It is not possible for us to receive the retribution for other people's deeds, nor can other people suffer the retribution for our deeds. If we plant the cause, we ourselves will reap its effect. A single evil act of karma can lead to boundless retribution. How much more so for a person who commits evil karma throughout his life!

We only care about our own bodies and are not concerned about the bodies of others. We only care about our own suffering but are not bothered about the suffering of others. We only seek peace and happiness for ourselves and fail to realize that others too seek the same. Because of ignorance, we discriminate between self and others, and give rise to thoughts of friends or foes; thus mutual resentment and animosity pervade the six paths. If we do not resolve these knots, when can we break away from the six paths? Suffering from kalpa to kalpa is truly pathetic. Thus let us bring forth a courageous mind, a mind of deep shame and remorse, to repent completely. Then, with a single thought we will surely evoke a response from the Buddhas of the ten directions, and our one bow can eradicate limitless knots of animosity. Let us all now with utmost, heartfelt sincerity, bow in full prostration and take refuge with the Greatly Kind and Compassionate Ones who are like fathers to those of us in this world.

Namo Maitreya Buddha
Namo Shakyamuni Buddha
Namo Moon Face Buddha
Namo Precious Lamp Buddha
Namo Precious Hallmark Buddha
Namo Superior Renown Buddha
Namo Renowned Deeds Buddha
Namo Infinite Sound Buddha
Namo *Wei Lan* Buddha
Namo Lion's Body Buddha
Namo Grasping the Meaning Buddha
Namo Invincible Buddha
Namo Grades of Merit and Virtue Buddha
Namo Moon Hallmark Buddha
Namo Attaining Strength Buddha
Namo Boundless Conduct Buddha
Namo Blossoming Flowers Buddha
Namo Cleansing Defilement Buddha
Namo Vision of All Meaning Buddha
Namo Courageous Strength Buddha
Namo Abundance and Contentment Buddha
Namo Blessings and Virtue Buddha
Namo Spontaneous in Timing Buddha
Namo Vast Resolve Buddha
Namo Revered Merit and Virtue Buddha
Namo Skillfully Quiescent Buddha
Namo Wealth Deva Buddha
Namo Sounds of Jubilation Buddha
Namo Great Strength Bodhisattva
Namo Ever-vigorous Bodhisattva

Namo Boundless Body Bodhisattva
Namo Guan Shi Yin Bodhisattva

Again, we take refuge with the Three Treasures of the ten directions to the ends of empty space. May you, with the power of the
Buddhas, the power of the Dharma, the power of the Bodhisattvas, and
the power of all sages and worthy ones enable all those who harbor
animosity in the four births and the six paths to come to this Bodhimanda.

Together, each and every one of us should whole-heartedly repent,
contemplate and state aloud, "I, _____, from time without beginning until now, have been entrenched in ignorance[3]. Because of this
body, I have created evil karma and knots of animosity when I was in
the heavenly realm, the human realm, the realm of asuras, the realm
of hells, the realm of hungry ghosts, and the animal realm. I now pray,
by the power of the Buddha, the power of the Dharma, the power of
the Bodhisattvas, and the power of all sages and worthy ones that all
those who harbor animosity, created throughout the three periods of
time and between beings in the four births and the six paths, whether
encountered or not, light or severe, be cleansed of their offenses,
become pure again through repenting and reforming, and never again
undergo suffering in the three realms. May they always be in the presence of Buddhas.

Furthermore, all of us in this assembly today, have created all
kinds of animosity in the evil paths from time without beginning until
now because of the causes and conditions of our evil body karma.
From the roots of the three poisons of hatred, greed or delusion, we
committed the ten evil deeds. We may have been fond of killing animals, such as cows or sheep. We may have killed each other due to
disputes over farmland, houses, or money.

Also, from time without beginning until now, we may have
deceived others by pretending to be doctors and administered
improper moxibustion, acupuncture, or other treatment for the sake
of profit and gain. Offenses such as these resulted in limitless

animosity against us. We now repent and reform of them all and beseech that they be eradicated.

Also, from time without beginning until now, we may have starved living beings, robbed them of their food, tormented them and made them suffer, or cut off their water supply. We now repent and reform of all such evil karma and the animosity resulting thereof and beseech that they be eradicated.

From time without beginning until now, we may also have killed animals and eaten their flesh; we may have indulged in the three poisons and whipped or flogged beings; we may have killed beings by poisoning their food. Offenses such as these have created boundless animosity. We now repent and reform of them all and beseech that they be eradicated.

Also, from time without beginning until now, we have stayed away from good teachers and drawn near to evil friends. Based on the three evil karmas of body, speech, and mind, we have committed all kinds of offenses. We may have unnecessarily indulged in killing the young, causing their premature death. We may have done it by draining or ruining marshes or ponds, or by blocking waterways such as ditches or canals, thus harming or killing waterborne creatures including tiny worms. We may have set fire to mountains and meadows, netted or trapped animals on land or in water, thus killing and harming all sorts of creatures. From offenses such as these, we have created boundless animosity. We now repent and reform of them all, and beseech that they be eradicated.

Also, from time without beginning until now, we have not been kind and compassionate, nor have we been impartial. We may have shortchanged others by manipulating scales and oppressed the disadvantaged. We may have destroyed the cities or towns of others, confiscated, robbed, or looted their belongings, and stolen their wealth for our own use. We may have been untrustworthy and may have harmed or killed each other. Offenses such as these caused boundless animosity. We now repent and reform of them all, and beseech that they be eradicated.

Also, from time without beginning until now, in mind or in deeds, we may have not been kind and compassionate. In the six paths, we inflicted misery upon living beings; we may have unjustifiably whipped or flogged our relatives and retinues; we may have bound or locked beings in dark cells; we may have tortured, impaled or severed their bodies, amputated or mutilated them, and skinned, roasted, or boiled them. With such offenses, we created boundless animosity. We now repent and reform of them all, and beseech that they be eradicated.

Also, from time without beginning until now, we have committed the three evil karmas of the body, the four evil karmas of speech, and the three evil karmas of the mind. We have committed the five rebellious acts and the four major offenses, as well as other types of unwholesome deeds. There has been no evil that we have not done. Young, brash, feeling blessed and fortunate, we were not fearful of spirits and ghosts and feared only that we could not outsmart others or that they were better than us.

On account of our nobility or lineage, we have been arrogant or oppressive towards others, thereby creating animosity. On account of erudition, we have been arrogant or oppressive towards others, thereby creating animosity. On account of literary skill, we have acted arrogantly or oppressively towards others, thereby creating animosity. On account of a luxurious lifestyle or family fortune, we have behaved arrogantly or oppressively towards others, thereby creating animosity. On account of eloquence or debating skill, we may have been arrogant or oppressive towards others, thereby creating animosity. All such animosity may have been created due to our disrespect of the fields of blessing of the Three Treasures and their revered images; or animosity may have been created with regard to our teachers, *acharyas*, or created with regard to our monastics of three seniorities; or animosity may have been created with regard to our fellow monastics or fellow practitioners, or created with regard to our parents or relatives. For all such limitless and boundless animosity, we now repent and reform of them all, and beseech that they be eradicated.

Also, from time without beginning until now, all sorts of bound-less animosity may have been created within the heavenly realm, the human realm, the asura realm, the realm of the hells, the animal realm, the hungry ghost realm, including the realms of all living beings in the ten directions. We now repent and reform of such offenses and beseech that they be eradicated.

Also, from time without beginning until now, we may have been jealous of others and may have been obsequious or devious in order to seek promotion. We may have shamelessly followed and drifted along with deviant views for the sake of fame or profit. Only Buddhas and great Bodhisattvas can see and understand completely all these knots of animosity, whether severe or light, whether many or few, as well as the causes and effects of our offenses.

May all Buddhas and Bodhisattvas kindly be mindful of us as we repent of the offenses we have committed throughout births and deaths without beginning. These are offenses we have committed our-selves, told others to do, or condoned their being done, including taking things without permission from the Three Treasures, whether we took them ourselves, told others to take them, or condoned their being taken, and whether or not these acts were concealed. Only Bud-dhas and Bodhisattvas see and know the magnitude and severity of all these offenses. These offenses warrant our falling into the evil des-tines of the hells, hungry ghosts or animals or warrant our lowly rebirth or rebirth in the border regions of the Buddhadharma. We now repent and reform of all the offenses that result in animosity and beseech that they be eradicated.

The spiritual powers of all Buddhas are inconceivable. May your kindness and compassion protect and save all living beings. May you witness and accept our repentance for our past offenses committed towards our parents, teachers, family members or retinues in the four births and the six paths and help us untie the knots of animosity. May all who suffer animosity in the six paths relinquish all their animosity and be joyful, be free of thoughts of friends or foes, and be unob-structed like empty space in everything they do.

From now until we accomplish bodhi, may we cut off all afflictions and purify the three karmas of body, speech, and mind so that all animosity will forever be extinguished. May we be reborn in any of the jeweled heavenly palaces, if we so wish; may we constantly practice the four limitless minds and six paramitas, constantly cultivate and be adorned with hundreds of blessings, and be replete with a myriad of wholesome qualities. May we dwell in proper samadhi and gain the indestructible vajra body. May we, within a single thought, pervasively respond to beings in the six paths in order to rescue them without exception, and together attain Buddhahood, the Proper and Equal Enlightenment.

Today, we are here in this Bodhimanda due to our shared karma. Together we have repented the karmic offenses of the body. Since our bodily karma has now been purified, we should work on the karmic mistakes we have made with our speech, which are also a source of animosity and trouble. That is why Buddhas warn us to not to engage in divisive speech, harsh speech, false speech, and frivolous speech. We should understand that flattery and words that are flowery but insubstantial stir up issues of right and wrong, create serious trouble, and bring about severe retribution. We in this world harbor venomous thoughts, speak vicious words, and do malevolent deeds, inflicting harm upon other beings. The victims of our malevolence harbor animosity and resentment and resolve to avenge the wrongs. They may succeed in this life or in later lives. Harboring such resentment and animosity throughout the six paths, many beings take endless revenge against each other. All these circumstances are caused by our past karma and do not come from nowhere.

We should understand that the three aspects of bodily karma and the four aspects of speech karma are the very source of evil. Worldly people who are not filial and loyal will enter Mount Tai of the underworld and undergo the retributions of being boiled or burned. Monastics who do not take delight in the Buddhadharma will always be reborn in evil places and be plagued by evil conditions. Thus we should understand that all such animosity fuels the three evil karmas.

Among the three evil karmas, the evil karma of speech is more readily committed and results in all kinds of dire retributions, trapping us in long dark nights with no dawn in sight, keeping us unaware of our suffering.

Today, we are here in this Bodhimanda due to our shared karma. The main reason we keep revolving in the cycle of the six paths is because of our speech karma. We have spoken casually or engaged in wanton speech. We have readily made eloquent excuses or hurt people with sharp words. We have used exaggerated or pretentious words. Our actions have contradicted our words. Thus we bring upon ourselves such evil retributions and can never be free throughout kalpas. How can each of us not be fearful and repent of these offenses?

From the time we first had consciousness until now, we have committed unwholesome speech karma. There is no evil that we have not uttered. We speak ill of our parents, teachers, relatives, retinues, and other beings of the four births and the six paths. Our words have been coarse and harsh; our speech destructive and violent. In gathering with friends, we have engaged in meaningless and unrighteous speech. We have fabricated something out of nothing or twisted something into nothing. What we saw, we denied seeing, and what we did not see, we claimed to have seen. What we heard, we denied hearing, and what we did not hear, we claimed to have heard. What we did, we denied doing, and what we did not do, we claimed to have done. We have committed all such upside-down speech, to the extent of claiming heaven to be earth, and vice versa.

In the process we benefited ourselves but hurt or harmed others and even slandered each other. Speaking of ourselves, we claimed all the good and virtue; speaking of others, we attributed all the evil we could, even criticizing sages and worthy ones, passing judgments on our parents and rulers, ridiculing our teachers and elders, and slandering good and wise advisors. Our speech was audacious, unrestrained, unscrupulous, and not in accord with the Way. In this life, we thus encounter calamities such as litigation, imprisonment, injuries or death. In future lives, we will have to undergo other retributions for infinite kalpas. An instance of light mocking or taunting can result in limitless grave offenses; how much the more when we utter sharp or harsh words, directed at all beings.

From time without beginning until now, our evil speech karma has resulted in animosity among heavenly beings, humans, asuras, hell-beings, hungry ghosts, animals, and among parents, teachers, elders, relatives and retinues. On behalf of them all, we now practice what Bodhisattvas practice, make the same vows that Bodhisattvas make, bow with respect and take refuge with the Greatly Kind and Compassionate Ones who are like fathers to those of us in this world.

> Namo Maitreya Buddha
> Namo Shakyamuni Buddha
> Namo Pure and Relinquishing Doubts Buddha
> Namo Boundless Support Buddha
> Namo Wonderful Bliss Buddha
> Namo Never Letting Others Down Buddha
> Namo Free of Attachments Buddha
> Namo Taksaka Buddha
> Namo Leader of the Multitudes Buddha
> Namo Light of the World Buddha
> Namo Many Virtues Buddha
> Namo Pusya Buddha
> Namo Boundless Awe-inspiring Virtue Buddha
> Namo Meaning and Principle Buddha
> Namo Medicine King Buddha
> Namo Severing Evil Buddha
> Namo Heat-free Buddha
> Namo Skilled in Subduing Buddha
> Namo Renowned Virtue Buddha
> Namo Blossoming Virtue Buddha
> Namo Courage and Virtue Buddha
> Namo Vajra Army Buddha
> Namo Great Virtue Buddha

Namo Mind of Quiescence Buddha
Namo Fragrant Elephant Buddha
Namo Narayana Buddha
Namo Skillfully Dwelling Buddha
Namo Never Resting Bodhisattva
Namo Wonderful Voice Bodhisattva
Namo Boundless Body Bodhisattva
Namo Guan Shi Yin Bodhisattva

Again, we take refuge with the Three Treasures of the ten directions to the ends of empty space. May the power of the Buddha, power of the Dharma, power of the Bodhisattvas, and power of the sages and worthy ones cause all living beings of the four births and the six paths to awaken and together come to this Bodhimanda. If there are living beings who desire to come but are hindered due to physical constraints, may the power of the Buddha, power of the Dharma, power of the Bodhisattvas, and power of the sages and worthy ones gather in their spirits and bring them to this Bodhimanda to repent of their evil speech karma.

From time without beginning until now, we may have been entrenched in ignorance, causing us to commit evil speech karma, which has generated animosity among beings throughout the six paths. May the spiritual power of the Three Treasures cause living beings of the four births and the six paths to eradicate forever all knots of animosity of the three periods of time.

From time without beginning until now, rooted in the three poisons of greed, hatred, or ignorance, we may have committed the ten evils. We have generated boundless offenses from the four evil speech karmas. We have uttered harsh speech, afflicting and upsetting our parents, teachers, relatives, retinues, and all other beings. We have created the karma of telling lies to our parents, teachers, relatives, retinues, and all other beings. What we saw, we denied seeing; what we did not see, we claimed to have seen. What we heard, we denied hearing; what we did not hear, we claimed to have heard. What we knew, we denied knowing; what we did not know, we claimed to have known. We may have lied because of arrogance or jealousy. Thus we have created all such boundless and limitless offenses. We now repent and reform of them all, and beseech that they be eradicated.

From time without beginning until now, we may have created divisive speech karma. Unable to take criticism, we may have retaliated by using divisive speech, false speech or fabrications, thereby causing bitterness, straining relationships, and creating break ups. We may also have caused contention between two families by our mocking, taunting or joking. We may have caused kin and loved ones to separate, thus destroying family relationships. We may have spread malice between superiors and subordinates. Thus we have created all such boundless and limitless offenses. We now repent and reform of them all, and beseech that they be eradicated.

From time without beginning until now, we may have committed the offense of frivolous speech by uttering meaningless words that have no benefit. We have afflicted our parents, teachers, elders, and fellow students. We have also afflicted or harmed other beings in the six paths. All such karma of speech has resulted in limitless animosity. We now repent and reform of them all, and beseech that they be eradicated.

We now pray, by the power of the Buddha, the power of the Dharma, the power of the Bodhisattvas, and the power of all sages and worthy ones that all animosity, created throughout the three periods of time between beings of the four births and the six paths be ultimately resolved. May all our offenses be severed and forever ended. May we never again create any animositythat would casue us to fall into the three evil paths. May we never again inflict misery upon beings in the six paths.

From this day forth, may we cast aside all animosity and be free of any thought of friends or foes. May all be united in harmony, like water and milk blended together. May we all have the happiness of those of the First Ground and forever become kin in Dharma and members of the compassionate family. From now until we attain bodhi, may we all be free from the retributions of the three realms, sever the karma of the three obstacles, and overcome the five fears. May we advance and deepen our cultivation and practice of the Mahayana Path, attain the four limitless minds and the six paramitas, and enter the Buddha's wisdom. May our ocean of vows be fulfilled. May we attain the six penetrations, the three insights, and thoroughly understand them all. May we gain the Buddha's threefold esoteric modes[4], be replete with the fivefold body, attain the vajra wisdom, and accomplish the fruition of All-Wisdom.

Today, we are here in this Bodhimanda due to our shared karma. We have now completed our repentance for the offenses of body and speech. We should next purify our mind karma. The reason living beings revolve in the cycle of birth and death and fail to attain liberation is because of accumulated mind karma which is deeply entrenched. The ten evils and five rebellious acts basically come from the mind. Thus the Buddha warned us that we must be free of greed, hatred, ignorance, and deviant views, which cause us to fall into the hells and suffer greatly. We should clearly see that the mind is the master of all consciousnesses, just like a king ruling over his officials. We should first know that all calamities originate from our mind. If we wish to repent and reform, we must first subdue our mind and next tame our thoughts.

Why is that? The sutras state, "If one can concentrate the mind, then there is nothing that cannot be achieved." We should know that clearing our thoughts is the source of liberation and purifying our mind is the foundation for advancement in practice. Having done that we will not fall into the evil paths and undergo severe retributions there.

Compared to eliminating body and mouth karma, eliminating mind karma is much more difficult because it is so subtle. The Tatagathas, great sages, and those with All-Wisdom have attained the stage of not needing to watch over their bodies, speech, and minds. However, deluded, ignorant ordinary people like us are unable to be mindful of and guard against the three karmas. If we do not overcome them, then it is impossible to realize goodness. That is why the sutras state, "Guard the mind like guarding a fortress; guard the mouth like a cap seals a bottle." How can we not watch over them carefully?

The body we have had from time without beginning have been borne of ignorance. With this ignorance we have given rise to emotional love which results in limitless rounds of birth and death, entailing all the suffering within each of the twelve links of dependent origination. Due to the eight deviations[5], we revolve endlessly, suffering the eight difficulties of the three evil destinies in the six paths, undergoing limitless suffering.

All this animosity is created by our mind karma. In thought after thought, our mind does not stop seeking and scheming for advantage. We stir up the six emotions in our mind, which drive our five sense faculties to create all kinds of evil karma, both severe and light. When things do not turn out as we wish, we become angry and malicious and may even harm or kill each other due to a lack of sympathy. When it comes to harming others, we may even feel we have not inflicted sufficient torment on them; however, when harm comes to us, we find it hard to even bear a minor pain or itch. When we see the faults of others, we gladly expose them. However, when we make mistakes, we conceal them. We should feel shame and remorse for holding such ideas. Thoughts of anger that arise are like a robber depriving us in our cultivation of the great Way. Therefore, the sutras state, "Anger and hatred are the greatest thieves of merit and virtue."

The *Avatamsaka Sutra* states, "Disciples of Buddha! To give rise to one thought of anger is the greatest of all evil." Why is that? When a thought of anger arises, one will be faced with hundreds of thousands of karmic obstructions, amongst which are:

- obstruction of not encountering conditions of bodhi,
- obstruction of not hearing the Dharma,
- obstruction of being reborn in the evil paths,
- obstruction of having many illnesses,
- obstruction of being slandered,

- obstruction of being born dull,
- obstruction of lacking proper mindfulness,
- obstruction of lacking wisdom,
- obstruction of drawing near bad advisors,
- obstruction of not delighting to see the worthy or wholesome,
- obstruction of being far apart from proper views,

even up to the point of being apart from the Buddha's proper teaching, entering a demonic state, going against good and wise advisors, being born with incomplete organs, being born in a family mired in evil karma, living in the border regions, and other similar obstacles that cannot be fully described.

From time without beginning until now, we have harbored boundless anger and evil in our mind. When a thought of anger arises, we become mean even to our relatives, how much the more to other living beings in the six paths. These afflictions totally overwhelm us so that we are not even aware of our anger or hatred. We may not be able to physically act on this malice, but mentally, there is nothing to restrain us. So when we are finally in a position to act, who can be spared from being victimized? Therefore, 'once the king becomes angry, corpses cover ten thousand miles.' From the time we harbor hatred, we become embroiled in emotional turmoil and may commit offenses such as flogging, beating, clubbing, and shackling. Then, where are our wholesome thoughts of "I will rely on wholesome instructions?" Rather, we are only afraid of not inflicting sufficiently severe torment or causing sufficiently deep misery. Thus, evil is pervasive among sentient beings, regardless of whether one is intelligent or ignorant, rich or poor. In this state of mind, we sentient beings feel no shame and do not seek to repent and reform.

Today, we are here in this Bodhimanda due to our shared karma. We should know that afflictions of hatred and anger are hidden deeply in the dark corners of our mind. We may wish to renounce these afflictions, but when we are faced with these states, without our even being aware, these afflictions have already flared up. As soon as our thoughts surface, we are in the company of evil, and in thought after thought, we become entangled in those states. When can we expect to be free from this suffering?

Great assembly, since we all know about the offense of hatred, how can we still remain as before and not repent and reform? Let each one of us bring forth utmost sincerity to repent and eradicate these offenses. With utmost, heartfelt sincerity, we bow in full prostration and take refuge with the Greatly Kind and Compassionate Ones who are like fathers to those of us in this world.

Namo Maitreya Buddha
Namo Shakyamuni Buddha
Namo Unburdened Buddha
Namo Moon Hallmark Buddha
Namo Lightning Hallmark Buddha
Namo Veneration Buddha
Namo Guarding with Awe-Inspiring Virtue Buddha
Namo Wisdom Sun Buddha
Namo Superior Benefit Buddha
Namo Summit of Mount Sumeru Buddha
Namo Subduing the Thief of Animosity Buddha
Namo Lotus Flower Buddha
Namo Worthy of Praise Buddha
Namo Stages of Wisdom Buddha
Namo Apart from Arrogance Buddha
Namo Narayana Buddha
Namo Ever Happy Buddha
Namo Shortage-Free Country Buddha
Namo Heavenly Renown Buddha
Namo Discerning Extreme Views Buddha
Namo Very Kind Buddha
Namo Much Merit and Virtue Buddha
Namo Jeweled Moon Buddha
Namo Lion Hallmark Buddha

Namo Delight in Dhyana Buddha
Namo Never Lacking Buddha
Namo Playfully Roaming Buddha
Namo Lion's Playfully Roaming Bodhisattva
Namo Lion's Swiftness and Vigor Bodhisattva
Namo Boundless Body Bodhisattva
Namo Guan Shi Yin Bodhisattva

Again, we take refuge with the Three Treasures of the ten directions to the ends of empty space. With their power of kindness and compassion and their power of countless and boundless self-mastery may the Three Treasures accept our repentance of these knots of animosity in our mind towards our parents, teachers, relatives and retinues throughout the four births and the six paths. We hope that all such knots of animosity, whether severe or light, whether acted upon or not, can be eradicated. Also, may any knot of animosity that has not been yet been tied never be tied in the future. May the power of the Three Treasures accept and gather us in and kindly protect us, so that we all can be liberated.

From time without beginning until now, because of the causes and conditions of our evil mind karma, we have been creating animosity, severe or light, with our parents, teachers, relatives and retinues of the four births and the six paths. Ashamed and remorseful, we now confess and repent and pray that all such animosity be eradicated.

From time without beginning until now, because of the roots of the three poisons, we give rise to greed; because of the fetters of greed, we commit the karma of greed, apparent or hidden, that pervades all of empty space and the dharma realm. We give rise to evil thoughts and covet belongings of others, including those of our parents, teachers, relatives and retinues, as well as those of all living beings, including heavenly beings or ascetic masters. Such offenses are boundless and countless. We now repent and reform of them all and beseech that they be eradicated.

From time without beginning until now, we have been committing the karma of hatred, our anger ablaze day and night without a moment's pause. We are easily infuriated with the slightest discomfort or provocation, and thus inflict all manner of distress and harm on living beings, such as clubbing, caning, flogging, drowning, herding and oppressing, starving, binding, imprisoning or hanging them upside-down, For offenses such as these, caused by hatred and boundless animosity, we now repent and reform of them all and beseech that they be eradicated.

From time without beginning until now, we have been adrift in ignorance, committing the karma of delusion. There is no evil that we do not do. Without proper wisdom, we believe in deviant teachings and accept deviant dharmas. Due to such karma of delusion, we have been creating limitless and boundless animosity with others. We now repent and reform of it all and beseech that they be eradicated.

From time without beginning until now, we have been committing the ten evils. There has been no animosity that we do not create and there has been no karma that we do not commit. In thought after thought, we have been grasping for conditions of advantage and benefit without a moment's pause. We incite the six emotions and commit all sorts of karmic entanglements. Whenever we disagree with any action or speech, our hearts seeth with malice and viciousness. Even slight mocks or taunts stir up thoughts of right and wrong. We are never straightforward in our dealings, always harboring crookedness and obsequiousness, without any sense of shame or remorse. Such offenses are boundless and countless and lead to great suffering in the six paths. We now repent and reform all of this and beseech that it be eradicated.

From time without beginning until now, we have committed unwholesome karma of body, speech, and mind. Such evil karma has resulted in our offenses and obstacles with respect to the Buddha, Dharma, Bodhisattvas, sages and worthy ones. These offenses and obstacles are boundless and limitless. Now with utmost sincerity, we repent and reform of them all, and beseech that they be eradicated.

From time without beginning until now, we have committed the ten evils: three with the body, four in speech, and three of the mind, including the five rebellious acts and the the offenses of breaking the four major precepts. There have been no offenses that we have not committed. We now repent and reform of them all and beseech that they be eradicated.

From time without beginning until now, our six sense faculties, together with the six sense objects, and the corresponding six consciousnesses, have given rise to deluded and upside-down thoughts, causing us to scheme and engage with external states, resulting in our committing all kinds of offenses. We now repent and reform of them all and beseech that they be eradicated.

From time without beginning until now, we have violated all three categories of precepts of gathering: the precepts of gathering in all proper deportment, the precepts of gathering in all wholesome Dharma, and the precepts of gathering in all living beings. After death, we will fall into the three evil paths. In the hells, we will undergo countless and boundless kinds of suffering, numerous as sand grains in the Ganges River. Thereafter, without understanding how or why, we are in the realm of hungry ghosts and suffer continuous hunger and afflictions. When in the animal realm, we undergo countless suffering, eating food that is not clean, drinking dirty liquids, and having to endure hunger and cold. When we are back in the human realm, we will be born into families with deviant views causing our minds to be obsequious and devious. Believing in deviant speech will cause us to deviate from the proper path. We will revolve endlessly in the sea of birth and death, without ever knowing when we can be free. The evil and animosity we create over the three periods of time are uncountable, and only the Buddhas know and understand them completely. We now repent and reform of all these offenses and retributions which the Buddhas clearly perceive, and beseech that they be eradicated.

Through this repentance today, may all Buddhas help us eradicate all the animosity that we have created, with their power of great kindness and compassion, great spiritual powers, and power of disciplining and harmonizing living beings to be in accord with the Dharma. We hope to ultimately be liberated from all animosity encountered and yet to be encountered among beings in the four births and the six paths, through the power of great kindness and compassion of all Buddhas, Bodhisattvas, sages and worthy ones.

From now until we attain bodhi, may all our karmic obstructions be cleansed, so that we will attain rebirth in pure lands instead of the evil paths. May we renounce the life of animosity and attain the wisdom-life. May we renounce this enmity-laden body and gain the vajra body. May we relinquish the suffering in the evil paths and gain the bliss of Nirvana. May we be aware of the suffering in the evil paths and bring forth the bodhi resolve. May the four limitless minds and the six paramitas always manifest; and may the four eloquences and six spiritual powers be used with as-you-wish mastery. May we be courageous and vigorous without rest, advancing and perfecting the practices of the Ten Grounds and then returning to take across boundless living beings.

Today, we are here in this Bodhimanda due to our shared karma. May we together with all other past and present living beings of the four births and the six paths to the ends of time, attain purity and liberation through the practice of this repentance. May we all be replete with wisdom and have full mastery of spiritual powers. From now until we attain bodhi, may all living beings always see the Buddhas' Dharma body pervading the ten directions to the ends of empty space. May we always see Buddhas' purple-golden bodies replete with thirty-two hallmarks and the eighty subsidiary fine features. May we also see their various transformation bodies that pervade the ten directions, rescuing living beings. May we always see the light from the Buddhas' white tuft, shining on all hell-beings and relieving them of their suffering.

Today, we are here in this Bodhimanda due to our shared karma. We also pray that from this day forth, with the pure merit and virtue from this repentance, we will all renounce the cycle of birth and death. May we not be reborn in the hells, where we would suffer being boiled, fried, scorched, scalded, burned and mashed. May we not be reborn in the realm of hungry ghosts, where we would suffer hunger and thirst with a needle-sized throat and drum-like belly. May we not be reborn as animals, to be herded, driven, or slaughtered to repay debts. If we are reborn as humans, may we not suffer the *"four hundred and four"* bodily sicknesses[6] or bear unspeakable heat or cold, or suffer beating, flogging, clubbing, cutting, poisoning, hunger or thirst, distress or tiredness.

Great assembly! From this day forth, may we all uphold the precepts purely and be free of defiled thoughts; may we practice benevolence and righteousness with a mind of gratitude; may we make offerings to our parents as we would to the World Honored Ones; may we serve all teachers as if they were Buddhas; may we honor and respect our rulers the same way we would the true Dharma body, and may we regard all other beings as if they were one with us.

Great assembly! From this day forth until we attain bodhi, may we also penetrate the profound meanings of Dharma, attain wisdom of fearlessness[7], and thoroughly understand the Mahayana and Proper Dharma. May we attain self-awakening without relying on others. May we be ever firm in our quest for the Buddha Way and return to rescue boundless living beings, so that they all accomplish the Proper Enlightenment of the Tathagatas.

Today, in this Bodhimanda, may all Tathagatas bear witness as we, visible and invisible beings present, make the following vows: May we be born where sages dwell. May we always be able to establish Bodhimandas and make offerings on a vast scale. May we greatly benefit all living beings. May we always be gathered in by the kindness and compassion of the Three Treasures. May we have the great strength to effectively teach and transform beings. May we always cultivate vigorously and not be attached to worldly pleasures. May we realize the emptiness of dharmas and skillfully transform friends and foes alike, so that they will never retreat from their resolve until they attain bodhi. From this day forth, we resolve to direct even a hair's breadth of goodness towards accomplishing all these vows.

If born as humans, may we be born in families that cultivate goodness. May we also establish Bodhimandas of Kindness and Compassion and make offerings to the Three Treasures. We will dedicate even a hair's breadth of goodness to all living beings. May we never be apart from teachers of Dharma and *acharyas*. May we naturally be vegetarians, sever thoughts of defilement, and be free of the need for spouses and children. May we be trustworthy, loyal, righteous, incorruptible, benevolent, forgiving, fair, and peaceful. May we be able to take a loss to benefit others and not seek fame or gain.

Should we fail to attain liberation by the end of this life and are reborn among ghosts and spirits, may we become wholesome mighty spirits who are great Dharma protectors able to save beings from suffering, and may we naturally have ample food and clothing.

Should we fail to attain liberation by the end of this life and fall into the animal realm, may we dwell deep in the mountains, eating only natural vegetation for food and be free of any suffering. If we have to come out, may we appear in an auspicious form and not be captured and held captive.

Should we fail to attain liberation by the end of this life, and fall into the hungry ghost realm, may we have peace of body and mind, be free of afflictions, be able to teach and transform fellow beings to enable them to give rise to shame and remorse and to bring forth the bodhi resolve.

Should we fail to attain liberation by the end of this life, and fall into the hells, may we naturally remember our own past lives, teach and transform fellow beings to enable them to give rise to shame and remorse and to bring forth the bodhi resolve.

We vow that we will forever be mindful of this bodhi resolve and continuously uphold it without cease. May all Buddhas, Bodhisattvas, and sages in ten directions kindly bear witness to our vows. May the heavenly beings, ascetic masters, four world-protecting heavenly kings, spirits who bless the good and punish the evil, spirits who guard and protect those who uphold mantras, dragon kings of the five directions, dragons and the rest of the eightfold division[8] bear witness as well. Again we bring forth utmost sincerity to take refuge with the Three Treasures.

Verses Praising the Buddha

Great Sage and World Honored One,
Is of lofty and dignified appearance.
His three insights thoroughly illuminate
And he is the King of all sages.
His transformation bodies save living beings.
He is dwelling in his bodhimanda,
Gods and humans admire and take refuge in him
His Dharma boundlessly nourishes and benefits us.
His Eight Voices⁹ are profound and pervasive,
Terrifying and stunning the demonic hordes.
His awe-inspiring virtue quakes the great thousand worlds;
The fragrance of his kind teaching is ever permeating.
With his power of kindness and compassion,
He universally gathers in all those of the ten directions,
So they forever leave the eight sufferings,
And reach the shore of bodhi.

Thus he is called Thus-Come One, Worthy of Offerings, One of Proper and Universal Knowledge, Perfect in Understanding and Conduct, Well-Gone One, One Who Understands the World, Unsurpassed Knight, Taming Hero, Teacher of gods and humans, Buddha, World-Honored One. He takes across numerous living beings and liberates them from the suffering of birth and death. By the spiritual powers of the Buddha and with the merit and virtue from this Repentance and the purity of praising the Buddha may all beings in the four births and the six paths, henceforth until all attain bodhi, have all of their wishes fulfilled and attain self-mastery.

Praise

The mind governs body and mouth,
Yet they are interrelated affecting each other;
We beings go through all six paths, creating grave offenses,
And incurring animosity that keep us deeply entangled.
Relying on the Buddha's boat of kindness,
Beings are ferried across the current of afflictions.

Namo Ground of Manifestation Bodhisattva, Mahasattva

(three times)

Concluding the Repentance

All Tathagatas have, in the past, practiced the *sixfold* mindfulness and the Dharmas of indescribably great compassion and kindness. Cultivating unceasingly, they attained indestructible bodies. Their kindness and compassion are expansive and profound, and their wisdom and expedients immeasurable. Cultivating throughout the *six* periods of time, they perfected the *six* paramitas. We look up to you, the Greatly Awakened Ones, and beseech that you will quickly bestow efficacious responses on us.

[Dharma Host]: On behalf of _____ [those who seek to repent], we practice this Repentance Dharma of Kindness and Compassion in the Bodhimanda. We have now successfully completed Roll Six, accomplishing its merit and virtue.

We burn rare and exotic Sea Shore incense and light the honeycombed array of candles. Arranged on the plates are seven kinds of precious gems; in the cups is the early spring tea from the royal garden. We offer these to all sages and worthy ones, as well as Dharma-protecting gods, and spirit guardians of this Bodhimanda. We dedicate all goodness amassed to universally benefit all sentient beings. On behalf of _____, [those who seek to repent] we pray that all of our lifetimes of karmic obstacles be cleansed and our bliss increased to be like that of the *six* heavens.

We bow and earnestly pray:

> May we attain purity of the *six* sense faculties to be like that of the brilliant sun in the clear sky and clarity of the *six* consciousnesses to be like the perfect autumn moon's reflection in water.
> May all contacts and sensations of the *six* sense faculties become causes for Prajna;
> May we transform all the *six* cravings for the *six* sense objects into the perfect and bright Fruition;
> May all in this and other worlds attain the *six* supreme results;
> May all in the human and heavenly realms perfect the *six* paramitas;
> May all of the four births and the *six* paths enter the gate of liberation;
> May all in the nine abodes of sentient beings and those in the three evil paths transcend the suffering from their drowning and deluded states.
> [Dharma host]: Our sincerity in repentance is not yet perfect, and our offenses grave beyond words. Thus I am taking the liberty to request that together, we continue to repent and reform.

Praise

> *The meritorious power of the Emperor of Liang Repentance Roll Six Enables the deceased and the disciples to eradicate offenses committed through the six sense faculties.*
> *May all realize the Bodhisattva's Ground of Manifestation.*
> *As the Repentance is chanted our offenses are blown away like flower petals in the wind.*
> *Offenses repented, enmity resolved,*

Wisdom and blessing increase as calamities are dispelled.
Liberated from suffering and reborn in the Trayastrimsha,
May we gather at the Dragon Flower's Three Assemblies
And receive a prediction personally from Maitreya Buddha.

Namo Dragon Flower Assembly of Bodhisattvas Mahasattvas

(three times)

Final praise

Emperor of Liang Repentance Roll Six now concludes.
We dedicate its merit to the four benefactors and the three realms.
May all in this assembly enjoy increased longevity and blessings,
May the Dharma water cleanse our offenses.
May the deceased be reborn in the Western Pure Land.
May the Bodhisattvas of the Ground of Manifestation compassionately gather us in.

Namo Ascending the Path to the Clouds Bodhisattva Mahasattva

(three times)

End Notes

1. **Six flavors:** bitter, sour, sweet, pungent, salty, acrid or without taste.
2. **Sixfold mindfulness:** recollection (mindfulness) of the virtues of the Buddha, the Dharma, the Sangha, the precepts, practicing renunciation, and the devas.
3. **Entrenchment of ignorance:** Ignorance is something innate and deeply embedded in the consciousness, which is difficult to remove, and which serves as the basis for the production of afflictions. Discussed at length in the *Śrīmālā-sūtra*, the *Sutra of Original Karma*, and Wonhyo's Doctrine of the Two Hindrances.

4. **Threefold esoteric modes**: In Buddhist practice, these three esoteric modes--mudras, mantras, and meditation—are funda-mental.

5. **Eight deviations**: the opposite of eight the proper paths, wrong view, wrong action, wrong thought, wrong speech, wrong effort, wrong livelihood, wrong mindfulness, and wrong samadhi.

6. **Four hundred and four bodily sicknesses**: the four hundred and four ailments of the body that are caused by the four elements of fire, wind, water, and earth. There are 202 fevers cause by fire and earth, and 202 chills caused by water and wind.

7. **Wisdom of fearlessness**: the Four Types of Fearlessness when speaking the Dharma,
    a) Fearlessness from total confidence in all dharmas
    b) Fearlessness from total extinction of any outflows
    c) Fearlessness when speaking about any defiled dharma that hinders or obstruct a practitioner.
    d) Fearlessness when proclaiming the transcendental dharmas

8. **Dragons and the rest of the eightfold division**: gods, dragons, yaksahs, asuras, garudas, mahoragas, gandharvas, kinnaras.

9. **Eight Voices**: The Buddha speaks Dharma with eight types of sounds.
    First, sonorous and crisp
    Second, gentle
    Third, appropriate
    Fourth, noble and wise
    Fifth, not *yin*
    Sixth, never facetious
    Seventh, deep and far-reaching
    Eighth, unending

ROLL SEVEN

Namo Buddhas and Bodhisattvas of the Dragon Flower Assembly
(*bow three times*)

Praise

He took one grain of wheat and sesame to fill his stomach.
But the immortals were mindful to make offerings to him.
And a shepherd-girl served him fragrant rice gruel and milk:
Offerings from the heavens' kitchen, indeed!
Then the Four Heavenly Kings held up a bowl of celestial food,
As they bowed from afar to Vulture Peak.
Finally, Cunda offered the Buddha his last meal.

Namo Universal Offering Bodhisattva Mahasattva (*three times*)

Listen respectfully

Seven Buddhas are the certifying hosts of the Repentance.
Seven analogies of the wonderful sutras guide us to the door of
liberation.
Seven treasures of precious Dharma jewels are replete with the
Seven bodhi shares.
The *chandana* forest is surrounded by *chandana* fragrance.
The Lion King lets out his lion roar.
All wishes will certainly be fulfilled and all prayers surely
answered.
Above we see his clouds of kindness spread vast and wide;
Just like the moon's reflection on all waters, his compassionate
face appears everywhere.

We bow before them and pray that they bear witness to our Repentance.

[Dharma Host]: On behalf of _____ [those who seek to repent], we practice this Kindness and Compassion Repentance Dharma in the Bodhimanda, and now we have come to Roll Seven. With all conditions fulfilled, we enter the Repentance Platform. May all faithful donors in the assembly deepen their faith and sincerity, and may all monastics cultivate in accord with the Dharma. Banners and painted images adorn the Bodhimanda; flowers, lamps, incense and fruits are in orderly display. We make these offerings and prostrate hundreds of times with utmost sincerity. We are earnestly mindful as we repent on behalf of our parents of many lifetimes, relatives, friends and foes from countless kalpas past who have sunk in the *seven* destinies and who thereafter have committed all kinds of evil deeds; those who have indulged in false thinking based on the *seven* kinds of emotions and who have acted recklessly; those who have given rise to the *seven* types of arrogance deceiving the worthies and lying to sages; those who have given rise to afflictions due to the *seven* kinds of outflows, turning their back on Awakening and uniting with defilement; those who have failed to uphold the *seven* categories of precepts, and those who have found it difficult to avoid committing the *seven* kinds of offenses.

Mindful that we have not repented for many kalpas, we are now fortunate to encounter the Buddha's teachings. Before the Buddhas, we now confess our offenses and cleanse and purify them in the great perfect mirror. Let us all now in this assembly read and chant the Repentance text. We hope to transcend the boundaries of the twelve links of dependent origination, and we also wish to have limitless and boundless compassion. May all Buddhas take pity on us and invisibly bless and protect us.

Throughout the worlds in the ten directions,
Before all lions among men in the past, present, and future,

With our body, speech, and mind entirely pure,
We bow down to them all, omitting none.

Commencement of the Repentance

We now begin the Repentance Dharma of Kindness and Compassion in the Bodhimanda. Together in this assembly, we single-mindedly return to and rely on all Buddhas of the three periods of time.

> Namo Buddhas of the past, Vipashyin Buddha
> Namo Shikhin Buddha
> Namo Vishvabhu Buddha
> Namo Krakucchanda Buddha
> Namo Kanakamuni Buddha
> Namo Kashyapa Buddha
> Namo our Fundamental Teacher Shakyamuni Buddha
> Namo Honored Future Buddha, Maitreya

Today, we are here in this Bodhimanda due to our shared karma. Ultimate virtue is vast, expansive and beyond description. However, to describe this virtue and the path to the Way, words have to be used. Doctrines form the stairway leading to the true principle, as well as a guide to the sagely state. Therefore, words are used to reveal the true principle; however, words are not the true principle. Though words reveal the principle, words cannot go beyond principle. Although words and principle are different, just as the paths of goodness and evil are greatly divergent, they function like shadow and form, echo and sound, seamlessly without any conflict.

For a beginner, one must use words to understand the Way. Only when one attains the state that is beyond-learning can one dispense with words and be in unity with principle. We should consider ourselves foolish mundane people, deluded and confused due to heavy karma, and thus we still need to rely on words to learn various Dharma-doors. Our understanding is rudimentary, and we cannot completely appreciate the wondrousness of the Dharma-doors. Our

insight is shallow, and we cannot penetrate the depths of their meanings. They are easy to talk about, but difficult to truly practice. Only
sages and the sagely can do both.

There may be criticism. "How can one rectify others if one fails to
rectify oneself first? How can one exhort others to be pure if one's
three karmas are defiled and turbid? If one is not pure, it is impossible
to make others pure. If one is not firm in cultivation, how can one
exhort others to be so?" If I fail to practice what I preach, then I will
only afflict others. Seeing that I have afflicted others, how can I not
stop behaving like this? As I keep reflecting on such matters, how can
I not feel ashamed of myself?

Those who criticize us are doing so because they are actually our
good and wise advisors. Thus we should listen with deference and
straighten our clothes, instead of trying to defend ourselves. Now
having received such criticism from those good and wise advisors, we
feel shame and repentant. Understanding that our offenses are heavy,
we dare not deceive the sages or conceal and cover up our faults.

Having said that, it has occurred to me, that if I were to destroy
the Repentance text we have compiled, I fear others will be deprived
of the opportunity to cultivate blessings. On the other hand, preserv-
ing this text may cause someone to slander the Dharma. Thus I am in
a dilemma, at a crossroad, and am not sure what to do next. Since my
original intention was wholesome, I should not allow anything to
obstruct this goodness. I should just proceed and establish this Repentance, exhaust my effort, and not fret over this dilemma. I will sincerely
rely on the Greatly Kind and Compassionate Ones who are like fathers
to those of us in this world.

Since the Repentance text is meant to be preserved, I should feel
ashamed, remorseful, and maintain an upright mindset. I sincerely
pray that the great assembly is not afflicted by what I have said. If
what I have said is in accord with principle, even just a bit of it, then
based on this dharma of Repentance, may members of the assembly
reform our past, cultivate for the future, and become good and wise
advisors. If what I have said is not agreeable with members of this

assembly, may you still practice the giving of happiness, and at minimum, not become bad advisors and remain members of our bodhi family.

Section 10 - Treasuring Our Good Fortune

Today, we are here in this Bodhimanda due to our shared karma. Having taken refuge with the Three Treasures, we know that we can rely on the Buddha, the One with utmost virtue. Cutting off our doubts and repenting, we can dispel both offenses and delusions. Furthermore, we have brought forth the bodhi mind and we both exhort and encourage ourselves, because we have untied the knots of past animosity and are now free and at ease. So, how can we not rejoice over this feeling of great fortune welling forth?

Let me now explain why. The sutras mention eight difficulties, which are:

1. The difficulties of the hells,
2. The difficulties of the hungry ghosts,
3. The difficulties of animals,
4. The difficulties of the remote border regions,
5. The difficulties of the Heaven of Longevity,
6. The difficulties of having many illnesses and disabilities although attaining a human body,
7. The difficulties of being born in a family of deviant views,
8. The difficulties of being born before or after a Buddha's time.

These eight difficulties make it challenging for beings to transcend the cycle of birth and death. We are all born in the Dharma Image Age. Although we will not encounter a Buddha during such a time, we still have reasons to feel fortunate.

Speaking of difficulties, we should know that difficulties result from offenses, and that offenses originate in the mind. Whenever there is doubt in our mind, what is not a difficulty becomes one.

Conversely, when there is no doubt in our mind, a difficulty is no longer a difficulty. How can we tell? The eighth difficulty is the one of being born before or after a Buddha's time. However, even when a person, for example, the old woman of the east gate, was born during the Buddha's time and dwelt in the area where the Buddha dwelt, she did not see the Buddha. Thus from this, we can see that being born in the time of a Buddha can also be a difficulty because of doubts in the mind.

It is also not necessarily the case that one will always encounter difficulties when born before or after the time of a Buddha. We should also understand that those born in the human or heavenly realms may also be in difficulties. If one has an unwholesome mind, the retributions would be onerous. Those blessed with residing for a time in the six desire heavens may also fall into the hells, while lowly beings in the animal realm may ascend the path to sagehood. Papiyan, for example, harbored evil thoughts which caused him to fall into the hells; the Dragon King heard the Dharma and attained the Way. With deviant minds, small difficulties become big, whereas proper minds are unobstructed by heavy difficulties.

Today, we are here in this Bodhimanda due to our shared karma. We should all understand that with obstacles in the mind, anything encountered becomes a difficulty. However, with a proper mind, what is a difficulty becomes a non-difficulty. The example of this eighth difficulty can be extended to other situations. Therefore, we know that the time before or after a Buddha can be a Proper Dharma period; and a border region or the animal realm can also be places for cultivation. If our mind is proper, then the eight difficulties do not exist; however, if we have doubts in our mind, then difficulties will be limitless. Reflecting on these principles, we have many reasons to feel fortunate. In our daily lives, we are unaware of our good fortune to be able to cultivate the proper Dharma. So now I would like express my humble view to illustrate the reasons why we should feel fortunate and thus further cultivate the resolve to transcend the world.

Why should we feel fortunate?

- The Buddha talked about the inevitability of falling into the hells, yet we have escaped this disaster. This is the first reason.
- We have avoided birth in the realm of hungry ghosts and are apart from all their suffering. This is the second reason.
- Birth in the animal realm is hard to avoid, yet we have avoided this retribution. This is the third reason.
- Those born in the border regions do not have the opportunity to learn the principles of benevolence, humaneness and righteousness. However, we now live in the central great country of China where the Dharma is widespread, and we are able to personally receive and learn the wondrous Teachings. This is the fourth reason.
- Those born in the Heaven of Longevity do not realize the need to plant blessings. Since we are not born in that heaven, we have the good conditions to be able to plant and nourish blessings. This is the fifth reason.
- The human body is hard to gain and if we lose it, we do not know when we may regain it. All of us should be grateful that we now have a human body. This is the sixth reason.
- Those with incomplete six sense faculties have difficulties planting roots of goodness. Now not only have we gained the purity of the complete six sense faculties, but we also are able to strive towards the profundity of the Dharma. This is the seventh reason.
- Those with worldly intelligence and eloquence are obstructed by these mundane abilities. Unobstructed by these, we are able to single-mindedly rely on the proper Dharma. This is the eighth reason.
- Being born before or after a Buddha is a difficulty; not seeing a Buddha in person is a big difficulty. Now we are already able to make the great and wholesome vow to save and rescue all living beings in the future. We do not take 'not seeing a Buddha' as a difficulty, because once we see the image of a Buddha

and once we hear the proper Dharma, we feel as if we are in the Deer Park hearing the Buddha first proclaiming the Dharma. Thus not seeing a Buddha is something we do not take as a difficulty. The Buddha said, "It is difficult to encounter a Buddha." However, we all see the Buddha's honored image. This is the ninth reason.

- The Buddha said, "It is difficult to hear the Dharma." We are now nourished by the sweet dew of Dharma. This is the tenth reason.

- The Buddha said, "It is difficult to renounce the householder's life." Now many are able to leave their loved ones and embarked on the path of cultivation. This is the eleventh reason.

- The Buddha said, "It is easy to benefit oneself but difficult to benefit others." Now with each prostration in veneration, we universally dedicate the merit and virtue to all beings in the ten directions. This is the twelfth reason.

- The Buddha said, "It is difficult to endure hardship and suffering." However we are now vigorous in cultivation and not lax in doing all good. This is the thirteenth reason.

- The Buddha said, "It is difficult to read and recite sutras." Now we are able to read and study sutras. This is the fourteenth reason.

- It is difficult to practice Chan meditation, but now there are those of us who can make our minds tranquil. This is the fifteenth reason.

Today, we are here in this Bodhimanda due to our shared karma. There are countless reasons we should all feel fortunate. The reasons are too numerous to fully express due to my lack of eloquence. Mundane people experience more suffering than happiness in their lives. For them, even momentary happiness or delight is hard to come by. In contrast, we are now much freer and less obstructed. All such non-obstructions are due to the blessings of the awe-inspiring powers of the Three Treasures throughout the ten directions.

Let us all now with utmost sincerity recollect this deep kindness and bow in full prostration with heartfelt sincerity. On behalf of all heads of nations as well as their citizens, parents, teachers, elders, monastics of the three seniorities, faithful donors, good and bad advisors, heavenly beings and ascetic masters, the four world-protecting heavenly kings, the intelligent and righteous spirits, celestial spirits, earth spirits, empty space spirits, spirits who bless the good and punish the evil, spirits who guard and protect those who uphold mantras, dragon kings of the five directions, dragons and the rest of the eightfold division, all great demon kings, five directional great demon kings, all other demon kings, King Yama and other lords of the underworld, great spirits in the five destinies, the guardian kings of the eighteen hells together with their officials, the limitless sentient beings, and all other beings with the Buddha nature in the three realms and six paths, we now sincerely take refuge with the Three Treasures of the ten directions to the ends of empty space.

May the Three Treasures kindly and compassionately gather us in, accept and protect us with their inconceivable spiritual powers, and enable all heavenly beings, ascetic masters, spirit kings, including all beings of the three realms and six paths, from this day forth, to transcend the sea of birth and death and arrive at the other shore, perfect their vows and practices, ascend the Ten Grounds, realize the vajra mind, and together accomplish Proper and Equal Enlightenment.

Section 11 Exhortation to Rely on the Three Treasures

Today, we are here in this Bodhimanda due to our shared karma. Each and every one of us should always be mindful of the Three Treasures. Why is that? If we were not mindful of the Three Treasures, we would not be able to bring forth the mind of kindness and sympathize with living beings. Without being constantly aware of the Three Treasures, how could we bring forth the heart of compassion to save all beings? Without thinking of the Three Treasures, how could we bring forth the mind of equanimity towards friends or foes? If we did not know of the Three Treasures, how could we to realize wonderful wisdom and attain the unsurpassed Way? Without mindfulness of the Three Treasures, how can we thoroughly understand the Two Emptinesses and Reality with No-mark?

The Buddha said, "The human body is hard to obtain," yet we now have a human body. The Buddha said, "It is hard to have faith," yet we have now given rise to faith.

Now all of us have come to rely on the Three Treasures. Our eyes do not see the hungry ghosts and hell beings, whose mouths spew fire and whose tongues are being pulled out. Our ears do not hear the sounds of suffering and torments of the hell beings and hungry ghosts. Our noses do not smell the stench from the pus and blood oozing from the splitting and flaying skin of hell beings and hungry ghosts. Our tongues do not taste any rotten or putrid food. Our bodies do not suffer the piercing cold of ice or the excruciating heat of being boiled in a cauldron or grilled over a fire. Our minds are constantly aware that the Buddha is the kindest and most compassionate father. He is our great physician king and his Dharmas are good medicine for the illnesses of all living beings. We know that sages and worthy ones are like a mother who is constantly by our side, attending to the sick. We are constantly aware of the Three Treasures protecting the world; wherever we are, we are conscious of this.

We understand that although we are unable to encounter the Buddha in person and have been born in the Dharma Ending Age, we have full faith, complete six sense faculties, and are free of high levels of distress or trouble. We are fortunate that we can live a more carefree and comfortable life. We are rarely obstructed in our daily activities. Such wonderful rewards are all due to conditions that we have planted in the past, as well as the blessings bestowed by the power of the Three Treasures. Furthermore, they aid us in bringing forth the bodhi resolve in this present life. All such benefits are too numerous to mention. So how could all of us fail to repay this kindness and make offerings to the Three Treasures?

Today, we are here in this Bodhimanda due to our shared karma. We should be aware that among all merit and virtue, making offerings to the Three Treasures is foremost. The sutras state, "Due to the merit from making even a small offering in the past, one enjoys rewards that endure for many kalpas and the remaining blessing will enable one to encounter the World-Honored One."

The sutras also mention, "If one wishes to repay the kindness of the Three Treasures, one may build monasteries or stupas, offer lamps, candles, banners, canopies, incense, flowers, bedding, and various other gifts. In the future, one will definitely receive blessings accordingly."

However, making these offerings does not truly amount to repaying the Buddha's kindness. The only way to repay the kindness of the Buddha is to bring forth the bodhi resolve, make the four great vows, create limitless affinities and conditions that create blessings to perfect the adorning hallmarks, and cultivate Pure Land practices. Truly, this is what the wise would do to repay the Buddha's kindness.

Today, we are here in this Bodhimanda due to our shared karma. We should all know that the kindness and compassion of the Buddhas is hard to repay. Even if a Bodhisattva Mahasattva were to sacrifice his body to repay this kindness, such a gesture would not even amount to one share in ten thousand. How much the less are we common folks able to repay the kindness of the Buddha! So we should all accord with the sutras and make benefiting all living beings our top priority. Let us all now, universally for the sake of countless living beings of the four births in the ten directions, bring forth utmost sincerity and take refuge with the Greatly Kind and Compassionate Ones who are like fathers to those of us in this world.

Namo Maitreya Buddha
Namo Shakyamuni Buddha
Namo Treasury of Virtue Buddha
Namo Deserving Fame Buddha
Namo Flower Body Buddha
Namo Great Voice Buddha

Namo Praised for Eloquence Buddha
Namo Vajra Pearl Buddha
Namo Limitless Lifespan Buddha
Namo Pearl Adornment Buddha
Namo Great King Buddha
Namo Lofty Virtuous Conduct Buddha
Namo Lofty Renown Buddha
Namo Hundreds of Lights Buddha
Namo Happiness and Delight Buddha
Namo Dragon Strides Buddha
Namo Wish and Vow Buddha
Namo Jeweled Moon Buddha
Namo Cessation-realized Buddha
Namo Joyful King Buddha
Namo Subduing and Taming Buddha
Namo Joyous Self-mastery Buddha
Namo Jewel Top Prominence Buddha
Namo Transcending Fear Buddha
Namo Jewel Treasury Buddha
Namo Moon Face Buddha
Namo Pure Name Buddha
Namo Boundless Body Bodhisattva
Namo Guan Shi Yin Bodhisattva

Again, we take refuge with the Three Treasures of the ten directions to the ends of empty space. We pray, with their power of kindness and compassion, their power of protecting and caring for living beings, their power of great expedients, their inconceivable powers they will enable all of us now repenting in this assembly, and all sentient beings throughout the Dharma Realm, constantly, everywhere, and in life after life to:

- always hear the names of the Three Treasures,
- always see the images of the Three Treasures,

- always, in body and mind, be illuminated by the Three Treasures,
- always, in body and mind, be guarded and protected by the kindness and compassion of the Three Treasures,
- always, in body and mind, be rescued and supported by the spiritual powers of the Three Treasures,
- always attain the wisdom of the Three Treasures, be awakened in body and mind, realize the patience of non-production, and certify to the True Mark.

We also vow that in life after life, in all places, we will

- constantly recognize the causes for the presence of the Three Treasures,
- constantly be mindful of the kindness of the Three Treasures,
- constantly praise the Three Treasures,
- constantly venerate the Three Treasures,
- constantly make offerings to the Three Treasures,
- constantly ensure that the Three Treasures be established and maintained,
- constantly support and protect the Three Treasures, and
- constantly perpetuate the Three Treasures.

This is how we should remind ourselves of the kindness of the Three Treasures and how to repay the kindness of the Three Treasures. This will enable us to attain purity of our six sense faculties, attain perfect clarity of the five eyes, so that the four limitless minds and four unobstructed wisdoms manifest spontaneously, and we attain as-you-wish self-mastery regarding the six spiritual powers and six paramitas. To the ends of time, may we benefit all sentient beings, and may we all accomplish and perfect all conduct and vows and together arrive at Proper Enlightenment.

Section 12 Encouragement from the Repentance Host

Today, we are here in this Bodhimanda due to our shared karma. We have all given rise to firm faith, brought forth the bodhi resolve, and vowed never to retreat from this resolve. This is an inconceivable resolve and aspiration. This very resolve and aspiration is praised by the Buddhas. As the Repentance Host, I deeply rejoice in this merit. I hope that throughout all future times, in life after life, until we realize bodhi, we will forever be kin in Dharma and be members of the compassionate family.

I myself [as the Repentance Host] established this Dharma assembly, and I feel humbled and shy. Why? Because I lack wisdom and understanding and am often not in accord with the practice. This brief revelation of my shortcomings may be sufficient to alarm and shock you. However, my position is trivial in the face of the crucial importance of this Repentance. My mind is filled with conflicting emotions – like that of ice and flaming coals. If we do not rely upon great causes and conditions, there is no way to attain the supreme and wondrous fruition. I recognize my errors and mistakes, yet I cannot refrain from doing good, hoping for the Buddhas and Bodhisattvas' kind and compassionate mindfulness, so that we can all be kin in Dharma. May I endeavor to trouble all of you to grace this Bodhimanda with your virtue!

Time and tide waits for no man; in the blink of an eye, old age arrives. We are all driven by our karmic conditions, and it is difficult to encounter such a supreme Dharma assembly. Thus, we should all encourage and exert ourselves in cultivation and at the same time, benefit others. We should stand out among ordinary people and not follow worldly trends so that we will not regret in the future. Once we hear the sound of Dharma, we receive great rewards for many kalpas. A single wholesome thought will bring everlasting benefit to ourselves and help us to fulfill all of our vows and wishes. So let each and every one of us now, with utmost sincerity, bow in full prostration and take refuge with the Greatly Kind and Compassionate Ones who are like fathers to those of us in this world.

Namo Maitreya Buddha
Namo Shakyamuni Buddha
Namo Awe-inspiring Virtue and Tranquil Cessation Buddha
Namo Attribute of Sensations Buddha
Namo Multitudes of Heaven Buddha
Namo Suyama Buddha
Namo Heaven Devotion Buddha
Namo Precious Assembly Buddha
Namo Treasured Strides Buddha
Namo Lion's Share Buddha
Namo Supreme and Lofty Conduct Buddha
Namo Human King Buddha
Namo Wholesome Mind Buddha
Namo Understanding the World Buddha
Namo Precious Awe-inspiring Virtue Buddha
Namo Vehicle of Virtue Buddha
Namo Enlightened Thought Buddha
Namo Adorned with Joy Buddha
Namo Fragrance and Charity Buddha
Namo Fragrant Elephant Buddha
Namo Multitude of Flames Buddha
Namo Hallmark of Kindness Buddha
Namo Wondrous Fragrance Buddha
Namo Sturdy Armor Buddha
Namo Awe-inspiring Virtue and Courage Buddha
Namo Pearl Armor Buddha
Namo Humane and Worthy Buddha
Namo Boundless Body Bodhisattva
Namo Guan Shi Yin Bodhisattva

Again, we take refuge with the Three Treasures of the ten directions to the ends of empty space. May all of us who are here in this Bodhimanda due to our shared karma, together with all sentient beings throughout the Dharma Realm, bring forth the same bodhi resolve and make the same bodhi vow. Henceforth, until the ends of time, and in life after life:

- May we always be in the retinue of the Three Treasures; be kin in Dharma of wisdom; be family members of kindness and compassion; cultivate together all the causes and realize the fruition – like echoes following sounds, or a shadow accompanying a form.
- May we adorn the Pure Lands, serving each and every Buddha.
- May we together strive to go everywhere to rescue and protect the world;
- May we together apply our strengths and efforts to take across beings.
- As there is no difference in our fundamental Dharma body, and we share the same vows and practices, may we together perfect the three bodies and four wisdoms and attain full mastery of the eight liberations and six spiritual powers.
- May we benefit all future living beings and together attain Proper Enlightenment.

Section 13 Making All-encompassing Vows

Today, we are here in this Bodhimanda due to our shared karma. With the merit and virtue from bowing this Repentance and from bringing forth the bodhi resolve as conditions, we now vow that all of the following beings in the ten directions throughout empty space enter the ocean of great vows and be replete with all merit and wisdom:

- all heavenly kings, heavenly beings, as well as their retinues;

- all leaders of ascetic masters, other ascetic masters, as well as their retinues;
- Lord Shakra, the four world-protecting heavenly kings, king spirits, spirit generals, as well as their retinues;
- the intelligent and righteous spirits, the celestial spirits, the earth spirits, the empty space spirits, spirits who bless the good and punish the evil, and spirits who guard and protect those who uphold mantras, all spirit kings and spirit generals as well as their retinues
- wondrous transformational dragon kings, *Nadobbaja* dragon kings, dragon kings of the five directions, dragons and the rest of the eightfold division, the leaders of the eightfold division, the generals of the eight divisions, as well as their retinues;
- asura kings, spirit kings, spirit generals, as well as their retinues;
- all rulers in the human realm, their ministers, generals, officials, their retinues, and the rest of the people;
- all bhikshus, bhikshunis, shikshamanas, shramaneras, shramanerikas as well as their fellow monastics and disciples in the ten directions;
- King Yama, other lords of the underworld, great spirits in the five destinies, all guardian kings of the eighteen hells, spirit kings, spirit generals, as well as their retinues;
- all beings in the hells, all hungry ghosts, all animals;
- all other beings in the future throughout empty space, big or small, together with their retinues; and
- all beings with lesser sentience who are not included in the above destinies and not specifically listed in our vows.

We again vow that all the countless and boundless beings, within or beyond the three realms, including all with name and form endowed with the Buddha nature, enter the ocean of great vows and be replete with all merit and wisdom.

Great assembly! Throughout all of empty space of the ten directions, may we now reverently rely on the power of great compassion and kindness of all Buddhas, on the power of the fundamental vows of all great Bodhisattvas, sages and worthy ones, and based on their:

- power of limitless and boundless wisdom,
- power of limitless and boundless merit and virtue,
- power of spiritual penetrations and self-mastery,
- power of protecting all beings,
- power of comforting all beings,
- power of enabling all heavenly beings and ascetic masters to end their outflows,
- power of gathering in and teaching all wholesome spirits,
- power of saving all hell beings,
- power of saving all hungry ghosts,
- power of preventing beings from falling into the animal realm and of freeing all therein, pray that all beings' wishes be fulfilled.

Great assembly! We also rely on:

- the power of this Repentance Dharma of Kindness and Compassion in the Bodhimanda,
- the power of taking refuge with the Three Treasures,
- the power of severing doubts and giving rise to faith,
- the power of repentance and making vows,
- the power of resolving animosity,
- the power of feeling fortunate and joyous,
- the power of heartfelt enthusiasm,
- the power of making resolves and dedicating the roots of goodness – to enable all beings's wishes to be fulfilled.
- Great assembly! We further rely on:
- the power of great kindness possessed by the seven Buddhas,
- the power of great compassion that all Buddhas of the ten directions share,

- the power of eradicating afflictions wielded by the thirty-five Buddhas,
- the power of subduing demons used by the fifty-three Buddhas,
- the power of rescuing all beings that the one hundred and seventy Buddhas employ,
- the power of gathering in all beings that the thousand Buddhas have,
- the power of protecting living beings that the twelve Bodhisattvas are endowed with, and
- the power of exhorting repentance that Boundless Body Bodhisattva and Guan Shi Yin Bodhisattva have perfected.

Now, we make the following vows:

May all living beings in the three realms and the six paths of the ten directions to the end of time, regardless whether they are big or small, ascending or descending in the realms of rebirth, who have name and form and the Buddha nature, henceforth, after this repentance, wherever they may be, gain all Buddhas' and Bodhisattvas' great vast wisdom and their inconceivable limitless self-mastery spiritual bodies. May they further gain the six paramita bodies to walk the path of bodhi, the four bodies of gathering-in and never giving-up on all beings, the great compassion body of eradicating all living beings' sufferings, and the great kindness body to bestow happiness on all living beings, the merit and virtue body to benefit all beings. May they also gain the wisdom body to inexhaustibly expound Dharma, the indestructible vajra body, the pure Dharma body that is free of birth and death, the expedient body manifesting the power of self mastery, and the accomplished body of *Anuttara-samyaksam-bodhi*. May all beings of the four births and the six paths be replete with all these bodies and perfect and accomplish the unsurpassed great wisdom body of all Buddhas.

Also, may all living beings of the ten directions, from this day forth, wherever they are, attain the following:

- a mouth that generates inconceivable merit and virtue, just as all Buddhas and Bodhisattvas do,
- a mouth that speaks kind words, carrying comfort and joy to all,
- a mouth from which issues sweet dew, bringing coolness to all,
- mouth that expresses truthfulness, speaking the proper and genuine Dharma,
- a mouth that truthfully relays speech, never uttering falsehoods even in dream-states,
- a mouth that expresses reverence, gaining the respect and veneration of Lord Shakra and the Four Heavenly Kings,
- a mouth that defines profundity, revealing the nature of Dharma,
- a mouth that offers firm encouragement, conveying never-retreating Dharma,
- a mouth that articulates with uprightness and straightforwardness, resulting in perfect eloquence,
- a mouth endowed with lovely precision, telling all according to karma and time,
- a mouth that communicates All-Wisdom, taking across all who are supposed to be liberated.

May all beings throughout the four births and the six paths be replete with all Buddhas' and Bodhisattvas' pure speech karma.

We further vow. May all living beings of the ten directions from this day forth, wherever they are, attain:

- the mind of inconceivable great wisdom of all Buddhas and Bodhisattvas,
- the mind that always leaves behind the weariness of afflictions,
- the courageous and keen mind,
- the mind of determination and resolve,
- the vajra mind,

- the never-retreating mind,
- the pure mind,
- the insightful mind,
- the mind that seeks goodness,
- the mind of adornment, and
- the vast and great mind.

May all living beings attain the power of great wisdom and comprehend all Dharma that is heard.

May they always have a mind of kindness towards others and sever all knots of animosity.

May they dwell in the sense of shame and always harbor the thought of regret and remorse.

May they, like all good and wise advisors, not have notions of a self.

May they always rejoice to see others practicing giving, upholding precepts, patience, vigor, samadhi, and wisdom.

May they treat friends or foes alike, regarding them as the same without any arrogance.

Section 14 Bowing to the Buddhas on behalf of Heavenly Beings

Today, we are here in this Bodhimanda due to our shared karma. We should be aware that heavenly beings, ascetic masters, and all wholesome spirits have been inconceivably virtuous and kind towards living beings, guarding and protecting them, wishing for them to be peaceful and safe and to tend towards goodness. How do we know this?

Because the Buddha has directed:
Dhrtarastra and the rest of the four heavenly kings
Kindly support those who uphold the sutras,
Enabling beings to hear the Compassionate Ones' names,
While being protected as would a king be by his ministers.

He also directed the dragon king Elapattra:
Kindly support those who uphold the sutras,
As if protecting your own eyes or caring for your own children,
And never be apart from them throughout the day and night.
He also directed rakshasa Yanpo,
Countless poisonous dragons, and dragon girls
To kindly support those who uphold the sutras,
As they would care for their own heads, fearing they might
come to injury.
He also directed king Virulaka
To kindly support those who uphold the sutras
– like a mother unwearyingly caring for her children –
Supporting and protecting them, at all times and places.

He also directed the dragon kings
Nada, Upanada, Sagara, and Utpalak,
To kindly support those who uphold the sutras,
And respectfully make offerings and bow to them,
Just as heavenly beings respect Shakra
Or filial sons respect their own parents.

May peace and happiness descend upon
This Bodhimanda of Kindness and Compassion,
and may all beings be guided to be kin in Dharma.
Whether born before or after the Buddha, may all attain samadhi and ultimately gain irreversibility.
May all hear the names of the Buddhas,
Guan Shi Yin Bodhisattva and Boundless Body Bodhisattva
whereupon their three karmic obstacles will melt away, and all
will be freed of evil.
May all attain the five eyes and accomplish bodhi.
May all the heavenly beings and kings of spirits care for all
beings always, encouraging them, and granting them awe-
inspiring powers.

Today, we are here in this Bodhimanda due to our shared karma. All these heavenly beings and kings of spirits have been protecting all beings with their virtue and kindness, but living beings do not aspire to repay this kindness.

Those of old would readily have given up their lives to repay the generosity of receiving a meal. How much more should we living beings strive to repay the kindness of heavenly beings, benevolent spirits, and generals of spirits of the eightfold division! Their kindness and benevolence is vast and boundless.

The reason that we can repent and make vows today is due to the heavenly kings' invisible spiritual aid which helps us to succeed. If it were not for their help, we would have already retreated in our resolve. Thus Bodhisattvas Mahasattvas always praise good and wise advisors who enable us to come to the Bodhimanda – it is due to great causes and conditions. Without good and wise advisors, how could we possibly see the Buddhas?

Even the Bodhisattvas Mahasattvas have said that the sacrifice of our very lives would not suffice to repay the vast and deep kindness of these heavenly kings. So how much the more should we mundane and ordinary people be grateful! How can we not have a mindset of repaying their kindness? Great assembly! Since we are not able to renounce our lives, should we not at least be vigorous in our cultivation so that, over time, we may repay their kindness? Let us all increase our effort and resolve, be mindful of this kindness, and repay it. We should not just drift aimlessly, for if we do that, we will be unable to find our way back. As mentioned previously, we are fortunate to have this rare opportunity of encountering this Dharma assembly. So what are we waiting for? If we miss out, who knows what realm we will fall into? Understanding all of this, we should be courageous and vigorous.

Everything is impermanent. For there to be success, there must also be failure. For there to be spring, there must also be winter. Time waits for no man. We cannot expect to live forever! Once we part, we do not know if we will ever meet again. Now, for the sake of all heavenly rulers and heavenly beings and their retinues throughout the ten directions of empty space, each one of us should apply great effort and with heartfelt sincerity bow in full prostration to the Greatly Kind and Compassionate Ones who are like fathers to those of us in this world.

Namo Maitreya Buddha
Namo Shakyamuni Buddha
Namo Well-gone Moon Buddha
Namo Brahma Self-mastery King Buddha
Namo Lion Moon Buddha
Namo Blessings and Awe-inspiring Virtue Buddha
Namo Proper Birth Buddha
Namo Invincible Buddha
Namo Contemplating the Sun Buddha
Namo Precious Name Buddha
Namo Great Vigor Buddha
Namo Mountain Light King Buddha
Namo Charitable and Brilliant Buddha
Namo Lightning Virtue Buddha
Namo Accumulating Virtue King Buddha
Namo Fame and Offerings Buddha
Namo Praising Dharma Buddha
Namo Precious Words Buddha
Namo Saving Lives Buddha
Namo Skilled in Precepts Buddha
Namo Skillfully Leading All Beings Buddha
Namo Mind in Samadhi Buddha
Namo Supreme Happiness King Buddha
Namo Lion Light Buddha
Namo Dispelling Darkness Buddha
Namo Bright Illumination Buddha
Namo Superior Renown Buddha
Namo Boundless Body Bodhisattva
Namo Guan Shi Yin Bodhisattva

Again, we take refuge with the Three Treasures of the ten directions to the ends of empty space. May you gather us all in with your power of kindness and compassion. May all heavenly rulers, heavenly beings, and their retinues of the ten directions throughout empty space:

- have the equanimity and wisdom of the contemplation of emptiness always spontaneously manifesting before them;
- attain the power of wisdom and expedients and pave for themselves the path of non-outflows;
- strengthen and illuminate their vows and practices of the Ten Grounds;
- cultivate the six paramitas and the four limitless minds;
- practice the Bodhisattava Path and enter the practices of Buddhas;
- save and never abandon living beings using the four great Bodhisattva vows;
- attain and sustain the four eloquences and delight in endlessly speaking the Dharma;
- use expedient methods to gather in, teach, and benefit all beings of the four births;
- together ascend to the Ground of the Dharma Clouds and realize ultimate fruition.

Section 15 Bowing to the Buddhas on behalf of Ascetic Masters

Today, we are here in this Bodhimanda due to our shared karma. Now on behalf of the leaders of ascetic masters, all other ascetic masters, and their retinues throughout empty space, I hope each one of us will bring forth our utmost, heartfelt sincerity, bow in full prostration, and take refuge with the Greatly Kind and Compassionate Ones who are like fathers to those of us in this world.

Namo Maitreya Buddha
Namo Shakyamuni Buddha
Namo King of Keen Wisdom Buddha
Namo Light of Pearl and Moon Buddha
Namo Awe-inspiring Light King Buddha
Namo Impeccable Discourses Buddha
Namo King of Radiance Buddha
Namo Pearl Wheel Buddha
Namo Teacher of the World Buddha
Namo Auspicious Hand Buddha
Namo Moon of Goodness Buddha
Namo Jeweled Flame Buddha
Namo Rahu Guardian Buddha
Namo Delight in Bodhi Buddha
Namo Light of Equanimity Buddha
Namo Ultimate Quiescence Buddha
Namo Most Wonderful in World Buddha
Namo Worry-free Buddha
Namo Ten Strengths Buddha
Namo King of Happiness and Strength Buddha
Namo Virtue and Strength Buddha
Namo Virtue Power Buddha
Namo Great Strength Buddha
Namo Treasury of Merit and Virtue Buddha
Namo True Practices Buddha
Namo Superior Peace Buddha
Namo Tisya Buddha
Namo Boundless Body Bodhisattva
Namo Guan Shi Yin Bodhisattva

Again, we take refuge with the Three Treasures of the ten directions to the ends of empty space. May you gather us all in with your power of kindness and compassion. May all leaders of ascetic masters, all other ascetic masters, and their retinues:

- be free from the defilements of sense objects;
- clean away their karmic obstacles;
- attain the serene, wondrous appearances and hallmarks of the Buddhas;
- spontaneously manifest the four limitless minds and the six paramitas;
- gain the as-you-wish self-mastery of the four unobstructed wisdoms and the six spiritual powers;
- freely enter, exit, or roam in the Bodhisattva state;
- reach the Ground of the Dharma Clouds and enter the vajra mind; and
- with inconceivable powers, return to take across beings in the six paths.

Section 16 Bowing to the Buddhas on behalf of Brahma Kings and Others

Today, we are here in this Bodhimanda due to our shared karma. Now on behalf of Brahma kings, Lord Shakra, and the four world-protecting heavenly kings and all their retinues, may all of us bring forth great sincerity, bow in full prostration, and take refuge with the Greatly Kind and Compassionate Ones who are like fathers to those of us in this world.

- Namo Maitreya Buddha
- Namo Shakyamuni Buddha
- Namo Great Light Buddha
- Namo Radiance of Lightning Buddha
- Namo Vast Virtue Buddha
- Namo Precious Jewels Buddha
- Namo Radiance of Blessings and Virtue Buddha
- Namo Armor-making Buddha
- Namo Hand of Accomplishment Buddha

- Namo Flower of Goodness Buddha
- Namo Gathering Treasure Buddha
- Namo Great Sea Buddha
- Namo Earth Guardian Buddha
- Namo Meaning and Principle Buddha
- Namo Skillful Contemplation Buddha
- Namo Wheel of Virtue Buddha
- Namo Jeweled Light Buddha
- Namo Benefits Buddha
- Namo Moon for the World Buddha
- Namo Beautiful Sound Buddha
- Namo Brahma Attributes Buddha
- Namo Foremost Teacher of Multitudes Buddha
- Namo Lion Conduct Buddha
- Namo Giving Despite Difficulty Buddha
- Namo Worthy of Offerings Buddha
- Namo Radiant Awe-inspiring Virtue Buddha
- Namo Great Light King Buddha
- Namo Boundless Body Bodhisattva
  Namo Guan Shi Yin Bodhisattva

Again, we take refuge with the Three Treasures of the ten directions to the ends of empty space. May you gather us all in with your power of kindness and compassion, so that the Brahma king, Lord Shakra, and the four world-protecting heavenly kings, together with their retinues, will:

- become ever clearer in their practice of the six paramitas and the four limitless minds;
- attain the four unobstructed eloquences and delight in ceaselessly speaking Dharma;
- gain the eight forms of self-mastery and perfect the six spiritual powers;
- manifest samadhi and dharani powers at will;

- kindly and compassionately bless all beings of the four births throughout the ten directions;
- perfect the hundred adornments and the myriad goodnesses from which the fine hallmarks arise;
- develop the three insights and open their five eyes;
- become Dharma-wheel kings, gathering in and transforming all beings in the six paths.

Praise

Free and without hindrances,
We are most fortunate.
Mindfulness of the Three Treasures' kindness is the true cause.
Together with sincere intention,
We now universally bow to the Honored One,
To repay the kindness of all heavenly gods.

Namo Ground of Traveling Far Bodhisattva Mahasattva
(three times)

Concluding the repentance

The *seven* Buddhas are kind and benevolent;
Those who take refuge will not fall into the eighteen hells.
Those who uphold the *seven* categories of pure precepts
Will be born in the Blissful Transformation Heaven.
May the Compassionate One certify our earnest sincerity
May you rescue all who have violated the *seven* categories of precepts.
May you enable them to be reborn on the *seven*-jeweled lotus dais.
May you bestow your boundless great compassion
And bear witness to sentient beings' humble requests.
[Dharma Host]: On behalf of _____ [those who seek to repent], we practice this Repentance Dharma of Kindness and

Compassion in the Bodhimanda. We have now successfully completed
Roll Seven, accomplishing its merit and virtue.

Lamps are lit as wisdom torches, and offerings are made as sincerely as the final one by Cunda. Wisps of fragrant incense rise from
the golden censer forming auspicious clouds. The flames from jade-
like candles blaze forth issuing propitious *qi,* while the bells chime
with melodious and sonorous rhymes of Dharma. Exquisite and rare
flowers and fruits are presented, together with Campaka and vegetarian dishes. All these we offer to the lofty and stately Well-Gone One.
We chant in praise the Gatha-verses of the sacred texts with voices
clear and far-reaching, extolling the heroic virtues of the Sagely Ones.
We enter the tranquil modes of dhyana contemplation, gathering in
all the various wondrous practices.

May you, sages of the Ten Grounds and Three Worthinesses bear
witness as we first dedicate this merit to bodhi and to all beings everywhere, many as the Ganges sands. May the four benefactors and all
in the three existences benefit from this kindness.

On behalf of _____ [those who seek to repent], may the
merit accrued enable everyone in this Repentance to be cleansed of all
karmic obstacles. May all attain great auspiciousness.

We bow and earnestly pray:

May the *seven* outflows cease completely, the *seven* factors of
awakening blossom, and in that way may the brilliant inherent
Nature be unveiled like a clear sky.

May the *seven* categories of precepts be purified and the *seven*
kinds of prohibitions cleansed, thus making the rough sea of
suffering tranquil.

May the mountain of *seven* kinds of arrogance be demolished
and the false thoughts arising from the *seven* emotions end.

May we obtain the Dharma treasury of the *seven* types of
wealth and take across all sentient beings on the *seven* paths.

May we transform the trees of swords into the fragrant forest
of *seven* jewels and transform the karma field into the sagely
realm of *seven* treasures.

[Dharma host]: I hope that everyone will continue to repent since we may not be spared completely from the retributions of any remaining karmic offenses.

Praise

The meritorious power of the Emperor of Liang Repentance Roll Seven
Enables the deceased and the disciples to eradicate the seven evils.
May all realize the Bodhisattva's Ground of Traveling Far.
As the Repentance is chanted our offenses are blown away like flower petals in the wind.
Offenses repented, enmity resolved,
Wisdom and blessing increase as calamities are dispelled.
Liberated from suffering and reborn in the Trayastrimsha,
May we gather at the Dragon Flower's Three Assemblies
And receive a prediction personally from Maitreya Buddha.

Namo Dragon Flower Assembly of Bodhisattvas Mahasattvas
(three times).

Final praise

Emperor of Liang Repentance Roll Seven now concludes.
We dedicate its merit to the four benefactors and the three realms.
May all in this assembly enjoy increased longevity and blessing,
May the Dharma water cleanse our offenses.
May the deceased be reborn in the Western Pure Land.
May the Bodhisattvas of the Ground of Traveling Far compassionately gather us in.

Namo Ascending the Path to the Clouds Bodhisattva Mahasattva
(three times)

ROLL EIGHT

Namo Buddhas and Bodhisattvas of the Dragon Flower Assembly
(*bow three times*)

Praise

Jewels are treasured in the world, from ancient times till now.
Coral and amber are threaded in silver,
Tridacna and carnelian form necklaces of pearls.
The Benefactor of Orphans and Solitary offers up the Garden.
The Gold Wheel Turning King speaks the Dharma;
It is perpetually preserved in the dragon palace.
Namo Universal Offering Bodhisattva Mahasattva (*three times*)

Listen respectfully

Having gone through the *eight* phases and having accomplished the Way, the World-Honored Buddha is like a full moon in space. The Well-gone Tathagata expounds the *eight* modes of teaching, like rain nurturing everything throughout worlds as many as the Ganges sands. Thus, many in the four births and seven destinies can ascend to the heavens; dragons and the rest of the eightfold division pay their respect. The *eighty*-four thousand great knights of Dharma assist in propagating the Buddhas' teaching. The *eight* great Bodhisattvas are ever vigilant guarding and protecting. The *eight* auspiciousnesses pervade the *eight* periods of time[1], and the *eight* liberations perfect the *eight* types of merit and virtue. The Buddhas' teaching, replete with spiritual insight and wondrous functions, pervasively responds to the needs of all beings. May the Buddhas bestow kindness on us and bear witness to this work of all Buddhas.

[Dharma Host]: On behalf of _____ [those who seek to repent], we practice this Repentance Dharma of Kindness and Compassion in the Bodhimanda. We have come to Roll Eight. With all conditions fulfilled, we now enter the Repentance Platform.

In accord with the Dharma, the faithful practice with ever increasing vigor;

Permeated in the Dharma, the monastics cultivate harmoniously in accord.

In the censer is lit the incense of precepts, samadhi, and wisdom;

In the vase are decoratively arrayed *mandarava* flowers.

Burning lamps sparkle in the tree of precious gems.

Golden plates present a variety of fruits.

We sincerely bow to all Buddhas replete with their golden hallmarks, as we remain focused in this Bodhimanda.

We confess all of our wrongdoings accumulated from innumerable lives past and pray that these offenses be eradicated.

We are earnestly mindful that from the time we first had consciousness until now, we have turned our backs on the *eightfold* proper path and strayed towards the *eight* deviant paths, thus creating numerous troubles for ourselves.

Pulled along by the *eight* greeds, we lose track of the *eight* liberations and rampantly give rise to delusional perceptions that can be likened to how someone with an eye disease sees illusory floating shapes when there are actually none. It is lamentable how easily we, being conditioned by our *eighth* consciousness and turned by the *eight* winds, become tainted by the *eight* defilements. Because of that it is to be feared that we may not be spared from the *eight* difficulties.

We now realize that we have not yet been able to repent of our offenses. Reflecting within, our hearts are filled with shame. This is because we have only managed to cultivate a small amount of goodness in the Mahayana teachings and harbored no more than an ounce of sincerity in our repentance before the Buddha images. Nevertheless, we still strive to confess our offenses and repent with utmost sincerity. Let all of us be mindful in this manner, with our attitude in accord. Now we respectfully bow to the Greatly Compassionate Ones and pray you will invisibly bless and protect us.

Thoughts numerous as dust motes in the worlds may be counted,
The waters in the oceans may be completely drunk,
Empty space may be measured and the wind tied still,
Yet the Buddha's merit and virtue cannot be told in full.

Commencement of the Repentance

We now begin the Repentance Dharma of Kindness and Compassion in the Bodhimanda. Together in this assembly, we single-mindedly return to and rely on all Buddhas of the three periods of time.

Namo Buddhas of the past, Vipashyin Buddha
Namo Shikhin Buddha
Namo Vishvabhu Buddha
Namo Krakucchanda Buddha
Namo Kanakamuni Buddha
Namo Kashyapa Buddha
Namo our Fundamental Teacher Shakyamuni Buddha
Namo Honored Future Buddha, Maitreya

Section 17 Bowing to the Buddhas on behalf of Asuras and All Wholesome Spirits

Today, we are here in this Bodhimanda due to our shared karma. Again, with utmost sincerity, we bow in full prostration to the Greatly Kind and Compassionate Ones who are like fathers to those of us in this world on behalf of:

All asura kings, asuras and their retinues throughout the ten directions to the ends of empty space;

All intelligent and righteous spirits, celestial spirits, earth spirits, empty space spirits, spirits who bless the good and punish the evil, spirits who guard and protect those who uphold mantras throughout the ten directions to the ends of empty space;

All spirit kings and generals of the eightfold division together with their retinues, and all other spirits with awe-inspiring virtue and great spiritual power, in this or other realms, near or far, north, south, east, west, the four intermediate directions, and zenith or nadir, pervading the whole of empty space and the Dharma Realm.

On behalf of all of them, we respectfully take refuge with the Greatly Kind and Compassionate Ones who are like fathers to those of us in this world.

Namo Maitreya Buddha
Namo Shakyamuni Buddha
Namo Precious Name Buddha
Namo Pure in the Assembly Buddha
Namo Boundless Name Buddha
Namo Genuine Light Buddha
Namo Sages' Heaven Buddha
Namo Wisdom King Buddha
Namo Vajra Assembly Buddha
Namo Skilled Obstructions Buddha
Namo Establishing Compassion Buddha
Namo Country of Flowers Buddha
Namo Dharma Meaning Buddha
Namo Wind Traveling Buddha
Namo Renowned for Wholesome Thoughts Buddha
Namo Abundant Brilliance Buddha
Namo Esoteric Assembly Buddha
Namo Upholding Virtue Buddha
Namo Beneficent Mind Buddha
Namo Fearless Buddha
Namo Persevering in Contemplation Buddha
Namo Dwelling in Dharma Buddha
Namo Fulfilling Pearl Buddha

Namo Virtue of Liberation Buddha
Namo Wonderful Body Buddha
Namo Wholesome Mind Buddha
Namo Universal Virtue Buddha
Namo King of Light Buddha
Namo Boundless Body Bodhisattva
Namo Guan Shi Yin Bodhisattva

Again, we take refuge with the Three Treasures of the ten directions to the ends of empty space.

May your power of kindness and compassion protect and guard all of the following:

- all asura kings, asuras and their relatives;
- all intelligent and righteous celestial spirits, earth spirits, empty space spirits;
- all spirits who bless the good and punish the evil;
- spirits who guard and protect those who uphold mantras;
- all spirit kings and generals of the eightfold division together with their retinues.

May all of them be freed from the defilement of sense objects and may all obstructing karmic conditions be cleared away.

May they bring forth the resolve for the Mahayana and cultivate the path of non-obstruction.

May they always dwell in the four limitless minds and the six paramitas.

May they gain mastery of the four unobstructed eloquences and six spiritual powers.

May they constantly, with kindness and compassion, save and protect all living beings.

May they practice the Bodhisattva Path, enter the Buddha's wisdom, attain the ultimate vajra mind, and accomplish Proper and Equal Enlightenment.

Section 18 Bowing to the Buddhas on behalf of Dragon Kings

Today, we who are here in this Bodhimanda due to our shared karma, again, with utmost sincerity, bow in full prostration on behalf of:

All inconceivable dragon kings and their retinues of the ten directions to the ends of empty space - such as wondrous transformational dragon kings, *Nadobbaja* dragon kings, dragon kings of the five directions, heavenly dragon kings, land dragon kings, mountain dragon kings, ocean dragon kings, sun palace dragon kings, moon palace dragon kings, star palace dragon kings, dragon kings for the seasons and time, blue ocean dragon kings, dragon kings protecting life forms, dragon kings protecting living beings including all other dragon kings with awe-inspiring virtue and great spiritual power - in this or other realms, near or far, north, south, east, west, the four intermediate directions, and the zenith and nadir, pervading the whole of empty space and the Dharma Realm. On behalf of all of them, we respectfully take refuge with the Greatly Kind and Compassionate Ones who are like fathers to those of us in this world.

Namo Maitreya Buddha
Namo Shakyamuni Buddha
Namo Wonderful Wisdom Buddha
Namo Brahma Wealth Buddha
Namo Sounds of Truth Buddha
Namo Proper Wisdom Buddha
Namo Gaining Strength Buddha
Namo Lion Resolve Buddha
Namo Flower Hallmarks Buddha
Namo Accumulating Wisdom Buddha
Namo Magnificent Teeth Buddha
Namo Treasury of Virtue Buddha
Namo Renown and True Buddha
Namo Rare Renown Buddha

Namo Superior Precepts Buddha
Namo Fearless Buddha
Namo Brilliance of Sun Buddha
Namo Brahma Longevity Buddha
Namo All Heavens Buddha
Namo Delight in Wisdom Buddha
Namo Jeweled Heaven Buddha
Namo Treasury of Pearls Buddha
Namo Widespread Virtue Buddha
Namo Wisdom King Buddha
Namo Free of Fetters Buddha
Namo Firm in Dharma Buddha
Namo Heavenly Virtue Buddha
Namo Boundless Body Bodhisattva
Namo Guan Shi Yin Bodhisattva

Again, we take refuge with the Three Treasures of the ten directions to the ends of empty space. May you gather us in with your power of kindness and compassion. We pray that all dragon kings, together with their retinues, gain greater brilliance and the self-mastery of spiritual powers.

- May they attain the realization of no-mark to eradicate their karmic conditions and obstructions.
- May they forever be apart from the evil destinies and always be reborn in the Pure Land.
- May they always attain the four limitless minds and the six paramitas.
- May they attain the as-you-wish mastery of the four unobstructed eloquences and six spiritual powers.
- May they rescue all beings with a heart of kindness and compassion.
- May they be adorned with sublime practices, advance through the Ground of Dharma Clouds, enter the vajra mind, and attain Proper and Equal Enlightenment.

Section 19 Bowing to the Buddhas on behalf of Demon Kings

Today, we are here in this Bodhimanda due to our shared karma. Again, with utmost sincerity, we bow in full prostration on behalf of all demon kings - the Five Directional Great Demon Kings, other demon kings of the north, south, east, west, the four intermediate directions, and the zenith and nadir - together with their retinues, pervading the whole of empty space. On behalf of all of them, we respectfully take refuge with the Greatly Kind and Compassionate Ones who are like fathers to those of us in this world.

Namo Maitreya Buddha
Namo Shakyamuni Buddha
Namo Brahma Muni Buddha
Namo Serene Conduct Buddha
Namo Diligence and Vigor Buddha
Namo Blazing Shoulders Buddha
Namo Great Awe-inspiring Virtue Buddha
Namo Campaka Flower Buddha
Namo Joyous Buddha
Namo Skillfully Leading All Beings Buddha
Namo Imperial Banner Buddha
Namo Great Loving Kindness Buddha
Namo Sumana Hue Buddha
Namo Multitude of Wonders Buddha
Namo Delighting Buddha
Namo Skillfully Defining Buddha
Namo Ox King Buddha
Namo Wondrous Arms Buddha
Namo Great Carriage Buddha
Namo Wish-fulfilling Buddha
Namo Light of Virtue Buddha
Namo Exquisite Sound Buddha

Namo Vajra Army Buddha
Namo Wealth and Honor Buddha
Namo Strong Practice Buddha
Namo Lion Power Buddha
Namo Pure Eye Buddha
Namo Boundless Body Bodhisattva
Namo Guan Shi Yin Bodhisattva

Again, we take refuge with the Three Treasures of the ten directions to the ends of empty space. May you protect and guard us with your power of kindness and compassion. We make this wish for all great demon kings, the Five Directional Great Demon Kings, and other demon kings, together with their retinues. From time without beginning until now:

- May all their karmic conditions and obstacles be purified;
- May all their karmic offenses be eradicated;
- May they be liberated from all suffering;
- May they always abide in the four limitless minds and the six paramitas;
- May they attain the as-you-wish mastery of the four unobstructed wisdoms and six spiritual powers;
- May they ceaselessly practice the Bodhisattva Path and take beings across before becoming Buddhas themselves.

Section 20 Bowing to the Buddhas on behalf of Rulers in the Human Realm

Today, we are here in this Bodhimanda due to our shared karma. We have completed our prostrations on behalf of all heavenly beings, ascetic masters, dragons and the rest of the eightfold division. Next, we continue to bow to the Buddhas to repay kindness on behalf of all rulers in the human realm, as well as our parents, elders, teachers, and all people. Why should we do so? Without rulers or heads of nations, living beings will not have a proper governing system to rely on. Rulers and heads of nations enable the citizens to have more settled lives, freedom of movement, and basic necessities such as water. They also provide many other benefits that are too numerous to speak of. Thus we, the great assembly, should all bring forth the mind of repaying their kindness.

There is a saying in the sutras, "If someone wishes to benefit and respectfully repay the kindness of others, enduring suffering throughout the six periods of the day and night, then this person should bring forth such a mind and practice kindness and compassion. Relying on the power of such vows, this person will be mindful of the kindness of the rulers who protect him, mindful of the kindness of donors who make offerings to him, mindful of the kindness of parents who raise him, mindful of the kindness of teachers who educate him, and mindful of the kindness of the Tathagatas who rescue him. Should this person bring forth utmost sincerity and be ever mindful without cease, he will quickly enter the Way."

Today, we are here in this Bodhimanda due to our shared karma. All Buddhas and great sages have been so kind as to earnestly guide us to the awareness of repaying the kindness of others. We rely on the rulers of nations, because they are able to make the Buddhadharma flourish in the time to come, able to generously make all kinds of offerings, including money and valuables, and able to influence all their subjects to be in awe of and take refuge with the Three Treasures.

Furthermore, they create an environment conducive for monastics to dwell peacefully and be focused on the Way. They are fully supportive of the monastic life, so that monastics are at ease, whether in walking, standing, sitting or reclining. They always extol the goodness of the monastics. They hope that monastics quickly transcend birth and death, expound limitless Dharma-doors, and set humans and heavenly beings on the right path. Since our rulers have such kindness for us, how could we not bow to the Buddhas on their behalf?

Let us all bring forth our utmost, heartfelt sincerity to take refuge with the Greatly Kind and Compassionate Ones who are like fathers to those of us in this world on the behalf of our rulers.

Namo Maitreya Buddha
Namo Shakyamuni Buddha
Namo Kashyapa Buddha
Namo Pure Mind Buddha
Namo Understanding Sequential Order Buddha
Namo Courage and Awe-inspiring Virtue Buddha
Namo Great Radiance Buddha
Namo Dazzling Sunshine Buddha
Namo Treasury of Purity Buddha
Namo Distinctly Awesome Buddha
Namo Non-diminishable Buddha
Namo Mystic Sun Buddha
Namo Moonlight Buddha
Namo Upholding Clarity Buddha
Namo Skillful Quiescent Practice Buddha
Namo Unmoving Buddha
Namo Requesting on a Grand Scale Buddha
Namo Dharma of Virtue Buddha
Namo Adornment King Buddha
Namo Outstanding Buddha
Namo Blazing Flame Buddha
Namo Blossoming Virtue Buddha
Namo Exquisite Embellishment Buddha
Namo Superior Goodness Buddha
Namo Superior Treasure Buddha
Namo Keen Wisdom Buddha
Namo Adorned Land Buddha
Namo Boundless Body Bodhisattva
Namo Guan Shi Yin Bodhisattva

Again, we take refuge with the Three Treasures of the ten directions to the ends of empty space. May you gather in all beings with your power of kindness and compassion.

Reverently, we pray:

May our heads of nations be healthy, their awesome influence widespread, the foundation of their rule ever strong and solid, their wisdom life ever enduring, and their kindness pervasive and boundless, causing all sentient beings to be loyal;

May Bodhisattvas respond and manifest in every part of the country;

May these heads of nations be extolled by heavenly beings; May they gain increasing strength and clarity in their practice of the four limitless minds and the six paramitas.

May they be endowed with the four unobstructed eloquences, delight in always speaking the Dharma, and attain the *eight* kinds of self-mastery and the six spiritual powers;

May the states of samadhi and dharani manifest as soon as they set their minds on them.

May their kindness and compassion benefit the world.

May their benevolence and virtue pervade and touch all in the six paths.

May they quickly perfect the myriad practices and attain Proper Enlightenment.

Section 21 Bowing to the Buddhas on behalf of Dukes, Princes and All Officials

Today, we are here in this Bodhimanda due to our shared karma. Again, with utmost sincerity, we bow in full prostration and take refuge with the Greatly Kind and Compassionate Ones who are like fathers to those of us in this world on behalf of His Highness the Crown Prince, all dukes, ministers, government officials and military officers, as well as their families and retinues.

Namo Maitreya Buddha
Namo Shakyamuni Buddha
Namo Sea-like Virtue Buddha
Namo Brahma Attributes Buddha
Namo Moon Canopy Buddha
Namo Myriad Flames Buddha
Namo King Wei Lan Buddha
Namo Renown Wisdom Buddha
Namo Enlightened Thought Buddha
Namo Light of Virtue Buddha
Namo Pervasive Sound Buddha
Namo Full Moon Buddha
Namo Flower Light Buddha
Namo Skilled in Precepts Buddha
Namo Lamp King Buddha
Namo Lightning Flash Buddha
Namo King of Light Buddha
Namo Radiance Buddha
Namo Praised for Being Complete Buddha
Namo Flower Treasury Buddha
Namo Pusya Buddha
Namo Sublime Physique Buddha
Namo Pure and Righteous Buddha
Namo Courageous and Awe-inspiring Army Buddha
Namo Blessings and Awe-inspiring Virtue Buddha
Namo Fortitude in Practice Buddha
Namo Rahu Deva Buddha
Namo Boundless Body Bodhisattva
Namo Guan Shi Yin Bodhisattva

Again, we return to and rely on the Three Treasures of the ten directions to the ends of empty space. May you protect and guard all with your power of kindness and compassion. We hope that His Highness the Crown Prince, all dukes, ministers, government officials and military officers, as well as their families and retinues will be healthy in body, peaceful in mind and have limitless wondrous functioning of wisdom.

- May they practice the Mahayana path, enter the Buddhas' wisdom, don the four great vows and not forsake any being.
- May they always abide in the four limitless minds and the six paramitas.
- May they be replete with the six spiritual powers and the three insights and be skilled in discerning beings' potential.
- May they be replete with the two adornments and have as-you-wish mastery in their spiritual powers.
- May they practice the kindness of the Tathagata and gather in, teach, and transform all beings throughout the six paths.

Section 22 Bowing to the Buddhas on behalf of All Parents

Today, we are here in this Bodhimanda due to our shared karma. Now we should be mindful of the kindness of our parents who raise us. They shower us with great care and love - holding us in their arms, cuddling, and nurturing us. They brave danger for the sake of our safety and well-being. As we grow up, our parents instruct us on benevolence and propriety, help us groom before we approach our teacher, and have aspirations for us that we be well-versed in the teachings of sages. In every thought, they wish for us to excel and become outstanding. They provide for all our needs, readily sacrificing the family's treasures. Constantly thinking and worrying about us, they sometimes cannot sleep peacefully and even fall sick. It is the most profound kindness in the world, second to none.

Thus the Buddha said, "Nothing in the world can compare to our parents' kindness."

Monastics who have renounced the householder's life, and who have yet to attain the Way, really need be diligent in cultivation, never abandon doing all good, and accumulate virtue without cease. In that way, monastics can definitely repay the kindness of our parents who had undergone so much hardship.

Now, on behalf of our parents in this life, all our parents and kin from the past, from the time we first had consciousness until now, let us together, with utmost, heartfelt sincerity, bow in full prostration and take refuge in the Greatly Kind and Compassionate Ones who are like fathers to those of us in this world.

Namo Maitreya Buddha
Namo Shakyamuni Buddha
Namo Accumulation of Wisdom Buddha
Namo Subduing and Taming Buddha
Namo Suchness King Buddha
Namo Flower Hallmarks Buddha
Namo Rahula Buddha
Namo Great Medicine Buddha
Namo Constellation King Buddha
Namo Medicine King Buddha
Namo Virtuous Hands Buddha
Namo Taksaka Buddha
Namo Renown Far and Wide King Buddha
Namo Sunlight Buddha
Namo Dharma Treasury Buddha
Namo Wonderful Intent Buddha
Namo Host of Virtues Buddha
Namo Vajra Assembly Buddha
Namo Wisdom Summit Buddha
Namo Skillfully Dwelling Buddha
Namo Mind Practice Buddha
Namo Brahma Sound Buddha
Namo Lion Penetration Buddha

Namo Thunder Sound Buddha
Namo Penetrating Attributes Buddha
Namo Peace and Tranquility Buddha
Namo Flourishing Wisdom Buddha
Namo Boundless Body Bodhisattva
Namo Guan Shi Yin Bodhisattva

Again, we take refuge with the Three Treasures of the ten directions to the ends of empty space. May you gather us in with your power of kindness and compassion. We hope that all our parents including relatives will, henceforth until they attain bodhi, have all their offenses eradicated.

- May they be liberated from all suffering and be cleansed of all tainted habits and fetters of afflictions.
  May they all attain purity forever.

- May they forever transcend the four evil paths, be reborn wherever they wish, draw near and serve Buddhas, and receive the Buddhas' predictions.
- May they never be apart from the four limitless minds and the six paramitas.
- May they gain as-you-wish mastery of the four unobstructed wisdoms and six spiritual powers.
- May they attain the Buddhas' ten powers, be adorned with all fine hallmarks and features, and together attain Buddhahood, the Proper and Equal Enlightenment.

Section 23 Bowing to the Buddhas on behalf of Parents from the Past

Today, we are here in this Bodhimanda due to our shared karma. Some of us who were orphaned when young, miss our parents greatly and have been thinking in vain of them because we have no possibility of ever encountering them again.

As we have not attained the spiritual penetration of the heavenly eye to see which paths they are in, we should spare no effort and hasten to create blessings on their behalf to repay their kindness. By unceasingly doing good like this, we will definitely succeed in doing so.

The sutras state, "Creating blessings for the deceased is like providing for travelers on a long journey." If the deceased have already been reborn in the human realm or in the heavens, what we have done will increase their merit and virtue. If the deceased are in the three evil paths, suffering the eight difficulties, the blessings created will help them forever transcend the multitudes of suffering. If the deceased are reborn in the time of a Buddha, they will receive the teachings of the Proper Dharma and immediately attain sudden awakening. Also, our parents of seven previous lives, as well as all relatives from kalpas past, will be able to eradicate all of their fears and worries and attain liberation. This is how a wise person practices compassion and filial respect to repay the kindness of one's deceased parents - it is the foremost method.

We should all now feel sorrow, remorse, weep, and bow in full prostration, as we fondly recollect the memories of our parents. On behalf of all our past parents, as well as relatives from kalpas past, we now take refuge in the Greatly Kind and Compassionate Ones who are like fathers to those of us in this world.

Namo Maitreya Buddha
Namo Shakyamuni Buddha
Namo Brahma King Buddha
Namo Ox King Buddha
Namo *Li Tuo Mu* Buddha
Namo Dragon Virtue Buddha
Namo Realilty Buddha
Namo Adornment Buddha

Namo Unfading Sound Buddha
Namo Blossoming Virtue Buddha
Namo Sound Virtue Buddha
Namo Lion Buddha
Namo Adorned Phrases Buddha
Namo Courage and Wisdom Buddha
Namo Accumulation of Flowers Buddha
Namo Blossoming Flowers Buddha
Namo Fortitude in Practice Buddha
Namo Amassing Virtue Buddha
Namo Superior Appearance Buddha
Namo Dazzling Brilliance Buddha
Namo Moon Lamp Buddha
Namo Awe-inspiring Virtue King Buddha
Namo Bodhi King Buddha
Namo Infinity Buddha
Namo Bodhi Eye Buddha
Namo Pervasive Body Buddha
Namo Land of Wisdom Buddha
Namo Boundless Body Bodhisattva
Namo Guan Shi Yin Bodhisattva

Again, we take refuge with the Three Treasures of the ten directions to the ends of empty space. May you with your power of kindness and compassion, rescue, protect, and gather in all beings. May you help eradicate all the karmic conditions for offenses of our parents and relatives of kalpas past, from now until they attain Buddhahood. May you also help them forever wipe out all their retributions of suffering and ultimately purify their fetters of afflictions.

- May they cut off the three kinds of obstructing karmic conditions and dispel the five fears.
- May they practice the Bodhisattva Path by expansively teaching and transforming all beings.

- May they apply the skills of the eight liberations in purifying their minds, and make the four great all-encompassing vows.
- May they also be able to wait upon the Buddhas in person, reverently receive the wonderful teachings, instantaneously end all their outflows, and freely traverse all Buddhalands within a thought.
- May they quickly accomplish their vows and practice and attain Proper Enlightenment.

Section 24 Bowing to the Buddhas on behalf of All Spiritual Teachers

Today, we are here in this Bodhimanda due to our shared karma. We have bowed to the Buddhas with utmost sincerity on behalf of our parents. We ought to now think of repaying the kindness of our Teachers of the Way. Why? Although our parents gave birth to us and brought us up, they are not able to help us quickly transcend the evil paths. Our teachers' kindness, on the other hand, is boundless. With their deep compassion, they exhort, guide, and encourage us to continually cultivate all goodness. They hope that we transcend birth and death and reach the other shore. Everything they do is to benefit us, enabling us to quickly eliminate the fetters of afflictions, see the Buddhas, and forever abide in the Unconditioned. Who could ever hope to repay such kindness from their supremely lofty virtue? Even if we were to cultivate the Way for our whole life just for the sake of benefiting ourselves, we would still be unable to repay the kindness of our teachers.

Therefore, the Buddha said, "Among teachers, foremost are teachers of the Way." It is because they not only take themselves across but others as well. It is all due to the kindness of our teachers that monastics have been able to leave the householder's life and receive full ordination. So, how could we all not cherish and keep in memory the kindness of our teachers?

Let us all bring forth utmost, heartfelt sincerity to bow in full prostration, and take refuge with the Greatly Kind and Compassionate Ones who are like fathers to those of us in this world on the behalf of our teachers of Dharma, *acharyas*, ordination certifying masters, monastics of the three seniorities, as well as their families and retinues.

Namo Maitreya Buddha
Namo Shakyamuni Buddha
Namo Supreme Buddha
Namo Pure Radiance Buddha
Namo Wisdom and Virtue Buddha
Namo Wonderful Voice Buddha
Namo Guiding Master Buddha
Namo Treasury of Non-obstruction Buddha
Namo Superior Giving Buddha
Namo Greatly Honored Buddha
Namo Wisdom Strength Buddha
Namo Great Flame Buddha
Namo Royal Monarch Buddha
Namo Power in Self-restraint Buddha
Namo Awe-inspiring Virtue Buddha
Namo Skilled in Clarity Buddha
Namo Renowned Buddha
Namo Upright and Adorned Buddha
Namo Free of Defilement Buddha
Namo Awe-inspiring Deportment Buddha
Namo Lion Army Buddha
Namo Celestial King Buddha
Namo Sublime Reputation Buddha
Namo Unique and Supreme Buddha
Namo Great Treasury Buddha
Namo Glowing with Blessings and Virtue Buddha
Namo Brahma Hearing Buddha

Namo Boundless Body Bodhisattva
Namo Guan Shi Yin Bodhisattva

Again, we take refuge with the Three Treasures of the ten directions to the ends of empty space. May you gather us in with your power of kindness and compassion. May you help cleanse the karmic offenses, eradicate the suffering, and dispel all the afflictions of our teachers of Dharma, *acharyas*, ordination certifying masters, monastics of the three seniorities, as well as that of their families and retinues, from now until they all attain Buddhahood.

- May they be reborn in the Buddhas' pure lands according to their wish.
- May they perfect all their bodhi vows and practices.
- May they practice limitless giving of wealth and Dharma.
- May they have limitless blessings and virtue, limitless peace and happiness, limitless longevity, and limitless wisdom.
- May they always dwell in the four limitless minds and the six paramitas.
- May they gain as-you-wish mastery of the four unobstructed wisdoms and the six spiritual powers.
- May they abide in the foremost Shurangama samadhi, and attain the vajra-indestructible body.
- May they never relinquish their fundamental vows to take living beings across.

Section 25 Bowing to the Buddhas on behalf of Monastics of the Ten Directions

Today, we are here in this Bodhimanda due to our shared karma. In line with our preceding prostrations, we now bow in full prostration and take refuge with the Greatly Kind and Compassionate Ones who are like fathers to those of us in this world on behalf of all of the following, those of the present and future, throughout the ten directions to the ends of empty space:

- All bhikshus, bhikshunis, shikshamanas, shramaneras, shramanerikas, as well as their families and retinues;
- All upasakas, upasikas, as well as their families and retinues;
- faithful donors, good and bad advisors, those with and those without affinities with us, together with their families and retinues;
- All in the human realm, together with their families and retinues.

Namo Maitreya Buddha
Namo Shakyamuni Buddha
Namo Lamp King Buddha
Namo Wisdom Summit Buddha
Namo Ascending to Heaven Buddha
Namo Earth King Buddha
Namo Ultimate Liberation Buddha
Namo Golden Crown Prominence Buddha
Namo Rahu Sun Buddha
Namo Undefeatable Buddha
Namo Mani Purity Buddha
Namo Light of Goodness Buddha
Namo Equal to Gold Buddha
Namo Planting-virtues Celestial King Buddha
Namo Dharma Canopy Buddha
Namo Arm of Virtue Buddha
Namo Angata Buddha
Namo Beautiful and Wonderful Wisdom Buddha
Namo Subtle Meaning Buddha
Namo Awe-inspiring Virtues Buddha
Namo Lion's Crown Prominence Buddha
Namo Attributes of Liberation Buddha

Namo Awe-inspiring Appearance Buddha
Namo Cutting off the Flow Buddha
Namo Wisdom Treasury Buddha
Namo Accumulation of Wisdom Buddha
Namo Praising Non-obstruction Buddha
Namo Boundless Body Bodhisattva
Namo Guan Shi Yin Bodhisattva

Again, we take refuge with the Three Treasures of the ten directions to the ends of empty space. With your power of kindness and compassion may you protect and guard:

- All bhikshus, bhikshunis, shikshamanas, shramaneras, shramanerikas, as well as their families and retinues;
- All upasakas, upasikas, as well as their families and retinues;
- Faithful donors, good and bad advisors, those with whom we have and with whom we do not have affinities, together with their families and retinues;
- All those in the human realm, together with their families and retinues.

- May you help eliminate all their afflictions, purify all their karmic conditions and obstacles, cleanse all their karmic offenses, and eradicate all their suffering, all of which have existed from time without beginning, enabling them to leave behind the three obstructive kinds of karma, and dispel the five fears.
- May they always dwell in the four limitless minds and the six paramitas. May they gain as-you-wish mastery of the four unobstructed wisdoms and six spiritual powers.
- May they practice the Bodhisattva Path, enter the Path of One Vehicle, and take across limitless living beings.

Section 26 Bowing to the Buddhas on behalf of All Past Monastics of the Ten Directions

Today, we are here in this Bodhimanda due to our shared karma. With a mind identical to that of all Buddhas, and with vows identical to that of all Buddhas, we now bow in full prostration and take refuge with the Greatly Kind and Compassionate Ones who are like fathers to those of us in this world on behalf of all past bhikshus, bhikshunis, shikshamanas, shramaneras, shramanerikas, upasakas, upasikas, and all beings who have lived in any human realm, together with their families and retinues, throughout the ten directions to the ends of empty space.

Namo Maitreya Buddha
Namo Shakyamuni Buddha
Namo Accumulation of Jewels Buddha
Namo Voice of Goodness Buddha
Namo Mountain King Hallmarks Buddha
Namo Dharma Summit Buddha
Namo Virtue of Liberation Buddha
Namo Wholesome and Sublime Buddha
Namo Body of Auspiciousness Buddha
Namo Words of Loving Kindness Buddha
Namo Beneficial Lion Buddha
Namo Aruna Buddha
Namo Dharma Lion Buddha
Namo Dharma Power Buddha
Namo Delight and Happiness Buddha
Namo Praising Unmoving Buddha
Namo Multi-faceted Understanding King Buddha
Namo Enlightening Buddha
Namo Wondrous Understanding Buddha
Namo Mind Abiding in Principles Buddha
Namo Radiating Brilliance Buddha

Namo Fragrance of Virtue Buddha
Namo Delighting-all Buddha
Namo Never Practicing in Vain Buddha
Namo Extinguishing Rage Buddha
Namo Superior Appearance Buddha
Namo Strides of Goodness Buddha
Namo Boundless Body Bodhisattva
Namo Guan Shi Yin Bodhisattva

Again, we take refuge with the Three Treasures of the ten directions to the ends of empty space. May you, with your power of kindness and compassion, rescue, protect, and gather in all beings. We now make vows for all past bhikshus, bhikshunis, shikshamanas, shramaneras, shramanerikas, upasakas, upasikas, as well as their families and retinues.

- May those suffering in the realm of hells immediately attain liberation.
- May those suffering in the realm of hungry ghosts immediately attain liberation.
- May those suffering in the realm of animals immediately attain liberation.
- May they all leave behind the eight difficulties, be born with the eight kinds of blessings, forever transcend the evil paths, and be reborn in the Pure Land.
- May they practice limitless giving of wealth and limitless giving of Dharma.
- May they be endowed with limitless blessings and virtue, limitless peace and happiness, limitless longevity, and limitless wisdom.
- May they always dwell in the four limitless minds and the six paramitas.
- May they gain as-you-wish mastery of the four unobstructed wisdoms and the six spiritual powers.

- May they always encounter Buddhas, listen to the Dharma, tirelessly cultivate the Bodhisattva Path with courage and vigor, continually advance in their cultivation until they accomplish *Anutara-samyak-sambodhi*, and vastly save all living beings.

Praise

Rulers of heavens, dragons and humans,
Meticulously protect the world.
Foremost is kindness of teachers and parents.
With the mind of repaying them,
We are resolved and sincere,
Painstakingly prostrating to all Buddhas in the Great Thousand
Worlds.

Namo Ground of No Movement Bodhisattva Mahasattva

(three times)

Concluding the Repentance

In the pool of *eight* virtues, thousands of flowers bloom, manifesting wondrous hallmarks.
In the realms of the *eight* sufferings, all gaze upward at the Honored One endowed with a myriad virtues.
With *eight* voices, the Buddhas vastly proclaim the wondrous Dharma of the *eight* patiences.
They universally rescue all undergoing severe retributions in the *eight* freezing-cold hells and *eight* blazing-hot hells.
They pity sentient beings, illuminating all with their great compassion and wisdom.
Their kindness touches humans and gods saddled with outflows.
Their blessing benefits all in infinitely many lands.
May all Buddhas kindly take pity on us and bear witness to this wondrous seed we plant.

[Dharma Host]: On behalf of _____ [those who seek to repent], we practice this Repentance Dharma of Kindness and Compassion in the Bodhimanda. We have now finished the recitation of Roll Eight.

The Bodhimanda abounds with "fire trees" decorated with bright lanterns. There are platters of offerings arrayed with various fresh and exotic fruits, and cups brimming with exquisite tea brewed from the shoots of early spring. Our spread of offerings is no less sincere than what Cunda made.

We offer all of these to the greatly awakened Golden Immortal, to the gods and deities of the ten continents and the three islands, to the sage-kings and wise rulers of the past, as well as to all loyal ministers, officers and soldiers who now reside in the ranks of gods and spirits.

May beings in the three realms throughout the ten directions, and all of the four births and the nine planes of existence, together benefit from this universal offering of Dharma. May all be liberated from the imprisonment of outflows.

With the superior benefit from bowing this repentance, we pray on behalf of _____ [those who seek to repent]. May all their karmic offenses be eradicated, and may they gain great auspiciousness.

We bow and earnestly pray:
May all relinquish the *eight* deviant views of sentient beings,
And walk the *eightfold* noble path which will lead us to freedom from outflows.
May the *eight* sufferings and misfortunes we are still due to undergo
Be immediately eradicated by the light of your kindness.
May the *eight* fields of blessings of the *eight* periods of time,
All be brought to perfection by immersing in the Dharma.
May we be imbued with and penetrate each and every Dharma, and
Roam in self-mastery through each and every land as numerous as motes of dust;

May all the waves arising in the ocean's vastness become
tranquil;
May the reflection of the moon be seen in the still water of
rivers and streams.
[Dharma host]: Should any aggregate still remain to be emptied,
We seek to accomplish by repenting and reforming.

Praise

The meritorious power of the Emperor of Liang Repentance Roll Eight
Enables the deceased and the disciples to eradicate the offenses of the
eight defilements.
May all realize the Bodhisattva's Ground of No Movement.
As the Repentance is chanted our offenses are blown away like flower
petals in the wind.
Offenses repented, enmity resolved,
Wisdom and blessing increase as calamities are dispelled.
Liberated from suffering and reborn in the Trayastrimsha,
May we gather at the Dragon Flower's Three Assemblies
And receive a prediction personally from Maitreya Buddha.

Namo Dragon Flower Assembly of Bodhisattvas Mahasattvas
(three times).

Final praise

Emperor of Liang Repentance Roll Eight now concludes.
We dedicate its merit to the four benefactors and the three realms.
May all in this assembly enjoy increased longevity and blessings,
May the Dharma water cleanse our offenses.
May the deceased be reborn in the Western Pure Land.
May the Bodhisattvas of the Ground of No Movement compassionately
gather us in.

Namo Ascending the Path to the Clouds Bodhisattva Mahasattva
(three times)

End Notes

1. **Eight periods of time:** Indian division of the day into eight
   time periods, four for day and four for night. The Sanskrit
   aṣṭan is transliterated as 頞瑟吒.

ROLL NINE

Namo Buddhas and Bodhisattvas of the Dragon Flower Assembly
(*bow three times*)

Praise

One hundred and eight
Dharanis, sutras, and other texts - a complete Dharma Treasury,
Including those texts related to
Medicine Master Buddha who quells disasters and lengthens life;
Vairocana Buddha, from whose mind arises the Yogacara School;
And Amitabha Buddha - all these texts of the Mahayana tradition
Wherein lies the story of the Dragon Girl of the south,
Who resolves on the path of bodhi and spontaneously realizes
Buddhahood.

Namo Universal Offering Bodhisattva Mahasattva (*three times*)

Listen respectfully

The Buddha's Way surpasses the *nine* heavens and Lord Shakra,
thus the Buddha is called Hero of the Worlds.
His merit exceeds that of all sentient beings in the *nine* planes
of existence, thus he is named Trainer of the World.
He rescues beings suffering in the *nine* realms of darkness here;
He draws beings in to the *nine* grades of lotuses there.
Within a thought, he transcends all *nine* successive stages of
samadhi.
Within the *nine* realms, he manifests physical forms to accord
with conditions.
His radiance envelopes the entire Dharma Realm, and

His Path surpasses that of all beings.

May the Buddha manifest his adornments derived from myriad practices and bear witness to the deeds we do for Buddhas throughout the *nine* periods of time.

[Dharma Host]: On behalf of _____ [those who seek to repent], we practice this Repentance Dharma of Kindness and Compassion in the Bodhimanda. We have come to Roll Nine. With all conditions fulfilled, we now enter the Repentance Platform.

We reverently offer arrays of incense and lamps, flowers and fruits. We humbly present platters of exotic delicacies. These offerings to the Three Treasures are a token of our single-minded devotion. Now we purify our minds, still our thoughts, and sincerely confess our faults before the Buddha, whose Dharma body is unmoving, whose Dharma nature is tranquil, whose Dharma eye is perfect and brilliant, and whose Dharma - each and every aspect of it - is pervasive.

The Buddha manifests his purple-golden hallmarks and radiates the bright fine light of white jade. We bow in reverence and take refuge with the Buddha. May the Buddha kindly take pity on us and gather us in as we strive to cleanse all remaining filth and continue to repent of all remaining offenses.

We are earnestly mindful that since past kalpas as numerous as dust motes, we have been adrift and lost, without the chance to return to the source. We have always been confused about the principle of cause and effect operating in the *nine* realms and have been covered by ignorance. We did not believe that the retribution of suffering awaits us in the *nine* springs of the underworld and thus entertained rampant deviant views.

We slighted the revered sutras of the *nine* divisions, thus wantonly committing all manner of offenses. We were entangled in the afflictions of the *nine* fetters, behaving recklessly and without restraint. We praised ourselves and slandered others; we harmed others to benefit ourselves. We deceived others by manipulating the weighing scales; we indulged in lust and wine causing us to drift in confusion. We did all these because of our greed for the fleeting pleasures of the mundane world and thus have not been spared from the extreme suffering of the dark paths. Realizing all this, we immediately repent. Fortunately we are able to evince reverence in our hearts and take refuge with the Buddha, the true and pure field of blessings. On behalf of _____ [those who seek to repent] we now rely on the Repentance Text. We respectfully bow to the Greatly Compassionate One and pray you will invisibly bless and protect us.

> On a white lotus dais is seated the Buddha of golden hallmarks,
> The red lotus blossoms reveal his purple-golden body.
> His noble and fine features are the divine among the divine.
> His vast states are indescribable - thus is the Sage among sages.

Commencement of the Repentance

We now begin the Repentance Dharma of Kindness and Compassion in the Bodhimanda.Together in this assembly, we single-mindedly return to and rely on all Buddhas of the three periods of time.

Namo Buddhas of the past, Vipashyin Buddha
Namo Shikhin Buddha
Namo Vishvabhu Buddha
Namo Krakucchanda Buddha
Namo Kanakamuni Buddha
Namo Kashyapa Buddha
Namo our Fundamental Teacher Shakyamuni Buddha
Namo Honored Future Buddha, Maitreya

Section 27 Bowing to the Buddhas on Behalf of Beings in the *Avici* Hell

Today, we are here in this Bodhimanda due to our shared karma. Starting from Section One on Taking Refuge up to this section, it has been repeatedly mentioned that despite the myriad varieties of dharma, contrasting like day and night, like merit and offenses, they can all be summed up into just two categories, dharmas of goodness or dharmas of evil. The dharmas of goodness lead beings to superior paths of humans and heavenly beings; whereas evil dharmas lead beings to deviated paths of the three evil destinies. If one cultivates humaneness and righteousness, one will tend towards superior destinies; if one harms and kills, then one will fall into inferior destinies.

Further, those who dwell in the superior paths are there due to their superior karma, not as a result of contention. They naturally enjoy wonderful bliss and tend towards supreme freedom and ease. On the other hand, those who fall into the inferior paths are there as a result of inferior karma. They live in flaming cities, within iron nets, eat iron pellets and hot iron, and drink molten copper or rocks. Their lifespans surpass the duration of the cosmos, lasting for infinite kalpas.

Moreover the suffering in the hells is so terrifying that no one would ever want to experience it. When our consciousness leaves our bodies, we plunge into the cities of hell, suffer the retribution of the revolving wheel of blades slicing us and the revolving grinders of fire destroying our bodies. There, even if we wish to quickly end our lives, we will find it impossible to do so and will have to continue to endure a life full of suffering. Suppose one day we are freed from the hells, we in turn fall into the realm of hungry ghosts where our mouths spurt fire, lingering on in a zombie-like state.

After that, we are reborn among animals and undergo a multitude of suffering. We may become prey to other predators that devour our flesh. We undergo uncountable cycles of short lifespans. We may be slaughtered, dismembered, and end up boiled in pots or fried in pans. Slices of our flesh may be laid on counters and slabs of our flesh hung and displayed. We may become tools of transportation, burdened with heavy loads for long hauls, driven over dangerous and rough terrain. Indeed, all of these are the grave suffering and misery we undergo. We lament throughout the long night and can hardly wait to see the light of dawn. Despite such crystal clear contrast between wholesome rewards and evil retributions, few believe in them. Because of our ego, we often give rise to doubts, and deluded by our doubts, we often shun goodness and instead tend towards evil.

That is why the Buddha mentioned ten factors that drag a person into the evil paths after death.

1. One's intention is not entirely wholesome.
2. One does not cultivate merit and virtue.
3. One is always gluttonous like a hungry tiger.
4. One always indulges in wine and sex and harbors venomous hatred.
5. One holds onto the habits of delusion and ignorance and refuses to listen to any remonstration; one gives free reign to wanton behavior, engaging in all manner of evil.
6. One delights in killing.
7. One bullies and takes advantage of the orphaned and weak.
8. One gangs up with evil people, encroaching and pillaging the territories of others.
9. One likes to make grandiose proclamations and is not truthful.
10. One lacks compassion towards all and creates various evil karma.

Behaving thus, it will not be long before one dies and falls into the evil paths.

Today, we are here in this Bodhimanda due to our shared karma. When we consider what the Buddha said, who among us could be spared? Since we cannot be spared, that means we will have our share of retributions in the hell realm. Recognizing this fact, each one of us should be wary and not be lax. We should cherish each passing minute and practice the Bodhisattva Path; we should diligently seek the Dharma and benefit all living beings. By doing so, we can eradicate our offenses as well as help others increase their blessings. This is what is meant by benefiting oneself and benefiting others and by being one with all.

Now let us all bring forth a courageous mind, a determined mind, a compassionate mind, a mind to take all beings across, and a mind to rescue all living beings. We pray that from now until the day we attain Buddhahood, we shall never forget these vows. We also look up to and beseech all Buddhas and great Bodhisattvas of the ten directions throughout empty space: May you enable all of us to accomplish deeds of benefiting others and to achieve our own vows, using your great spiritual powers, your power of great compassion, your power of rescuing beings from hells, your power of guiding and taking across hungry ghosts, your power of extricating animals from the animal realm, your power engendered by great spiritual mantras, and your awesome and mighty great power.

With heartfelt sincerity, we bow in full prostration. With our bodhi resolve, with our bodhi practice, and with our bodhi vows, we now take refuge with the Greatly Kind and Compassionate Ones who are like fathers to those of us in this world on behalf of all the following suffering beings who are:

- in the *Avici* Hell,
- in the Hells of Pitched Darkness,
- in the eighteen Hells of Freezing Cold,
- in the eighteen Hells of Blazing Heat,
- in the eighteen Hells of Wheels of Blades,
- in the Hells of Forests of Swords,
- in Hells of Fire Carts,
- in the Hells of Boiling Excrement,
- in the Hells of Cauldrons of Seething Broth,

and in all other similar hells and their eighty-four thousand subsidiary hells.

Namo Maitreya Buddha
Namo Shakyamuni Buddha
Namo Praising with Majestic Voice Buddha
Namo Pure Vows Buddha

Namo Sun Deva Buddha
Namo Delight in Wisdom Buddha
Namo Disciplining the Body Buddha
Namo Strength in Awesome Virtue Buddha
Namo Kshatriya Buddha
Namo Vehicle of Virtue Buddha
Namo Superb Gold Buddha
Namo Topknot of Liberation Buddha
Namo Delight in the Dharma Buddha
Namo Dwelling in Practice Buddha
Namo Renouncing Arrogance Buddha
Namo Wisdom Treasury Buddha
Namo Pure Practices Buddha
Namo Chandana Buddha
Namo Worry-free Renown Buddha
Namo Stately and Sublime Body Buddha
Namo Prime Minister Buddha
Namo Lotus Flower Buddha
Namo Boundless Virtue Buddha
Namo Heaven's Light Buddha
Namo Wisdom Flower Buddha
Namo *Pin Tou Mo* Buddha
Namo Abundance of Wisdom Buddha
Namo Lion Playfully Roaming Bodhisattva
Namo Lion Swiftness and Vigor Bodhisattva
Namo Earth Treasury Bodhisattva
Namo Boundless Body Bodhisattva
Namo Guan Shi Yin Bodhisattva

Again, we take refuge with the Three Treasures of the ten directions to the ends of empty space. We pray that the Three Treasures will, through the power of compassion, help save, extricate, and guide all beings who are suffering in the *Avici* Hell, the Hells of Total Darkness, the Hells of Wheels of Blades, the Hells of Fire Carts, the Hells of

Boiling Excrement, and all other hells as well as their subsidiary hells. We pray, by virtue of the power of the Buddhas, the power of the Dharma, the power of all Bodhisattvas, and the power of all virtuous sages that all hell beings be immediately liberated and never again fall into any of these different hells.

We also pray for all their karmic offenses to be eradicated and that they never again create the karma of hells.

- May they renounce rebirths in the hells and attain birth in the Pure Land.
- May they renounce the hell life and attain the wisdom life.
- May they renounce the hell body and attain the vajra body.
- May they renounce the suffering of hells and attain the bliss of Nirvana.
- May they be mindful of the suffering in hells and bring forth the bodhi mind.
- May they spontaneously manifest the four limitless minds and the six paramitas.
- May they gain self-mastery of the four unobstructed eloquences and the six spiritual powers.
- May they be replete with wisdom and exert courageous vigor to practice the Bodhisattva Path without pause or rest.
- May they quickly attain the Ten Grounds, gain entry to the vajra mind, and realize Proper and Equal Enlightenment.

Section 28 Bowing to the Buddhas on behalf of Those in the Hell of River of Ash and the Hell of Iron Pellets

Today, we are here in this Bodhimanda due to our shared karma. Again with utmost sincerity we now bow in full prostration. With our minds resolved on bodhi, we take refuge with the Greatly Kind and Compassionate Ones who are like fathers to those of us in this world on behalf of all beings suffering in

- the Hell of River of Ash,
- the Hell of Forest of Swords,
- the Hell of Forest of Thorns,
- the Hell of Copper Pillars,
- the Hell of Iron Traps,
- the Hell of Iron Nets,
- the Hell of Iron Caverns,
- the Hell of Iron Pellets,
- the Hell of Sharp Stones,

and all such hells of the ten directions to the ends of empty space.

Namo Maitreya Buddha
Namo Shakyamuni Buddha
Namo Brahma Wealth Buddha
Namo Jeweled Hands Buddha
Namo Roots of Purity Buddha
Namo Comprehensive Shastras Buddha
Namo Superior Shastras Buddha
Namo Pusya Buddha
Namo Tiṣya Buddha
Namo Presence of the Sun Buddha
Namo Transcending the Mire Buddha
Namo Attaining Wisdom Buddha
Namo *Mo Luo* Buddha
Namo Most Auspicious Buddha
Namo Dharma Bliss Buddha
Namo Striving for Victory Buddha
Namo Wisdom Buddha
Namo Goodness and Sage Buddha
Namo Nets of Light Buddha
Namo Lapis Lazuli Treasury Buddha
Namo Renowned Buddha
Namo Beneficial Stillness Buddha

Namo Teaching and Transforming Buddha
Namo Brillliance of Sun Buddha
Namo Skilled in Clarity Buddha
Namo Superb Brilliance of a Multitude of Virtues Buddha
Namo Precious Virtue Buddha
Namo Lion Banner Bodhisattva
Namo Lion Deeds Bodhisattva
Namo Earth Treasury Bodhisattva
Namo Boundless Body Bodhisattva
Namo Guan Shi Yin Bodhisattva

Again, we take refuge with the Three Treasures of the ten directions to the ends of empty space. May you, with your power of kindness and compassion, rescue and extricate all beings now suffering in the Hell of Ash River and all other hells, so that these beings may all:

- be liberated,
- have all their bitter retributions eradicated,
- be purified of all their hell karma,
- renounce the hell bodies and attain the vajra body,
- renounce the suffering of hells and attain the bliss of Nirvana,
- be mindful of the sufferings of hells and bring forth the resolve for bodhi, and
- escape the burning house, and together with all the Bodhisattvas, attain Buddhahood, the Proper Enlightenment.

Section 29 Bowing to the Buddhas on behalf of Those in the Hell of Drinking Molten Copper, the Hell of Charcoal Pits, and Other Hells

Today, we are here in this Bodhimanda due to our shared karma. Once again with utmost sincerity, we bow in full prostration, and with our sincere bodhi mind, take refuge with the Greatly Kind and

Compassionate Ones who are like fathers to those of us in this world on behalf of all beings suffering in all hells of the ten directions to the ends of empty space, including:

- the Hell of Drinking Molten Copper,
- the Hell of Crushing and Squeezing,
- the Hell of Howling and Screaming,
- the Hell of Loud Howling and Screaming,
- the Hell of Blazing Heat,
- the Hell of Extreme Blazing Heat,
- the Hell of Charcoal Pits,
  the Hell of Burning Forests,

and all other such immeasurable and boundless subsidiary hells.

Namo Maitreya Buddha
Namo Shakyamuni Buddha
Namo Moon of Humanity Buddha
Namo Rahu Buddha
Namo Sweet Dew-like Understanding Buddha
Namo Wonderful Intent Buddha
Namo Great Brilliance Buddha
Namo Master-of-all Buddha
Namo Delight in Wisdom Buddha
Namo Mountain King Buddha
Namo Tranquil Cessation Buddha
Namo Accumulation of Virtue Buddha
Namo Celestial King Buddha
Namo Wonderful Voice Buddha
Namo Wonderful Flower Buddha
Namo Dwelling in Principles Buddha
Namo Accumulation of Awe-inspiring Merit and Virtue Buddha
Namo Peerless Wisdom Buddha
Namo Sound of Sweet Dew Buddha
Namo Hand of Goodness Buddha

Namo Keen Wisdom Buddha
Namo Contemplating Principles of Liberation Buddha
Namo Triumphant Sound Buddha
Namo *Li Tuo* Practice Buddha
Namo Principle of Goodness Buddha
Namo Free of Fault Buddha
Namo Practicing Goodness Buddha
Namo Steadfast, Courageous, and Vigorous Bodhisattva
Namo Vajra Wisdom Bodhisattva
Namo Earth Treasury Bodhisattva
Namo Boundless Body Bodhisattva
Namo Guan Shi Yin Bodhisattva

Again, we take refuge with the Three Treasures of the ten directions to the ends of empty space. May you, with your power of kindness and compassion, rescue and extricate all beings now suffering in all the hells, such as the Hell of Drinking Molten Copper and the like, so that all these beings may:

- have their karmic offenses eradicated,
- be free of all their suffering,
- be liberated,
- never fall into the hells again,
- renounce rebirths in the hells and attain rebirth in the Pure Land,
- renounce the hell life and attain the wisdom life,
- spontaneously manifest the four limitless minds and the six paramitas,
- attain the as-you-wish mastery of the four unobstructed eloquences and six spiritual powers,
- escape from the paths of hell and attain the path to Nirvana, and
- accomplish Proper Enlightenment identical to all Tathagatas.

Section 30 Bowing to the Buddhas on behalf of Those in the Hell of Military Weaponry, the Hell of Copper Cauldrons, and Other Hells

Today, we are here in this Bodhimanda due to our shared karma. Again with utmost sincerity, we bow in full prostration and with the power of our bodhi resolve, take refuge with the Greatly Kind and Compassionate Ones who are like fathers to those of us in this world on behalf of all beings suffering in all hells of the ten directions to the ends of empty space, including:

- the Hell of Thought,
- the Hell of Black Sand,
- the Hell of Nailing the Body,
- the Hell of the Well of Fire,
- the Hell of Stone Mortars,
- the Hell of Boiling Sand,
- the Hell of Military Weaponry,
- the Hell of Starvation,
- the Hell of Copper Cauldrons, and all other countless hells.

Namo Maitreya Buddha
Namo Shakyamuni Buddha
Namo Flower Treasury Buddha
Namo Wonderful Light Buddha
Namo Delight in Speaking Buddha
Namo Skillfully Rescuing Buddha
Namo Leader of Multitudes Buddha
Namo Transcending Fear Buddha
Namo Sun of Eloquence Buddha
Namo Renowned Buddha
Namo Radiance of Jeweled Moon Buddha
Namo Superior Resolve Buddha
Namo Fearless Buddha

Namo Great Vision Buddha
Namo Brahma Sound Buddha
Namo Voice of Goodness Buddha
Namo Rescuing with Wisdom Buddha
Namo Peerless Resolve Buddha
Namo Vajra Army Buddha
Namo Resolve for Bodhi Buddha
Namo King of Trees Buddha
Namo Panthaka Sound Buddha
Namo Power of Blessings and Virtue Buddha
Namo Strength in Virtue Buddha
Namo Sagely Devotion Buddha
Namo Strength and Practice Buddha
Namo Amber Buddha
Namo Delight in Knowledge Buddha
Namo Renouncing Hindrances of *Skandhas* Bodhisattva
Namo Tranquil Sense Faculties Bodhisattva
Namo Earth Treasury Bodhisattva
Namo Boundless Body Bodhisattva
Namo Guan Shi Yin Bodhisattva

Again we take refuge with the Three Treasures of the ten directions to the ends of empty space. May you, with your power of kindness and compassion, rescue and protect all beings now suffering in the Hell of Military Weaponry as well as all other hells and their susubsidiary hells. May all these beings:

- immediately be liberated today and have all their sufferings removed and eradicated forever,
- leave the conditions of the hells and be reborn with wisdom,
- bring forth the bodhi resolve upon recalling all the suffering in the hells,
- cultivate the Bodhisattva practice without rest,
- enter the path of the One Vehicle and fulfill the practice of the Ten Grounds,

- gain spiritual powers and then return to guide all sentient beings, so together they can all realize Buddhahood, the Proper Enlightenment.

Section 31 Bowing to the Buddhas on behalf of Those in the Hell of the Flaming Cities, the Hell of Mountains of Blades, and Other Hells

Today, we are here in this Bodhimanda due to our shared karma. Again with utmost sincerity, we bow in full prostration, and with the power of our bodhi resolve, take refuge with the Greatly Kind and Compassionate Ones who are like fathers to those of us in this world on behalf of all beings suffering in all hells of the ten directions to the ends of empty space, including

- the Hell of Flaming Cities
- the Hell of Stone Caves,
- the Hell of Being Scalded with Boiling Liquids
- the Hell of Mountains of Blades,
- the Hell of Tigers and Wolves,
- the Hell of Iron Beds,
- the Hell of Blazing Hot Winds,
- the Hell of Spurting Fire,
- and all other such countless and immeasurable subsidiary hells.

Namo Maitreya Buddha
Namo Shakyamuni Buddha
Namo Thunder-sound Cloud Buddha
Namo Eye of Goodness and Devotion Buddha
Namo Goodness and Wisdom Buddha
Namo Fully Endowed Buddha,
Namo Amassing Virtue Buddha

Namo Great Sounds Buddha

Namo Dharma Attributes Buddha

Namo Wisdom Sound Buddha

Namo Empty Space Buddha

Namo Temple Sounds Buddha

Namo Discerning Wisdom Sounds Buddha

Namo Light of Merit and Virtue Buddha

Namo Sage-King Buddha

Namo Intention of the Multitudes Buddha

Namo Wheel of Eloquence Buddha

Namo Skillfully Tranquil Buddha

Namo Moon Face Buddha

Namo Sun Renown Buddha

Namo Undefiled Buddha

Namo Amassing Merit and Virtue Buddha

Namo Hallmark of Blossoming Virtue Buddha

Namo Land of Eloquence Buddha

Namo Precious Giving Buddha

Namo Loving-kindness Moon Buddha

Namo Untowering Buddha

Namo Superior Wisdom Bodhisattva

Namo Never Leaving the World Bodhisattva

Namo Earth Treasury Bodhisattva

Namo Boundless Body Bodhisattva

Namo Guan Shi Yin Bodhisattva

Again, we take refuge with the Three Treasures of the ten directions to the ends of empty space. May you, with your power of kindness and compassion, gather us in. May all beings suffering in the Hell of Mountains of Blades and all other hells be liberated immediately. By the power of the Buddhas, the power of the Dharma, the power of Bodhisattvas, the power of sages and the worthy ones may all beings who are now suffering and those who are about to suffer be liberated and forever eradicate their karma of the hells of the ten directions. From now until they attain Buddhahood, may they

- never again fall into the three evil destinies,
- life after life always encounter the Buddhas,
- be replete with wisdom, purity, and self-mastery,
- be courageous and vigorous without rest, advancing in cultivation until they perfect the Ten Grounds,
- attain the vajra mind,
- enter the fruition of the Wisdom of All Modes, and
- by the power of the Buddha, attain as-you-wish self-mastery.

Section 32 Bowing to the Buddhas on behalf of Those in the Realm of Hungry Ghosts

Today, we are here in this Bodhimanda due to our shared karma. Again with utmost sincerity we now bow in full prostration on behalf of beings in the realm of hungry ghosts - hungry spirits, hungry ghosts, as well as their retinues - in the ten directions to the ends of empty space. With the power of our bodhi resolve we take refuge with the Greatly Kind and Compassionate Ones who are like fathers to those of us in this world on behalf of these beings.

Namo Maitreya Buddha
Namo Shakyamuni Buddha
Namo Lion Power Buddha
Namo King Self-mastery Buddha
Namo Limitless Purity Buddha
Namo Equal Samadhi Buddha
Namo Indestructible Buddha
Namo Eradicating Defilement Buddha
Namo Unfailing in Skillful Means Buddha
Namo Beyond Seduction Buddha

Namo Wondrous Face Buddha
Namo Disciplining through Wisdom, Then Abiding Buddha
Namo Dharma Master King Buddha
Namo Great Heaven Buddha
Namo Profound Meaning Buddha
Namo Without Limit Buddha
Namo Dharma Power Buddha
Namo Offerings from the Worlds Buddha
Namo Flower Light Buddha
Namo Offerings from the Three Periods Buddha
Namo In Accord with Sun Treasury Buddha
Namo Offerings from the Heavens Buddha
Namo One with Superb Wisdom Buddha
Namo Genuine Crown Prominence Buddha
Namo Sweet Dew of Faith Buddha
Namo Vajra Buddha
Namo Steadfast Buddha
Namo Medicine King Bodhisattva
Namo Medicine Superior Bodhisattva
Namo Earth Treasury Bodhisattva
Namo Boundless Body Bodhisattva
Namo Guan Shi Yin Bodhisattva

Again, we take refuge with the Three Treasures of the ten directions to the ends of empty space. May you, with your power of kindness and compassion, gather in the beings in the realm of hungry ghosts which include hungry spirits, hungry ghosts, and their retinues throughout the north, south, east, west, the four intermediate directions, zenith and nadir, pervading the ten directions.

- May they all be liberated from their suffering, and may all their karmic offenses be eradicated.
- May their bodies and minds be pure, refreshed, free from all afflictions, and be full and content, no longer experiencing hunger or thirst.

- May they savor the flavor of sweet dew and open their wisdom eye.
- May they spontaneously manifest the four limitless minds and the six paramitas.
- May they attain as-you-wish mastery of the four unobstructed eloquences and six spiritual powers.
- May they also transcend the realm of hungry ghosts and attain Nirvana.
- And may they accomplish Proper Enlightenment identical to that of the Tathagatas.

Section 33 Bowing to the Buddhas on behalf of Those in the Animal Realm

Today, we are here in this Bodhimanda due to our shared karma. Once again with utmost sincerity, we bow in full prostration on behalf of all beings and their retinues from the four births in the realm of animals, whether big or small, whether in water, land, or space, throughout the north, south, east, west, the four intermediate directions, zenith and nadir, pervading the ten directions. And with the power of kindness and compassion we take refuge with the Greatly Kind and Compassionate Ones who are like fathers to those of us in this world on behalf of these beings.

Namo Maitreya Buddha
Namo Shakyamuni Buddha
Namo Radiance from Jeweled Shoulders Buddha
Namo Ridra Strides Buddha
Namo Following the Sun Buddha
Namo Purity Buddha
Namo Strength from Understanding Buddha
Namo Amassing Merit and Virtue Buddha
Namo Replete with Virtue Buddha

Namo Lion Conduct Buddha
Namo Outstanding Buddha
Namo Blossoming of Giving Buddha
Namo Pearl's Radiance Buddha
Namo Lotus Flower Buddha
Namo Delight in Wisdom Buddha
Namo Panthaka Adornment Buddha
Namo Never Practicing in Vain Buddha
Namo Dharma Producing Buddha
Namo Radiant Hallmark Buddha
Namo Bliss of Contemplation Buddha
Namo Delight in Liberation Buddha
Namo Aware of Principles Buddha
Namo Ever-vigorous Bodhisattva
Namo Never Resting Bodhisattva
Namo Earth Treasury Bodhisattva
Namo Boundless Body Bodhisattva
Namo Guan Shi Yin Bodhisattva

Again, we take refuge with the Three Treasures of the ten directions to the ends of empty space. May you, with your power of kindness and compassion, gather in all beings and their retinues from the four births in the realm of animals, throughout the north, south, east, west, the four intermediate directions, zenith and nadir, pervading the ten directions.

- May all of their karmic offenses be eradicated, and may they be liberated from their suffering.
- May they all renounce the evil destinies and accomplish the fruition of the Way.
- May they attain peace and happiness in body and mind, just like that experienced in the Third Dhyana Heaven.
- May they spontaneously manifest the four limitless minds and the six paramitas.

- May they gain as-you-wish mastery of the four unobstructed eloquences and the six spiritual powers.
- May they transcend the animal realm and attain Nirvana.
- May they attain the vajra mind and realize Proper and Equal Enlightenment.

Section 34 Bowing to the Buddhas on behalf of Sentient Beings of the Six Realms

From the causes and conditions generated from the merit and virtue of bowing to the Buddhas may we now make the following vows on behalf of all heavenly beings, ascetic masters, dragons and the rest of the eightfold division:

- May all beings of the ten directions to the ends of time and space, including those of the four births and the six paths, from now until they attain bodhi, no longer commit any wrong or evil that would cause them to undergo pain and suffering.
- May they no longer perpetrate the ten evil deeds and the five rebellious acts that would cause them to fall into the three evil destinies.
- May all beings also attain the Bodhisattva Mahasattva's pure karma of body, speech, and mind, and
- May all of them bring forth the Bodhisattva's great resolve,
  - o a resolve like the great earth, which generates all roots of goodness,
  - o a resolve like the vast ocean, which can uphold all Buddhas' Dharma of wisdom,
  - o a resolve like Mount Sumeru, which enables all beings to firmly dwell in bodhi,
  - o a resolve like a precious *mani* jewel, which is far apart from afflictions,
  - o a vajra resolve, which is decisive in all Dharmas,

- o a steadfast resolve, which is beyond harm from any demon or externalist,
- o a lotus-like resolve, which can transcend the defilement of any worldly dharma,
- o a resolve like an *udumbara* flower, which is hard to encounter in kalpas,
- o a resolve like the sun in the clear sky, which eliminates all obstructions of delusion and illusion,
- o a resolve like empty space, which is beyond measure by any being.

We further pray that all beings of the four births and the six paths, henceforth,

- contemplate the nature of consciousness,
- contemplate the nature of understanding with resolute faith,
- renounce frivolous speech and always contemplate words of Dharma,
- practice giving without a trace of stinginess,
- in thought after thought be courageous, vigorous, and fearless,
- dedicate the merit they cultivate to all beings,
- never fall back on deviant paths but always focus on the One Vehicle,
- regard all good as illusions and all evil as dreams,
- renounce and end the cycle of birth and death and swiftly transcend the three realms,
- contemplate and clearly understand the profound and wondrous Dharma,
- possess an abundance of resources to generously make offerings to Buddhas,
- possess an abundance of resources to generously make offerings to Dharma,

- possess an abundance of resources to generously make offerings to all Bodhisattvas,
- possess an abundance of resources to generously make offerings to all sages and worthy ones.

If there are living beings in the future who do not have these vows, we pray that they too shall all enter the sea of these great vows and instantaneously accomplish merit, virtue and wisdom. By the power of the Buddha, may they attain as-you-wish self-mastery and accomplish Proper Enlightenment identical to that of the Tathagatas.

Section 35 Wary and Mindful of Impermanence

Today, we are here in this Bodhimanda due to our shared karma. Together we have bowed, repented, and made vows on behalf of all beings in the six realms. We should now awaken to the impermanence of this world. Therefore, we should be mindful that all blessings and suffering are the consequences of past causes. We should take this to heart and always be mindful that: effect follows cause, just like a shadow following form, or an echo following sound. These consequences are never off by a hair's breadth, and no one can escape them.

The retribution of good and evil never errs and cannot be personally altered by willful means. May all in this Repentance assembly awaken to the reality of impermanence, help ourselves by cultivating diligently, and never be lax or fail to apply effort. The wise ones always lament that even if one lived for millions of years enjoying the five desires of wealth, sex, food, fame, and sleep, one is still unable to avoid the suffering of the three evil paths. How much the less, when our lifespan is only about a hundred years, and our productive years are not even half of that! Hence, hard-pressed with such a short lifespan, how could we possibly afford to be lax?

Moreover, the world is illusory and delusive, decaying and disappearing before long. What exists now will eventually come to an end just as one at the pinnacle will eventually fall; being together is followed by separation; birth is followed by death. When it is time for death, none of those who deeply love and cherish us can take our place, whether they are fathers, mothers, siblings, spouses, or relatives. Neither a high position, nor ample salary and benefits, or glory, status, aristocracy, or wealth can prolong our lives. Nor can it be done by pleading and beseeching or life-vitalizing food! The unseen forces of death determine that no one can stay beyond one's time. The sutras state: "Death is the termination of one's life force." With one's last breath, the spirit passes on, leaving the body to decay.

Thus, at the point of death, the sentient and insentient merge and become one. All that comes into being must end in death. When dying, one suffers great agony and distress. Surrounded by wailing and howling relatives - whether by blood or marriage, close or distant - one becomes terrified, not knowing where to go or who to rely on. When one's energy is spent, one's body becomes cold, and all the good or evil done throughout one's life unfolds before one's eyes. Those who have done good gain the assistance and protection of heavenly beings; those who have done evil are herded and driven by ox-headed hell guardians.

The ox-headed wardens and rakshasas are never lenient or forgiving. Neither caring parents nor filial children can rescue the dying from these ox-headed wardens or rakshasas. Loving couples too, cannot do anything except watch helplessly as their spouse dies. As the life force expires, one experiences the wind cutting one's body like slicing blades, causing indescribable pain and agony. At that point, the dying feel sharp and shattering pain. An endless multitude of afflictions and pain simultaneously converge. The person becomes overwhelmingly terrified as if crazy or drunk. Even if this person has a single thought of doing good to create a hair's breadth of merit, with the mind filled with hatred and resentment, it is impossible for him to do so. Such are the suffering and afflictions the dying one has to undergo, and no one else can take his place.

The *Nirvana Sutra* states that the deceased travels on a treacherous path without aid or provisions. The journey is long and endless, and one is alone, travelling all day long, on a path shrouded in complete darkness. Having entered the underworld, punishments are meted out without discrimination; once in, there is no escaping. When alive, if one does not cultivate blessings, when dead, one will end up in places of suffering, full of agony, excruciating pain, and extreme bitterness, misery for which there is no remedy. All such horrific scenes are not just mentioned here in order to instill fear in everyone.

Today, we are here in this Bodhimanda due to our shared karma. The retributions of life and death are like a wheel revolving endlessly. After passing away, we become ghosts, destitute and existing in solitude, unseen and beyond the reach of those looking for us. Thus, when alive, we should exhaust all efforts and patiently endure toil and hardship to diligently cultivate the four limitless minds and the six paramitas, to aid us in our passing. We should refrain from being complacent, believing we will always be strong and healthy. Let us all now with utmost, heartfelt sincerity, bow in full prostration, and take refuge with the Greatly Kind and Compassionate Ones who are like fathers to those of us in this world.

Namo Maitreya Buddha
Namo Shakyamuni Buddha
Namo Oceanic Erudition Buddha
Namo Holding up a Flower Buddha
Namo Not Following the World Buddha
Namo Joyful Assembly Buddha
Namo Peacock's Call Buddha
Namo Never Retreating into Oblivion Buddha
Namo Severing the Defilement of Emotional Love Buddha
Namo Beneficial Awe-inspiring Deportment Buddha
Namo Unmoving Buddha
Namo Pervading Heavens Buddha
Namo Treasured Strides Buddha

Namo Flower-hand Buddha
Namo Awe-inspiring Virtue Buddha
Namo Destroying the Thief of Resentment Buddha
Namo Wealthy and Erudite Buddha
Namo Land of Wonder Buddha
Namo Radiant Flower Buddha
Namo Lion's Wisdom Buddha
Namo Moonrise Buddha
Namo Dispelling Darkness Buddha
Namo Lion Playfully Roaming Bodhisattva
Namo Lion Swiftness and Vigor Bodhisattva
Namo Boundless Body Bodhisattva
Namo Guan Shi Yin Bodhisattva

Again, we take refuge with the Three Treasures of the ten directions to the ends of empty space. May you, with your power of kindness and compassion, care for and protect all of us. We pray each and every one in the Repentance assembly, from today until we reach Buddhahood will:

- eradicate all causes of offenses and their immeasurable retributions of suffering;
- ultimately remove all entangled karmic afflictions;
- always be able to personally participate in all Buddhas' Dharma assemblies;
- practice the Bodhisattva Path and be reborn as they wish;
- diligently cultivate in accord with the four limitless minds and the six paramitas;
- be replete with the four limitless eloquences and the six spiritual powers;
- attain hundreds of thousands of samadhis as soon as the mind is set on them;
- be able to enter each and every gateway of dharani;
- and finally, quickly realize Buddhahood, Proper Enlightenment.

Section 36 Bowing to the Buddhas on behalf of Laborers and Others

Today, we are here in this Bodhimanda due to our shared karma. Again with utmost sincerity, we bring forth the mind of kindness and compassion, and without differentiating between friends or foes, bow on behalf of all of the following, including all of their family members and associates:

- all workers who are involved in the process of bringing food from the fields to the kitchen and on to the dining table;
- manual laborers including volunteers;
- those who engage in charitable deeds as well as those who support such deeds;
- all prisoners everywhere, locked up or in solitary confinement, tormented with suffering, worries, afflictions, and undergoing all manner of punishment. Contemplating their plight, we see that although they have a human body in this world, they enjoy little happiness but suffer greatly. They are never free but are always handcuffed, chained, shackled, or bound. Their punishment may be due to offenses committed in their present lives or as retribution due to past offenses. They ought to be free but lack the opportunity to plead their case. They may be sentenced to death and lack someone to rescue or protect them.

On behalf of all these beings, their families and associates, we now take refuge with the Greatly Kind and Compassionate Ones who are like fathers to those of us in this world.

Namo Maitreya Buddha
Namo Shakyamuni Buddha
Namo Sequential Practice Buddha
Namo Lamp of Blessings and Virtue Buddha
Namo Rectifying through Sounds Buddha

Namo Gautama Buddha
Namo Power and Strength Buddha
Namo Well-settled in Body and Mind Buddha
Namo Moon of Goodness Buddha
Namo Blossoming Mind of Enlightenment Buddha
Namo Most Auspicious Buddha
Namo Skilled Awe-inspiring Virtue Buddha
Namo Strength of Wisdom and Virtue Buddha
Namo Lamp of Goodness Buddha
Namo Steadfast in Practice Buddha
Namo Heavenly Sound Buddha
Namo Peace and Bliss Buddha
Namo Sun Face Buddha
Namo Delight in Liberation Buddha
Namo Clarity in Precepts Buddha
Namo Abiding in Precepts Buddha
Namo Undefiled Buddha
Namo Lion Banner Bodhisattva
Namo Lion Deeds Bodhisattva
Namo Boundless Body Bodhisattva
Namo Guan Shi Yin Bodhisattva

Again, we take refuge with the Three Treasures of the ten directions to the ends of empty space. May you, with your power of kindness and compassion, from now until they attain Buddhahood, care for and protect all current manual laborers together with their retinues.

- May all their karmic hindrances and sufferings be eradicated.
- May they be blessed with longevity, peace and happiness, both in body and mind.
- May they be forever free from calamities, disasters, afflictions and hindrances.
- May they bring forth the Mahayana resolve and cultivate Bodhisattva practices.

- May they perfect the six paramitas and four limitless minds, renounce the suffering of birth and death, and attain the bliss of Nirvana.

As to those confined in prison or captivity, held in fetters, and tormented by suffering, illness, worry, and being ill at ease, together with their retinues and relatives:

- May all of their suffering be eradicated by the merit, virtue, and awe-inspiring power generated by our bowing to the Buddhas.
- May the various causes of all this evil karma be eradicated as well.
- May they be freed from imprisonment, gain entry into wholesome dharmas, enjoy longevity and infinite wisdom, and find eternal bliss in body and mind like that experienced in the third stage of dhyana.
- May they never forget the suffering of imprisonment, be mindful of the Buddhas' kindness, rectify their own evil-doing and cultivate goodness, bring forth the Mahayana resolve, and practice the Bodhisattva Path until they attain the vajra mind. Thereafter, may they return to rescue all other beings so that all ascend towards Proper Enlightenment and gain mastery of spiritual powers.

Section 37 Dedication of Merit

Today, we are here in this Bodhimanda due to our shared karma. Having brought forth the bodhi resolve and carried out what needs to be done, we ought to now dedicate all the accumulated merit and virtue. Why? It is because we living beings are attached to karmic rewards, are unable to renounce them, and thus find it difficult to gain liberation. By dedicating the merit from even the smallest blessing or a hair's breadth of goodness, we gradually gain detachment from these rewards. This in turn leads us toward liberation and brings us the ease of self-mastery. Hence, the sutras praise and encourage the practice of dedicating merit, as it will bring about great benefit. Henceforth, everyone is encouraged to dedicate all merit without attachment. Let us all now with utmost sincerity, bow in full prostration and take refuge with the Greatly Kind and Compassionate Ones who are like fathers to those of us in this world.

Namo Maitreya Buddha
Namo Shakyamuni Buddha
Namo Steadfast in Transcending Buddha
Namo Anjana Buddha
Namo Enhanced Benefits Buddha
Namo Fragrant Radiance Buddha
Namo *Wei Lan* Radiance Buddha
Namo King of Mindfulness Buddha
Namo Paramitas Alms-bowl Buddha
Namo Unobstructed Attributes Buddha
Namo Faith in Precepts Buddha
Namo Ultimate Wondrous Path Buddha
Namo Delighting in Truth Buddha
Namo Understanding the Dharma Buddha
Namo Possessing Awe-inspiring Virtue Buddha
Namo Ultimate Quiescence Buddha
Namo Superior Kindness Buddha
Namo Great Kindness Buddha
Namo Sweet Dew King Buddha
Namo Meru Radiance Buddha
Namo Extolling Sages Buddha
Namo Vast Illumination Buddha
Namo Manjushri Bodhisattva
Namo Samantabhadra Bodhisattva
Namo Boundless Body Bodhisattva
Namo Guan Shi Yin Bodhisattva

Again, we take refuge with the Three Treasures of the ten directions to the ends of empty space. May you, with your power of kindness and compassion, care for and protect all of us so that we will perfect our practices and vows. Henceforth, until we attain bodhi, may we who are here in this Bodhimanda with our shared karma, never retreat or regress from the Bodhisattva Path, and may we liberate living beings before we ourselves attain Buddhahood. For those of us who are trapped in *samsara* and have not attained the Way, may the power of these vows enable us to always be pure in the karma of body, speech, and mind, wherever we may be born.

May we constantly bring forth the gentle and supple mind, the harmonious mind, the mind of vigor, the quiescent mind, the true mind, the unscattered mind, the mind free of greed and stinginess, the great supreme mind, the great compassionate mind, the peacefully dwelling mind, the joyful mind, the mind to rescue all beings, the mind that guards and protects all beings, the mind that guards the bodhi resolve, and the mind that resolves to be equal with Buddhas. These are the vast, supreme, and wonderful minds that we vow to bring forth. May we be focused in our efforts to be erudite, renounce desire and cultivate samadhi, and bring benefit and peace to all beings. May we never renounce our vows for bodhi and together attain Proper Enlightenment.

The Dharma of Dedicating Merit on behalf of Others

Today, we are here in this Bodhimanda due to our shared karma. Let all of us kneel and put our palms together. Let us be mindful and follow the Dharma host as we now make these dedications on behalf of others:

We dedicate all the merit from the virtuous deeds performed by all the heavenly beings and ascetic masters of the ten directions, so that, together, we return to the path leading to Proper Enlightenment.

We dedicate all the supreme and wholesome deeds performed by the dragons, ghosts, and spirits of the ten directions so that, together, we return to the Path of the One Vehicle.

We dedicate all the karma cultivated by people and kings of the ten directions striving for bodhi so that, together, we return to the unsurpassed Way.

We dedicate all the wholesome karma, however minute, cultivated by beings in the six realms, so that together we return to the unsurpassed Way.

We dedicate to the Buddha Way all the merit generated by all Buddhist disciples of the ten directions: all bhikshus, Arhats of all four stages who are free of attachments, those seeking the path of Sages Enlightened by Conditions, all who take beings across whether visibly or invisibly to understand the Dharma of causes and conditions, and other Dharmas.

We dedicate to living beings all the merit generated by all Bodhisattvas of the ten directions who read, recite, and uphold sutras, exit or enter dhyana, exhort beings to do myriad deeds of goodness, and base themselves on the threefold foundations of precepts, samadhi, and wisdom, so that together we return to the unsurpassed Way.

Furthermore, we now exhort beings in the heavens and human realms, who are on the Sagely Way or who have done various good deeds, to dedicate their merit so that together we return to the unsurpassed Way. May they dedicate to all living beings their blessings, however minute, from resolving on bodhi and practicing repentance, whether practicing themselves or exhorting others to practice.

As long as a single being has not attained Buddhahood, we vow never to renounce the bodhi resolve; only after every being accomplishes Buddhahood will we realize Proper Enlightenment. We beseech all Buddhas, Bodhisattvas, and other sages of non-outflows, to bear witness to our vows and gather us in, both in this life and in future lives.

Today, we are here in this Bodhimanda due to our shared karma. With utmost sincerity, we bow in full prostration. Together, we dedicate all the merit on behalf of all:

- heads of nations such as kings, emperors, and presidents,

- parents and relatives,
- spiritual mentors, elders, and fellow students,
- faithful donors, as well as all good and bad advisors,
- the four world-protecting heavenly kings,
- demon kings throughout the ten directions,
- intelligent and righteous spirits, celestial spirits, earth spirits, empty space spirits, spirits who bless the good and punish the evil, spirits who guard and protect those who uphold mantras, together with the dragon kings of the five directions, dragons and the rest of the eightfold division;
- visible or invisible spirits and souls, and
- living beings of the ten directions to the ends of empty space.

May all heavenly beings, ascetic masters, dragons and the rest of the eightfold division and all other living beings, henceforth, until they attain bodhi, always understand the Reality of No-mark, and be free of any attachment.

Praise

> *Severe retributions in the three evil paths,*
> *Torment us with unbearable suffering.*
> *One single thought and misfortunes befall.*
> *Be forewarned everything is impermanent.*
> *Sincerely pray to the Physician King,*
> *May he kindly forever teach and transform us.*

Namo Ground of Perfected Wisdom Bodhisattva Mahasattva
(three times)

Concluding the Repentance

> The Guiding Master of the *nine*-grade lotuses,
> Is attended upon by gods of six heavens and *nine* tiers.
> The Benevolent One of the *nine* realms,
> Is followed by Arhats of the *nine* kinds who study under him.

We sincerely pray the Sage of Compassion
Forever dwells in the *nine*-level palaces,
Rescuing the multitudes of beings,
So together we ascend the *nine*-grade lotus daises.
His merit surpasses those in the *nine* existences;
His Way excels that of the *nine* heavens.
We look up to the Greatly Enlightened One,
May he bear witness to our Repentance.

[Dharma Host]: On behalf of _____ [those who seek to repent], we have been chanting the efficacious text from the oceanic treasury and are now concluding Roll Nine. Having started at dawn and ending at dusk, we are now about to finish generating its merit. Respectfully, we come before and take refuge with the Sagely Ones.

We have burned exotic Seashore Chandana incense, offered rare fruits from the exquisite garden and flavorful tea to dispel torpor, lit lamps to shatter the darkness, offered exotic flowers revealing the wondrous mysteries of Heaven, and carried out chanting that resembles celestial melodies. We are sincere in our sixfold mindfulness and are focused in our *chan* contemplation.

Summing up all the merit and virtue, we universally dedicate them to *Anuttara-samyaksam-bodhi*. May all Bodhisattvas Mahasattvas, Hearers, Arhats, heavenly beings, rulers of heaven and earth in control of *yin* and *yang*, dragons and the rest of the eightfold division who help maintain the balance of Nature, bear witness to our sincerity and enable all of us to dwell in true and eternal bliss.

On behalf of _____ [those who seek to repent], we bow this Repentance in order to eradicate various karmic hindrances, attain everlasting auspiciousness, immediately ascend the *nine* grades of lotus daises, and quickly arrive at the Lotus Land. We bow in prostration, praying that all karmic offenses of the *nine* fetters be resolved and that everyone transcends many kalpas of suffering in the *nine* dark destinies.

We bow and earnestly pray:

May everyone be free of the *nine* kinds of view delusions of the *nine* grounds and quickly arrive in the Pure Land of the *nine* grades of lotuses and their *nine* subdivisions. May everyone excel in the *nine* merits and be adorned with the *nine* virtues. [Dharma host]: We have tried to be as sincere as we could, but fear our sincerity may still fall short. Thus I am taking the liberty to request that together, we continue to repent and reform.

Praise

The meritorious power of the Emperor of Liang Repentance Roll Nine
Enables the deceased and the disciples to eradicate the nine fetters.
May all realize the Bodhisattva's Ground of Perfected Wisdom.
As the Repentance is chanted our offenses are blown away like flower
petals in the wind.
Offenses repented, enmity resolved,
Wisdom and blessing increase as calamities are dispelled.
Liberated from suffering and reborn in the Trayastrimsha,
May we gather at the Dragon Flower's Three Assemblies
And receive a prediction personally from Maitreya Buddha.

Namo Dragon Flower Assembly of Bodhisattvas Mahasattvas
(three times)

Final Praise

Emperor of Liang Repentance Roll Nine now concludes.
We dedicate its merit to the four benefactors and the three realms.
May all in this assembly enjoy increased longevity and blessing,
May the Dharma water cleanse our offenses.
May the deceased be reborn in the Western Pure Land.
May the Bodhisattvas of the Ground of Perfected Wisdom compassionately gather us in.

Namo Ascending the Path to the Clouds Bodhisattva Mahasattva
(three times)

Roll Ten

Namo Buddhas and Bodhisattvas of the Dragon Flower Assembly
(*bow three times*)

Praise

We make offerings of garments,
Silk, satins, brocaded fabrics,
And gold-embroidered vests,
All exquisite beyond description.
Dragon Girl weaves a gold-threaded handkerchief
While King Prasenajit offers a kasaya;
All are brought about by the spiritual powers
And past vows of Asvaghosa Bodhisattva.

Namo Universal Offering Bodhisattva Mahasattva. (*three times*)

Listen respectfully

The Benevolent One with *ten* titles,
Realizes Proper Enlightenment on a precious lotus.
The Taming Hero with *ten* bodies,
Turns the Dharma wheel within a dust mote.
His brilliant light shines throughout the *ten* directions;
His skill-in-means surpasses all of the *Ten* Grounds.
Perfect in the *ten* paramitas,
He is the Great King of the *ten* vows.
Looking up, we pray for your vast compassion.
May you watch over us with caring eyes.

[Dharma Host]: On behalf of _____ [those who seek to repent], we practice this Repentance Dharma of Kindness and

Compassion in the Bodhimanda. Now we have come to Roll Ten. With all conditions fulfilled, we now enter the Repentance Platform. Reverently and wholeheartedly, we meticulously present *ten* kinds of offering to the Three Treasures of the *ten* directions. Immersing ourselves in all *ten* rolls of Repentance texts and cultivating in accord with the *ten*fold Repentance Dharma, we free ourselves from offenses of the *ten* entanglements.

We are earnestly mindful of the retributions we now undergo, resulting from the causes planted in kalpas past. Ignorant of planting proper causes that come from the *ten* good deeds, we committed the *ten* evil deeds resulting in our karmic hindrances. We become caught in the *ten* entanglements, which hook and lock us up in a continuous chain. We become tainted and driven by the *ten* kinds of bad habits, like moths darting towards fire. Thus our karma keeps growing and branching out, taking on myriads of patterns and forms, which in turn become the source of limitless offenses.

We have always been satiated with greed, and have been unable to let go of emotional love and egotistical views. The fire of hatred burns our bodhi seeds; the winds of karma devastate our forest of merit and virtue. Years pass in vain before we recognize our faults; time flies before we awaken to our misdeeds. How fortunate we are to have this esoteric Repentance Dharma that reveals to us a clear path of cultivation. Relying on the Sangha, we now read and chant the sacred texts, perform the Buddha's work to its perfect grandeur, and generate limitless Dharma benefits. In thought after thought, we restrain and rein in our mind; in every move and aspect, we reinforce and redouble our sincerity. May all Buddhas bestow their kindness, and invisibly bless and protect us.

> *He universally contemplates limitless kalpas in one thought,*
> *Neither coming, going, nor dwelling anywhere.*
> *Thoroughly knowing all phenomena of the three periods of time,*
> *Surpassing all expedient means, he accomplishes the ten powers.*

Commencement of the Repentance

We now begin the Repentance Dharma of Kindness and Compassion in the Bodhimanda.

Together in this assembly, we single-mindedly return to and rely on all Buddhas of the three periods of time.

> Namo Buddhas of the past, Vipashyin Buddha
> Namo Shikhin Buddha
> Namo Vishvabhu Buddha
> Namo Krakucchanda Buddha
> Namo Kanakamuni Buddha
> Namo Kashyapa Buddha
> Namo our Fundamental Teacher Shakyamuni Buddha
> Namo Honored Future Buddha, Maitreya

Section 38 Bodhisattvas' Dharma of Dedication of Merit and Virtue

Today, we are here in this Bodhimanda due to our shared karma. We have toiled and endured various hardships bowing this Repentance, thus cultivating limitless roots of goodness. It is therefore fitting that each one of us brings forth the following thoughts:

I dedicate the roots of goodness that I have cultivated to benefit all living beings so they may attain ultimate purity. May these roots of goodness help eradicate the boundless suffering and afflictions of hell-beings, hungry ghosts, and animals, and spare them from further meetings with King Yama.

May this Repentance Dharma:

- be a great dwelling for all living beings, eradicating their suffering of the *skandhas*;
- be a great guardian and protector of beings, freeing them from afflictions;

- be their great refuge, enabling them to be free from fear;
- be their place of rest, settling them on the path towards the ground of wisdom;
- be their secure abode, enabling them to dwell in ultimate peace and security;
- be a great beacon, dispelling the darkness of ignorance;
- be a great brilliant lamp, enabling them to dwell securely in the radiance of ultimate purity;
- be a great guiding master, enabling them to attain expedient means and realize the pure wisdom body.

Today, we are here in this Bodhimanda due to our shared karma. All these Dharmas are the Bodhisattvas Mahasattvas' practices of dedicating all their roots of goodness for the sake of friends and foes. Bodhisattvas are free of discriminating thoughts. In their contemplation of equanimity they consider themselves as one with all living beings and are free of notions of friends and foes. They always regard living beings with eyes of compassion. Even when faced with living beings who harbor hateful or heinous thoughts towards them, the Bodhisattvas are like a vast ocean that cannot be ruined by any type of poison - they remain genuine good and wise advisers, disciplining and harmonizing these beings and explaining the profound Dharma for them.

Even when faced with beings who are deluded, lack wisdom and gratitude, and who do not know how to repay kindness, thus committing immeasurable evil, Bodhisattvas remain undisturbed in their resolve for the Way - just like a brilliant sun in the sky that universally shines on beings and does not hide its light from the blind.

Bodhisattvas are also like this in their resolve for the Way - they do retreat or relinquish their practices just because living beings are difficult to tame and subdue, nor do they forsake the roots of goodness. With regard to their roots of goodness, Bodhisattvas Mahasattvas are pure in their faith and continually nurture their mind of great compassion. They dedicate these roots of goodness to all beings everywhere, doing it profoundly, not just verbally.

With regard to living beings, Bodhisattvas Mahasattvas bring forth a happy and joyful mind, a bright and pure mind, a gentle and supple mind, a kind and compassionate mind, a caring and cherishing mind, a mind that gathers in, a mind that benefits, a mind that brings peace and delight, and the supreme mind, and further they dedicate their roots of goodness to living beings.

Similarly, we should now respectfully emulate these Bodhisattvas Mahasattvas and dedicate our roots of goodness, both in speech and in mind. We dedicate all of our merit and virtue, wishing that living beings will:

- attain rebirth in the Pure Lands or other pure destinies;
- be replete with merit and virtue that cannot be ruined by the mundane world;
- be inexhaustible in their merit, virtue and wisdom;
- be well-adorned in body, speech, and mind;
- always behold the Buddhas, listen and embrace their teachings of Proper Dharma with indestructible faith, cast away the nets of doubt, and retain all the teachings without forgetting any;
- purify their body and speech karma, with minds constantly and peacefully abiding in the supreme and wonderful roots of goodness;
- never be impoverished but be always replete with the seven kinds of wealth;
- learn what all Bodhisattvas learn, attaining roots of goodness;
- accomplish equanimity, wonderful liberation, and Wisdom of All Modes;
- attain eyes of loving kindness towards all living beings;
- be pure in their body faculties and be intelligent and eloquent in speech;
- practice all kinds of goodness;

- be free of any defilement or attachment, enter the profound Dharma, and gather in all living beings;
- dwell where Buddhas dwell - the place of no dwelling.

We make the same dedications as all Bodhisattvas Mahasattvas of the ten directions, dedications that are as expansive as the Dharma nature, and ultimate, like empty space.

May all of us_____ [those who seek to repent] fulfill our vows and our bodhi resolve, and may all beings of the four births and the six paths also have their wishes fulfilled.

Again, we bow in full prostration with utmost respect and take refuge with the Greatly Compassionate Ones who are like fathers to those of us in this world.

Namo Maitreya Buddha
Namo Shakyamuni Buddha
Namo Awe-inspiring Virtue Buddha
Namo Clarity in Vision Buddha
Namo Wholesome Practices and Rewards Buddha
Namo Wholesome Joy Buddha
Namo Worry-free Buddha
Namo Jeweled Radiance Buddha
Namo Awe-inspiring Deportment Buddha
Namo Delight in Blessing and Virtue Buddha
Namo Ocean of Merit and Virtue Buddha
Namo Eradicating Attributes Buddha
Namo Breaking away from Demons Buddha
Namo Eradicating Demons Buddha
Namo Transcending the Path of Decline Buddha
Namo Indestructible Resolve Buddha
Namo Water King Buddha
Namo Cleansing Demons Buddha
Namo Superior among Multitude Kings Buddha
Namo Cherished Radiance Buddha

Namo Lamp of Blessings Buddha
Namo Attributes of Bodhi Buddha
Namo Sound of Wisdom Buddha
Namo Ever-vigorous Bodhisattva
Namo Never Resting Bodhisattva
Namo Boundless Body Bodhisattva
Namo Guan Shi Yin Bodhisattva

Again, we take refuge with the Three Treasures of the ten directions to the ends of empty space. We beseech the Three Treasures to gather us in with their power of kindness and compassion, enabling us to perfect and accomplish our dedication of merit and virtue.

There may come a time when we are burdened with immeasurable grave and evil karmic offenses deserving the retributions of boundless and limitless suffering, trapped in the evil paths, unable to extricate ourselves, thus causing us to go against the bodhi resolve that we brought forth today, go against the bodhi practices, and go against the fundamental vows of bodhi. We now beseech the Bodhisattvas of All Grounds throughout the ten directions, as well as other sages, not to forsake their fundamental vows and once again help rescue us from suffering in the three evil paths, enabling all of us to attain liberation.

May you never abandon living beings even if you have to endure hardship. May you shoulder the heavy burdens of living beings, fulfill your vows of equanimity, and liberate all living beings from *samsara* - birth, old age, sickness, death, worry, distress, suffering, afflictions, as well as limitless other woes and agonies. May you thus enable all beings to attain purity, be replete with roots of goodness, and attain ultimate liberation.

May all beings break free from the multitudes of demons, stay away from unwholesome friends, and be close to wholesome friends and kin. May all beings accomplish the karma of purity, completely end all suffering, perfect limitless Bodhisattva vows and practices, joyfully behold Buddhas, attain All-wisdom, and then return to save and liberate all other living beings.

Section 39 Making Vows about Sense Faculties

Today, we who are here in this Bodhimanda due to our shared karma, having dedicated our merit, should proceed to make vows. A thorough review will reveal that all evil is committed because of our six sense faculties; they are the very source of all troubles and disasters. However, these six sense faculties are also the source of limitless blessing. *The Srimala Sutra* states, "Guard your six sense faculties, purify your karma of body, speech, and mind." Based on this teaching, we can surmise that the proper use of the six sense faculties form the basis from which all goodness arise. Therefore, we should make great vows about our six sense faculties.

Making Vows about the Eye Faculty

Today, we are here in this Bodhimanda due to our shared karma. We vow that all beings of the four births and the six paths throughout the ten directions, henceforth until they attain bodhi:

- will not behold sights that lead to insatiable greed, desire, deception, and delusion;
- will not behold any fawning, flattery or other corrupt behavior;
- will not behold any fancy events that lead to temptation;
- will not behold ugly sights of anger, hatred, or contention;
- will not behold sights of beating, fighting, tormenting, or other forms of harming or injuring others;
- will not behold sights of slaughtering, slicing, or other forms of mutilating the bodies of living beings;
- will not behold the dark sights of ignorance, doubt, and lack of faith;

- will not behold sights of arrogance, disrespect, and lack of humility;
- will not behold the ninety-six deviant views.

Instead, may all beings always be able to:

- behold the eternally-abiding tranquil Dharma body that pervades the ten directions;
- behold the Buddha's purple-golden body with the thirty-two major hallmarks and eighty subsidiary characteristics;
- behold heavenly beings and ascetic masters making offerings of treasures and showering flowers;
- behold the five-colored light emanating from the mouths of those proclaiming the Dharma to liberate living beings;
- behold the Buddhas' transformation bodies that appear everywhere throughout the ten directions;
- behold Buddhas emitting light from the flesh prominence at the crowns of their heads to gather in beings with whom they have affinities;
- behold all Bodhisattvas, Pratyekabuddhas, Arhats and other sages of the ten directions;
- always join other beings and their retinues when they behold Buddhas;
- behold the formless and wordless teachings that give rise to multitudes of goodness;
- behold the flower of enlightenment that results from the sevenfold purities;
- behold the wondrous fruition of liberation;
- behold this Dharma Assembly joyfully praising and respectfully embracing the Dharma;
- behold the disciples of the fourfold assembly gathered together, listening to the Dharma with earnestness and reverence;

- behold the practices of giving, upholding precepts, patience and vigor;
- behold the practices of meditative stillness, contemplation, and wisdom;
- behold all beings attaining the patience of non-production and joyfully receiving predictions from Buddhas;
- behold all beings ascending the ground of vajra wisdom, dispelling the darkness of ignorance, and attaining the position of *avaivartika,* where those who will succeed in
- becoming Buddhas abide;
- behold all beings never retreating but always immersed in the stream of Dharma.

Having made these vows about our eye faculty, let us all now with utmost sincerity, bow in full prostration and take refuge with the Greatly Kind and Compassionate Ones who are like fathers to those of us in this world.

Namo Maitreya Buddha
Namo Shakyamuni Buddha
Namo Skilled in Cessation Buddha
Namo Brahma Attributes Buddha
Namo Joy of Wisdom Buddha
Namo Divine Attributes Buddha
Namo Like a King within the Multitude Buddha
Namo Earth Guardian Buddha
Namo Cherishing the Sun Buddha
Namo Moon of Rahu Buddha
Namo Radiant Flower Buddha
Namo Superior Medicine Master Buddha
Namo Maintaining Strength Buddha
Namo Radiance of Blessings and Virtue Buddha
Namo Radiance of Joy Buddha
Namo Pleasant Voice Buddha

Namo Self-mastery in Dharma Buddha
Namo Brahma Sound Buddha
Namo Wonderful Voice Bodhisattva
Namo Great Strength Bodhisattva
Namo Boundless Body Bodhisattva
Namo Guan Shi Yin Bodhisattva

Again, we take refuge with the Three Treasures of the ten directions to the ends of empty space. May you protect and guard all with your power of kindness and compassion and enable us to fulfill our wishes and perfect our bodhi vows.

Making Vows about the Ear Faculty

Again, may all of us here in this Bodhimanda due to our shared karma, together with all other beings of the four births and the six paths throughout the ten directions, henceforth until we all attain bodhi:

- never hear the sounds of crying or weeping caused by worry or suffering;
- never hear the sounds of suffering in the *Avici* Hell;
- never hear the thundering and rumbling sounds of boiling liquids in the hells;
- never hear the terrifying sounds of splitting, tearing, and cutting from the Hells of Mountain of Blades and Trees of Swords;
- never hear sounds of the limitless, unceasing pain and suffering in the Eighteen Hells;
- never hear the sounds of hungry ghosts tormented and famished by hunger and thirst, begging in vain for food;
- never hear the sounds of the joints of hungry ghosts burning while they are moving, which resemble the sounds of five hundred carriages rolling;
- never hear the suffering cries of animals with huge bodies five *yojanas* in extent, bitten by little worms;

- never hear the suffering sounds of those reborn as camels, mules, horses and oxen that are always over-loaded, whipped or harshly beaten for reneging on their debts from past lives;
- never hear the sounds of the eight kinds of suffering, which include being apart from those you love, being together with those you hate, and so forth.
- never hear the suffering sounds of the four hundred four illnesses;
- never hear the sounds of anything unwholesome or evil;
- never hear the distracting sounds of entertainment coming from musical instruments such as bells, conchs, drums, stringed instruments, harps, or the bewitching chimes of beautiful jade ornaments.

Instead, may all beings henceforth always be able to:

- hear the sounds of Buddhas proclaiming Dharma with the eight types of voices;
- hear the sounds that reveal the truth of impermanence, suffering, emptiness, and no-self;
- hear the sounds of the eighty-four thousand paramitas;
- hear the sounds of the empty nature of the myriad phenomena;
- hear Buddhas expound the Dharma in one voice, yet hear and awaken according to each one's potential;
- hear the sounds of the teachings that all beings have inherent Buddha nature and that the Dharma body abides eternally;
- hear about the practices of patience and vigor by Bodhisattvas of the Ten Grounds;
- hear sounds about attaining non-production, skillfully entering the Buddha's wisdom, and transcending the three realms;
- hear about how Bodhisattvas who have realized the Dharma body enter the stream of Dharma, contemplate both mundane

and ultimate truths, and in thought after thought, perfect the myriad practices;

- hear about the fruition of Pratyekabuddhas and Arhats of all four stages in the ten directions;
- hear Lord Shakra expounding *prajna* to celestial beings;
- hear the next-to-be Buddhas, the Tenth-Ground Mahasattvas in the Tushita Heaven, expounding the practices of the ground of non-retreat;
- hear about how myriad goodness leads to the realization of Buddhahood;
- hear the sounds of all Buddhas praising and rejoicing in living beings' practices of the ten good deeds;
- hear the Buddhas' praise: "Good indeed! This person will soon attain Buddhahood."

Having made these vows about our ear faculty, let us all again now with utmost sincerity, bow in full prostration and take refuge with the Greatly Kind and Compassionate Ones who are like fathers to those of us in this world.

Namo Maitreya Buddha
Namo Shakyamuni Buddha
Namo Deeds of Goodness Buddha
Namo Never Erring in Thoughts Buddha
Namo Generous Giving Buddha
Namo Renowned and Praise-worthy Buddha
Namo Multitude of Hallmarks Buddha
Namo Widespread Virtue Buddha
Namo Ease of Self-mastery in the World Buddha
Namo Tree of Virtue Buddha
Namo Severing Delusion Buddha
Namo Without Limit Buddha
Namo Moon of Goodness Buddha
Namo Attributes of Infinite Eloquence Buddha

Namo Jeweled Moon Bodhisattva
Namo Moonlight Bodhisattva
Namo Boundless Body Bodhisattva
Namo Guan Shi Yin Bodhisattva

Again, we take refuge with the Three Treasures of the ten directions to the ends of empty space. May you protect and guard all with your power of kindness and compassion and enable us to fulfill our wishes and perfect our bodhi vows.

Making Vows about the Nose Faculty

Again, we are here today in this Bodhimanda due to our shared karma. Together with all other beings of the four births and the six paths throughout the ten directions, henceforth, until we attain bodhi, may we:

- never smell the odor of any food that involves killing;
- never smell the odor of hunting or setting fire to kill living beings;
- never smell the odor of steaming, boiling, or frying creatures;
- never smell the stench from the thirty-six parts of a human body, which is just a foul-smelling skin-bag;
- never smell the enticing scents of lavish silken crepe and embroidered feminine clothing;
- never smell the odor of flesh being stripped, torn, and burned in the hells;
- never smell the odor of hungry ghosts drinking urine, pus, blood, or eating excrement;
- never smell the stench of animals;
- never smell the putrid sores of the neglected or the bedridden;
- never smell foul and filthy urine and stool;
- never smell the odors of decaying and swollen worm-infested corpses;

Instead, may all of us in the six paths, henceforth always be able to:

- smell the priceless incense of ox-head sandalwood that pervades the worlds of the ten directions;
- smell the fragrance of the five-colored *udumbara* flower;
- smell the fragrances of the flowers and trees in the Garden of Joy in the Trayastrimsha Heaven;
- smell the fragrance of Dharma spoken in the Tushita Heaven;
- smell the fragrance of roaming at ease in the Wonderful Dharma Hall in the Trayastrimsha Heaven;
- smell the fragrance of living beings of the ten directions, who uphold the five precepts, do the ten good deeds, and practice the sixfold mindfulness;
- smell the fragrance of the beings of the seven expedients, who practice the sixteen contemplations;
- smell the fragrance of virtuous Learners, and those Beyond-Learning, as well as Pratyekabuddhas throughout the ten directions;
- smell the fragrance of non-outflow Arhats of the Four Fruitions or Four Accesses;
- smell the fragrance of countless Bodhisattvas on the Grounds of Happiness, Transcending Defilement, Emitting Light, Blazing Wisdom, Difficult to Surpass, Manifestation, Traveling Far, No Movement, Perfected Wisdom, and Dharma Clouds.
- smell the fragrance of all sages' fivefold Dharma body of precepts, samadhi, wisdom, liberation, and knowledge and views of liberation;
- smell the bodhi fragrance of all Buddhas;
- smell the fragrance of the thirty-seven wings of enlightenment, the twelve dependent origination contemplations, and the six paramitas;
- smell the fragrance of the Buddhas' threefold mindfulness of great compassion, the ten powers, the fourfold deliverance from fear, and the eighteen unique dharmas;

- smell the fragrance of eighty-four thousand paramitas;
- smell the fragrance of the Dharma body, which is eternally abiding, infinite, wondrous to the utmost and which pervades the ten directions.

Having made these vows about our nose faculty, let us all now again with utmost sincerity bow in full prostration and take refuge with the Greatly Kind and Compassionate Ones who are like fathers to those of us in this world.

Namo Maitreya Buddha
Namo Shakyamuni Buddha
Namo Ridra Dharma Buddha
Namo Worthy of Offerings Buddha
Namo Transcending Worries Buddha
Namo Peace and Happiness Buddha
Namo Wishes of the World Buddha
Namo Cherishing the Body Buddha
Namo Wondrous Abundance Buddha
Namo Utpala Buddha
Namo Flower Tassels Buddha
Namo Light of Boundless Eloquence Buddha
Namo Faith in Sages Buddha
Namo Vigorous in Virtue Buddha
Namo Wonderful Virtue Bodhisattva
Namo Vajra Treasury Bodhisattva
Namo Boundless Body Bodhisattva
Namo Guan Shi Yin Bodhisattva

Again, we take refuge with the Three Treasures of the ten directions to the ends of empty space. May you gather all in with your power of kindness and compassion and enable us to fulfill our wishes and perfect our bodhi vows.

Making Vows about the Tongue Faculty

Again, we are here today in this Bodhimanda due to our shared karma. Together with all other beings of the four births and the six paths throughout the ten directions, henceforth, until we attain bodhi, may we:

- never taste the meat of creatures who have been harmed or killed;
- never taste the meat of those who have died naturally;
- never taste the blood or marrow of any being;
- never taste the poisons of foes or karmic creditors;
- never taste any flavor that triggers greed, attachment, or afflictions in living beings.

Instead, may all of us in the six paths, henceforth always be able to:

- taste the hundred kinds of ambrosia;
- taste the natural foods of the heavens;
- taste the fragrant rice in the Land of Abundant Fragrance;
- taste the flavor of the food of the Buddhas;
- taste the flavors of cultivating the Dharma body through precepts, samadhi, and wisdom;
- taste the joy of Dharma and the bliss of Dhyana;
- taste the exquisite flavors that nourish our wisdom life through the myriad types merit and virtue;
- taste the one and equal flavor of liberation;
- taste the supreme flavor of Buddhahood and the ultimate bliss of Nirvana.

Having made these vows about our tongue faculty, let us all now again with utmost sincerity, bow in full prostration and take refuge with the Greatly Kind and Compassionate Ones who are like fathers to those of us in this world.

Namo Maitreya Buddha

Namo Shakyamuni Buddha
Namo Sincere and Genuine Buddha
Namo Celestial Lord Buddha
Namo Delightful and Sonorous Voice Buddha
Namo Pure Faith Buddha
Namo Vijiradha Buddha
Namo Mind of Blessings and Virtue Buddha
Namo Blazing Flame Buddha
Namo Boundless Virtue Buddha
Namo Collective Accomplishment Buddha
Namo Lion's Travel Buddha
Namo Unmoving Buddha
Namo Pure and Clear Faith Buddha
Namo Treasury of Empty Space Bodhisattva
Namo Sadapralapa Bodhisattva
Namo Boundless Body Bodhisattva
Namo Guan Shi Yin Bodhisattva

Again, we take refuge with the Three Treasures of the ten directions to the ends of empty space. May you take pity on us, protect and guard all of us with your power of kindness and compassion, and enable us to fulfill our wishes and perfect our bodhi vows.

Making Vows about the Body Faculty

Again, we are here in this Bodhimanda due to our shared karma. Together with all other beings of the four births and the six paths throughout the ten directions, henceforth, until we attain bodhi, may we:

- never feel the seductive tactile sensations associated with the five desires;
- never feel boiling water, burning charcoal, or freezing ice;
- never feel the flaming sensation on the heads of hungry ghosts or experienced by hell beings whose mouths are burned and scorched by molten copper;

- never feel the pain and suffering of animals whose bodies and limbs are skinned, ripped, and torn apart;
- never feel the suffering and afflictions of the four hundred four illnesses;
- never feel unbearable scorching heat or freezing cold;
- never feel the bites of mosquitoes, gnats, fleas and other insects;
- never feel the harm of knives, clubs, or poison;
- never experience hunger, thirst, or any other torments.

Instead, may our bodies always:

- feel the sensation of wonderful celestial garments;
- experience the feeling of natural sweet dew;
- feel a refreshingly cool and pleasant ambiance that is neither too warm nor too cold;
- feel neither hunger nor thirst, illness or affliction, but only a sense of well-being and vitality;
- never feel the suffering caused by knives or clubs;
- feel peaceful and at ease, whether asleep or awake, and be free of worries or fears;
- feel the gentle breeze of the Buddhas' Pure Lands of the ten directions;
- feel the body and mind purified in the seven-jeweled pools in the Buddhas' Pure Lands of the ten directions;
- never feel the suffering of aging, sickness, and death;
- fell free to fly to and attend Dharma lectures with Bodhisattvas;
- feel the eight sensations of self-mastery of the Buddhas' Nirvana.

Having made these vows about our body faculty, let us all now again with utmost sincerity, bow in full prostration and take refuge with the Greatly Kind and Compassionate Ones who are like fathers to those of us in this world.

Namo Maitreya Buddha
Namo Shakyamuni Buddha
Namo Clarity in Practice Buddha
Namo Dragon's Voice Buddha
Namo Upholding the Wheel Buddha
Namo Accomplished in Wealth Buddha
Namo Beloved by the World Buddha
Namo Dharma Name Buddha
Namo Unlimited Cherished Names Buddha
Namo Appearance of Clouds Buddha
Namo Wisdom Path Buddha
Namo Wondrous Fragrance Buddha
Namo Empty Space Sound Buddha
Namo Empty Space Buddha
Namo Transcending the Three Realms Bodhisattva
Namo Bhadrapala Bodhisattva
Namo Boundless Body Bodhisattva
Namo Guan Shi Yin Bodhisattva

Again, we take refuge with the Three Treasures of the ten directions to the ends of empty space. May you protect, guard and gather us in with your power of kindness and compassion and enable us to fulfill our wishes and perfect our bodhi vows.

Making Vows about the Mind Faculty

Again, we are here in this Bodhimanda due to our shared karma. Together with all other beings of the four births and the six paths throughout the ten directions, henceforth, until we attain bodhi, may we:

- always be mindful of the perils of greed, desire, anger, and delusion;
- always be mindful of the perils of killing, stealing, sexual misconduct, lying, frivolous speech, divisive speech, and harsh speech;

- always be mindful that killing one's father, mother, or an Arhat; shedding the Buddha's blood; disrupting the harmony of the Sangha; slandering the Buddha, Dharma and Sangha; and disbelieving in cause and effect are all offenses that will send one directly into the *Avici* Hell;
- always be mindful that there is rebirth after death and accompanying retributions;
- always be mindful to avoid those who are a bad influence and instead draw near to wholesome friends;
- always be mindful not to consult the ninety-six kinds of deviant teachers or accept their dharma;
- always be mindful that the three outflows, the five hindrances, and the ten entanglements are all obstructions;
- always be mindful of the terrifying perils of the three evil destinies wherein the cruel cycles of birth and death and the retributions of severe suffering occur;
- always be mindful that all livings beings are endowed with the Buddha Nature;
- always be mindful that Buddhas are compassionate fathers and unsurpassed physician king, that the sacred Dharma is the effective antidote for all living beings' illnesses, and that all sages and worthy ones are like mothers caring for sick living beings;
- always be mindful that we should take refuge with the Three Treasures, receive the five precepts, and practice the ten good deeds and other practices such as these that will result in superior blessings in the human and heavenly realms;
- always be mindful that since we have not ended birth and death, we should cultivate the seven kinds of expedient contemplations such as the stage of heating-up, and the stage of preeminence in the world;
- always be mindful to cultivate the sixteen kinds of contemplations of the Four Noble Truths and thereafter, to practice the sixteen sagely minds that lead to non-outflow, such as patience with suffering.

- always be mindful that the Four Noble Truths, which are impartial and free of attributes, can lead us to attain the Four Fruitions;
- always be mindful of the general and specific attributes of all dharmas;
- always be mindful of the twelve links of dependent origination, and the law of cause and effect spanning the three periods of time - both of which revolve incessantly;
- always be mindful to cultivate the six paramitas and the eighty thousand practices;
- always be mindful to eradicate the eighty-four thousand wearisome defiling afflictions;
- always be mindful to realize Non-production, as that realization will definitely help end birth and death;
- always be mindful of a Bodhisattvas' progressive stages of realization of the Way, starting from the ten abidings and continuing with the subsequent stages;
- always be mindful to use the vajra mind to break through the darkness of ignorance and attain the unsurpassed fruition of Buddhahood;
- always be mindful that, with the attainment of the ultimate illumination of totality, the myriad virtues are perfected, the myriad burdens and troubles end, and great Nirvana is realized;
- always be mindful of the Buddhas' ten powers, four fearlessnesses, and the rest of the eighteen unique dharmas, their immeasurable wisdom, their infinite wholesome dharmas, and their limitless merit and virtue.

Having made these vows about our mind faculty, let us all now with utmost sincerity, bow in full prostration and take refuge with the Greatly Kind and Compassionate Ones who are like fathers to those of us in this world.

Namo Maitreya Buddha
Namo Shakyamuni Buddha
Namo Celestial King Buddha
Namo Purifying-pearl Buddha
Namo Good Wealth Buddha
Namo Lamp's Flame Buddha
Namo Precious Sound Buddha
Namo Supreme Ruler of People Buddha
Namo Rahu Guardian Buddha
Namo Peace and Tranquility Buddha
Namo Lion Resolve Buddha
Namo Precious Renown Buddha
Namo Attaining Benefits Buddha
Namo Pervasive View Buddha
Namo Asvaghosa Bodhisattva
Namo Nagarjuna Bodhisattva
Namo Boundless Body Bodhisattva
Namo Guan Shi Yin Bodhisattva

Again, we take refuge with the Three Treasures of the ten directions to the ends of empty space. May you protect, guard, and gather us in with your power of kindness and compassion and enable us to fulfill our wishes and perfect our bodhi vows.

Making Vows about Our Mouth Faculty

Again, we are here in this Bodhimanda due to our shared karma. Together with all other beings of the four births and the six paths throughout the ten directions, henceforth, until we attain bodhi, may we:

- never slander or disparage the Three Treasures;
- never slander people who propagate the Dharma nor talk about their mistakes and offenses;

- never say that good deeds do not bring good rewards and that bad deeds do not result in bad retributions;
- never say that the death of beings is nihilistic and there is no rebirth;
- never say anything that is harmful or detrimental;
- never discuss the externalists or their teachings;
- never encourage others to commit the ten evil deeds or the five rebellious acts;
- never gossip about others' mistakes or offenses;
- never talk about meaningless or frivolous worldly affairs;
- never tell others to believe in deviant teachers or evil ghosts or spirits;
- never comment on the good or bad of others;
- never scold or curse parents, teachers, elders, or wholesome friends;
- never advise others to commit offenses or prevent others from cultivating blessings.

Instead, may we:

- always praise the Three Treasures;
- always praise those who proclaim and propagate the Dharma, extolling their merit and virtue;
- always explain to others the retributions of good and evil deeds;
- always say that a being's soul will not be annihilated after death;
- always use wholesome speech to benefit others;
- always expound the Tathagatas' Twelve Divisions of sacred texts;
- always state that living beings are endowed with the Buddha Nature and can attain Nirvana, with the four qualities of permanence, bliss, true self and purity;

- always instruct others to be filial to their parents and respectfully attend to their teachers and elders;
- always encourage others to take refuge with the Three Treasures, receive and uphold the five precepts, cultivate the ten good deeds, and practice the sixfold mindfulness;
- always praise the benefits of reading, reciting, and memorizing sutras;
- always talk about all manner of good deeds;
- always advise others to draw near to good and wise advisers and to avoid those who are bad or evil;
- always speak about the immeasurable merit and virtue of the various stages of fruition from the ten abidings up to Buddhahood;
- always encourage others to cultivate the Pure Land practices and adorn one's ultimate fruition;
- always exhort others to diligently venerate the Three Treasures;
- always encourage others to create or set up Buddha images and make various offerings;
- always exhort others to do good deeds with the same urgency as if saving one's head that is on fire, and
- always exhort others to ceaselessly help those who are distressed, impoverished, and in need.

Having made these vows about our mouth faculty, let us all now with utmost sincerity, bow in full prostration and take refuge with the Greatly Kind and Compassionate Ones who are like fathers to those of us in this world.

Namo Maitreya Buddha
Namo Shakyamuni Buddha
Namo Blossom of the World Buddha
Namo Lofty Summit Buddha
Namo Accomplished in Boundless Eloquence Buddha

Namo Discerning Knowledge and Views Buddha
Namo Lion's Tooth Buddha
Namo Ridra Strides Buddha
Namo Blessings and Virtue Buddha
Namo Dharma Lamp and Canopy Buddha
Namo Maudgalyayana Buddha
Namo Worry-free Land Buddha
Namo Contemplative Thoughts Buddha
Namo Delight in Bodhi Buddha.
Namo Lion Playfully Roaming Bodhisattva
Namo Lion Swiftness and Vigor Bodhisattva
Namo Boundless Body Bodhisattva
Namo Guan Shi Yin Bodhisattva.

Again, we take refuge with the Three Treasures of the ten directions to the ends of empty space. May you protect, guard, and gather us in with your power of kindness and compassion and enable us to fulfill our wishes and perfect our bodhi vows.

Dharma-doors of Cultivation

We also vow that all beings of the four births and the six paths throughout the ten directions henceforth accomplish all these Dharma-doors of Cultivation:

- the Dharma-door of reverence and respect –so as to have deep faith in the Three Treasures;
- the Dharma-door of being steadfast – so as to never be skeptical;
- the Dharma-door of diligently repenting - so as to eradicate the evil committed;
- the Dharma-door of remorse - so as to attain purity;
- the Dharma-door of guarding the body - so that it will not be defiled by the three evil karmas of killing, stealing, and lust;

- the Dharma-door of guarding one's speech - so as to be completely free of the four kinds of speech offenses: frivolous speech, divisive speech, harsh speech, and false speech;
- the Dharma-door of guarding one's mind - so as to calm it and attain purity;
- the Dharma-door of bodhi - so as to fulfill all our vows and resolves;
- the Dharma-door of compassion - so as not to harm any living being;
- the Dharma-door of kindness – so as to influence others to establish virtue;
- the Dharma-door of happiness – so as to never belittle or slander others;
- the Dharma-door of utmost sincerity – so as to never deceive others;
- the Dharma-door of relying on the Three Treasures - so as to eliminate the three evil destinies;
- the Dharma-door of being genuine – so as to never be pretentious;
- the Dharma-door of renouncing harm – so as to never be arrogant or slight others;
- the Dharma-door of renouncing fetters of the mind – so as to be without hesitation and procrastination;
- the Dharma-door of non-contention – so as to eliminate thoughts of fighting, or arguing, or litigation; and,
- the Dharma-door of the One Worthy of Offerings and Proper Enlightenment – so as to always uphold equanimity.

Also, may living beings perfect the practices of immeasurable Dharma-doors, including:

- Dharma-door of reflection on mental tendencies, by contemplating thoughts as illusory;

- Dharma-door of severing discursive thoughts, by discarding the roots of that which is unwholesome;
- Dharma-door of the full attainment of spiritual powers, by feeling light and at ease in both body and mind;
- Dharma-door of roots of faith, by never retreating;
- Dharma-door of roots of vigor, by never forsaking being inspired by and intent upon goodness;
- Dharma-door of roots of mindfulness, by skillfully creating wholesome karma leading to the Way;
- Dharma-door of roots of samadhi, by focusing the mind on the proper path;
- Dharma-door of roots of wisdom, by contemplating suffering, impermanence, and emptiness;
- Dharma-door of faith-power, by overpowering intimidating demonic forces;
- Dharma-door of vigor-power, by always advancing without ever retreating;
- Dharma-door of mindfulness-power, by never forgetting or forsaking mindfulness;
- Dharma-door of samadhi-power, by eliminating all false thoughts;
- Dharma-door of wisdom-power, by skillfully dealing with whatever comes or goes;
- Dharma-door of the bodhi-share of vigor, by accumulating practices of the Buddha Path;
- Dharma-door of proper concentration, by attaining samadhi; and,
- Dharma-door of the pure nature, by never delighting in lesser Vehicles.

May all living beings accomplish all Bodhisattvas Mahasattvas' one hundred and eight Dharma-doors. These include:

- purifying the Buddhalands;

- exhorting and transforming those who are stingy or jealous;
- liberating those in the evil destinies and the eight difficulties;
- gathering in and transforming those who are hateful, angry, litigious, or contentious;
- diligently cultivating all good deeds and influencing and encouraging everyone not to be lax or lazy;
- having the samadhi and spiritual power to gather in beings troubled by scattered thoughts.

Having made these vows, let us all now, with utmost sincerity, bow in full prostration and take refuge with the Greatly Kind and Compassionate Ones who are like fathers to those of us in this world.

Namo Maitreya Buddha
Namo Shakyamuni Buddha
Namo Heavenly Reverence of Dharma Buddha
Namo Cutting-off Strength Buddha
Namo Ultimate Strength Buddha
Namo Wisdom Flower Buddha
Namo Firm Voice Buddha
Namo Peace and Bliss Buddha
Namo Wonderful Meaning Buddha
Namo Delight in Purity Buddha
Namo Countenance of Penance and Remorse Buddha
Namo Wondrous Crown Prominence Buddha
Namo Desiring Bliss Buddha
Namo Rucika Buddha
Namo Medicine King Bodhisattva
Namo Medicine Superior Bodhisattva
Namo Boundless Body Bodhisattva
Namo Guan Shi Yin Bodhisattva.

Again, we take refuge with the Three Treasures of the ten directions to the ends of empty space. May you protect, guard, and gather in all beings of the four births, the three realms, and the six paths with your power of kindness and compassion. May you enable them to perfect their wisdom, spiritual powers, and wish-fulfilling self-mastery from the merit and virtue of bringing forth the bodhi resolve and from the vows made during today's Repentance Dharma of Kindness and Compassion in the Bodhimanda.

Section 40 Sincere Requests

Today, we are here in this Bodhimanda due to our shared karma. We have already made vows on behalf of living beings of the four births and the six paths. And we trust that you great Bodhisattvas with your kindness and compassion will gather in and take care of all living beings. From the causes and conditions that have lead to creating merit and virtue while repenting and making vows here in this Bodhimanda today, may you with the power of your great kindness and compassion enable all living beings to:

- delight in seeking the unsurpassed field of blessings and deeply believe that making offerings to Buddhas brings about immeasurable rewards;
- have devout faith in Buddhas and attain immeasurable rewards of purity.

May living beings:

- harbor no thoughts of stinginess but readily and unreservedly make great offerings in the presence of Buddhas;
- cultivate the unsurpassed field of blessings in the presence of Buddhas, renounce any aspirations for the Two Vehicles, cultivate the Bodhisattva Path, and gain the Tathagata's unobstructed liberation and Wisdom of All Modes;
- plant inexhaustible roots of goodness in the presence of Buddhas and thus attain the Buddhas' limitless merit, virtue, and wisdom;

- assimilate profound wisdom, emulating the pure, unsurpassed King of Wisdom;
- have self-mastery in traveling and attain the Buddhas' unobstructed spiritual powers to go anywhere;
- embrace the Mahayana, obtain immeasurable Modes of Wisdom, and dwell steadfastly therein;
- perfectly accomplish the foremost field of blessings, from which wells forth stages of All-wisdom;
- never harbor any thought of hatred or loathing toward the Buddhas but instead plant roots of goodness and joyfully seek the Buddha's wisdom;
- be able to go to all the magnificent Buddhalands using wonderful expedient means, and within a single thought, tirelessly enter the profound Dharma realm;
- attain boundless bodies and be able to travel tirelessly throughout the worlds of the ten directions;
- accomplish vast bodies that can go wherever they please, attain all the Buddhas' spiritual powers to adorn the ultimate other shore, and within a single thought, manifest the Tathagatas' complete mastery of spiritual powers that pervade empty space.

Having made these great vows, which are as vast as the Dharma nature and as ultimate as empty space, we pray that living beings will fulfill all their wishes and perfect their bodhi vows. Together, with utmost sincerity, we now bow in full prostration.

Since we ourselves have to undergo retributions involving suffering and may be unable to rescue other living beings, we do humbly entrust them all to the following Bodhisattvas:

- the limitless and boundless non-produced Dharma-body Bodhisattvas extending to the ends of empty space;
- the limitless and boundless non-outflow form-body Bodhisattvas extending to the ends of empty space;

- the limitless and boundless Bodhisattvas resolved on bodhi extending to the ends of empty space;
- Great Master Asvaghosa Bodhisattva who made the Dharma flourish during the Proper Dharma Age;
- Great Master Nagarjuna Bodhisattva who made the Dharma flourish during the Dharma Image Age;
- Boundless Body Bodhisattva extending to the ends of empty space in the ten directions;
- Guan Shi Yin Bodhisattva extending to the ends of empty space in the ten directions; as well as
- Manjushri Bodhisattva,
- Samantabhadra Bodhisattva,
- Lion Playfully Roaming Bodhisattva,
- Lion Swiftness and Vigor Bodhisattva,
- Lion Banner Bodhisattva,
- Lion Deeds Bodhisattva,
- Resolute Vigor Bodhisattva,
- Vajra Wisdom Bodhisattva
- Renouncing *Skandhas* and Hindrances Bodhisattva
- Tranquil Sense Faculties Bodhisattva,
- Wisdom Superior Bodhisattva,
- Never Leaving the World Bodhisattva,
- Medicine King Bodhisattva,
- Medicine Superior Bodhisattva,
- Empty Space Treasury Bodhisattva,
- Vajra Treasury Bodhisattva,
- Ever-vigor Bodhisattva,
- Never Resting Bodhisattva,
- Wonderful Voice Bodhisattva,
- Wonderful Virtue Bodhisattva,
- Precious Moon Bodhisattva,
- Moonlight Bodhisattva,
- Sadapralapa Bodhisattva, and
- Transcending the Three Realms Bodhisattva.

Again we beseech all the Bodhisattvas Mahasattvas of the ten directions to the ends of empty space, based on their fundamental vow-power to liberate living beings, to gather in the endless and limitless numbers of living beings throughout the ten directions.

- May the Bodhisattvas Mahasattvas never abandon any living being, but instead regard them as good and wise advisers without discrimination.
- May all living beings be grateful for the kindness of the Bodhisattvas, draw near to them, and make offerings to them.
- May the Bodhisattvas compassionately gather in all livings beings and enable them to have integrity and be straightforward. May beings always follow and never be apart from the Bodhisattvas.
- May all living beings accord with and never transgress any of the Bodhisattvas' teachings, attain solid and unwavering resolve, never be apart from good and wise advisers, and attain the indestructible mind free of defilement.
- May all living beings renounce everything, even their own lives, for the sake of good and wise advisers and never go against their teachings.
- May all living beings cultivate great kindness and stay away from all evil.
- May they receive and uphold the Buddha's proper Dharma once they hear it.
- May all living beings have the Bodhisattvas' roots of goodness and karmic rewards, attain ultimate purity in their Bodhisattva practices and vows, perfect their spiritual powers, and attain as-you-wish self-mastery.
- May they thereby ride on the Mahayana and never become weary or lax until they perfect the ultimate Wisdom of All Modes.
- May they ride the vehicle of wisdom, reaching secure and tranquil places; may they acquire the unobstructed Vehicle, accomplishing ultimate self-mastery.

- May all the following practices:
  - taking refuge with the Three Treasures,
  - severing doubts and deepening faith,
  - repenting and reforming,
  - bringing forth the resolve,
  - revealing the retributions,
  - leaving the hells,
  - resolving animosity and feeling fortunate,
  - making vows and dedication, and
  - finally entrusting all living beings to the Bodhisattvas,

from the beginning until the end of this Repentance, together with all the merit and virtue generated, be dedicated to all living beings throughout the ten directions to the ends of empty space.

We now look up and pray that Maitreya, the future Buddha, World-Honored One, bear witness to our vows and practices, and that the Buddhas of the ten directions kindly and compassionately guard and protect us, so that both our repentance and vows will be accomplished.

May all living beings be born in the land of this compassionate one who is a like fathers to us , attend his first Dharma assembly, and awaken to the Way upon listening to the Dharma. May all be completely endowed with the merit and virtue, as well as the wisdom that are identical to that of the Bodhisattvas. May everyone gain entry into the vajra mind and accomplish Proper and Equal Enlightenment.

Praying to and Praising the Buddhas

Honored are the Buddhas with ten titles, which include Tathagata, Worthy of Offerings, One of Proper and Pervasive Knowledge. They rescue immeasurable living beings and extricate them from the suffering of birth and death. May the merit and virtue attained from repenting and bowing to the Buddhas enable all living beings to fulfill their vows and their bodhi resolve.

May our vows be identical to that of all Buddhas and great Bodhisattvas of the ten directions to the ends of empty space.

Just as the vows of all Buddhas and Bodhisattvas are limitless and boundless, as vast as the Dharma nature, as ultimate as empty space, and extend throughout all kalpas to the end of time, so too are our vows.

1. Just as living beings are limitless and boundless, so too are our vows.
2. Just as worlds are limitless and boundless, so too are our vows.
3. Just as empty space is limitless and boundless, so too are our vows.
4. Just as the Dharma nature is limitless and boundless, so too are our vows.
5. Just as Nirvana is limitless and boundless, so too are our vows.
6. Just as the Buddhas' manifestations in the worlds are limitless and boundless, so too are our vows.
7. Just as the Buddhas' wisdom is limitless and boundless, so too are our vows.
8. Just as our scheming thoughts are limitless and boundless, so too are our vows.
9. Just as our discriminatory thoughts are limitless and boundless, so too are our vows.
10. Just as the mundane ways, the transcendental ways, and the ways of wisdom are limitless and boundless, so too are our vows.

Only when all the above ten circumstances come to an end will our vows end. We now pay homage to the sages of all Three Vehicles.

Praise

We have endured the hardship of bowing this Repentance.
May the Buddhas now bestow their kindness upon us,
To aid us in fulfilling our vows regarding the six sense faculties

And to help us persevere in each and every practice.
We dedicate all to the realization of bodhi,
Entrusting living beings to the Guiding Teachers
Who can take everyone across.

Namo Bodhisattvas Mahasattvas of the Ground of Dharma Clouds
(three times)

Concluding the Repentance

The Buddha's *ten* bodies are fine and splendorous,
Majestic and unmoving like a purple-golden mountain.
The Benevolent One, honored with the *ten* titles,
His hallmarks vast, perfect, and jade-like,
Uses his spiritual powers to universally respond.
His wondrous edifying teaching knows no restriction.
May he pour his unobstructed perfect radiance down upon us
And bear witness to the effort we have put into this last Roll.
Respectfully, we bow to the Enlightened Ones of the *ten*
directions;
We repent of our offenses from the *ten* evils.

[Dharma Host]: On behalf of _____ [those who seek to repent], we practice this Repentance Dharma of Kindness and Compassion in the Bodhimanda. We have now successfully completed Roll Ten. May all reap the perfect and abundant fruition of its goodness.

In this Bodhimanda:
Lamps are lit, blazing forth radiance;
Flowers are arrayed, sublime and adorned;
Tea is prepared and fruits presented.
These are all offerings from our sincere hearts.
Extolling Buddhas' meritorious deeds extensively and
Revering Buddhas as numerous as dust motes,
We make our resolve resolute; our dedication, sincere.

May the Greatly Enlightened Ones of the ten directions,
The sacred and splendorous Dharma of the Tripitaka,
Pratyekabuddhas with the five eyes,
Arhats with the six spiritual powers,
Gods in the heavens and sages on earth,
Spiritual ones in the water and worthy ones on land,
All of whom encompass the four domains,
Being boundless and efficacious, and bestowing blessings,
Examine our sincerity, we who are ordinary ones, and
Bear witness to the wholesome seeds we have planted.

We now further pray on behalf of _____ [those who seek
to repent] so that they can all cleanse their subtle offenses and
amass boundless blessings.
We bow and earnestly pray:
May we be instantly freed from the *ten* fetters and be liberated
from the ten entanglements;
May we perfect the *ten* resolves and fulfill the *ten* vows, so we
become like a bright moon shining in the clear sky;
May we cultivate the Ten Grounds and sever the *ten* obstacles,
so we become like flowers blossoming in the Garden of
Enlightenment;
May we find the gate to liberation in each and every dust mote,
and may every place reveal the workings of True Suchness;
May friends and foes, sages and ordinary beings everywhere
receive benefit, so that all can realize the wondrous way to
Nirvana from the wholesome conditions of this Repentance.
[Dharma host]: Having done just minimal repentance, we fear
our subtle delusions may not be removed. Thus I am taking the
liberty to request that together, we continue to repent and
reform.

Praise

*The meritorious power of the Emperor of Liang Repentance Roll Ten
Enables the deceased and the disciples to eradicate offenses of ten
entanglements.
May all realize the Bodhisattva's Ground of Dharma Clouds.
As the Repentance is chanted our offenses are blown away like falling
flowers
Offenses repented, enmity resolved,
Wisdom and blessing increase as calamities are dispelled.
Liberated from suffering and reborn in the Trayastrimsha,
May we gather at the Dragon Flower's Three Assemblies
And receive a prediction personally from Maitreya Buddha.*

Namo Dragon Flower Assembly of Bodhisattvas Mahasattvas *(three times)*.

Final praise

*Emperor of Liang Repentance Roll Ten now concludes.
We dedicate its merit to the four benefactors and the three realms.
May all in this assembly enjoy increased longevity and blessings.
May the Dharma water cleanse our offenses.
May the deceased be reborn in the Western Pure Land.
May the Bodhisattvas of the Ground of Dharma Clouds compassion-
ately gather us in.*

Namo Ascending the Path to the Clouds Bodhisattva Mahasattva *(three times)*

Now let us chant the Buddha's name and dedicate the merit in
the same manner as before.

*The Buddha is just like empty space dwelling in the world;
Just like the lotus untouched by water.*

To the Buddha I return and rely, vowing that all living beings
understand the great way profoundly and bring forth the bodhi
mind.

To the Dharma I return and rely, vowing that all living beings deeply enter the sutra treasury and have wisdom like the sea. To the Sangha I return and rely, vowing that all living beings from together a great assembly, one and all in harmony.

End Notes

1. **Eighteen unique dharmas:** (also Eighteen Unshared Dharmas) because they are unshared by those of the Two Vehicles and by Bodhisattvas. Only the Buddha is:
   a) Faultless in body.
   b) Faultless in speech.
   c) Faultless in mindfulness.
   d) Has no perception of difference.
   e) Has no unconcentrated thoughts.
   f) There is nothing he does not know that has not already been cast aside.
   g) His zeal never decreases.
   h) His vigor never decreases.
   i) His concentration never decreases.
   j) His wisdom never decreases.
   k) His liberation never decreases.
   l) His knowledge and vision of liberation never decreases.
   m) All his bodily karma accords with the practice of wisdom.
   n) All his karma of speech accords with the practice of wisdom.
   o) All his karma of mind accords with the practice of wisdom.
   p) With his wisdom, he has unhindered knowledge of the past.
   q) With his wisdom, he has unhindered knowledge of the future.
   r) With his wisdom, he has unhindered knowledge of the present.

GLOSSARY

This glossary is an aid for readers unfamiliar with the Buddhist vocabulary. Definitions have been kept simple and are not necessarily complete. Skt.: Sanskrit word; py: pinyin romanization of Chinese word.

Amitābha Buddha: (Skt.) The Buddha of the Western Land of Ultimate Bliss. He is known as Amitābha "infinite light" and Amitāyus "infinite life."

Ānanda: (Skt.) One of the ten great disciples of the Buddha Śākyamuni, Ānanda was the Buddha's first cousin and his attendant. He also compiled and edited the *sutras*. His name means rejoicing, because he was born on the day the Buddha realized Buddhahood. His father also rejoiced and gave him that name. The entire country celebrated the Buddha's enlightenment on that day. With his flawless memory, Ānanda was able to remember all the *sutras* the Buddha spoke and was foremost among the Buddha's disciples in erudition.

anuttarā-samyak-saṃbodhi: (Skt.) The unsurpassed, proper and equal, right enlightenment of all Buddhas.

Arhat (Skt.) An enlightened sage who has awakened by contemplating on the Four Noble Truths. There are four stages of arhatship. (Also Hearer, Sound Hearer, shravaka, *śrāvaka*)

asura: (Skt.) A "being who likes to fight," one of the eightfold division of ghosts and spirits, found among gods, human beings, animals, and ghosts. Examples of evil *asuras* are thieves, robbers, gunmen, tigers, lions, and wolves. *Asuras* in the heavens have the blessings of the gods but not the authority.

Avalokiteśvara Bodhisattva (Skt.) One of the four Bodhisattvas of
greatest importance in Mahāyāna Buddhism, Avalokiteśvara is the
Bodhisattva of Compassion and the disciple and future successor
of the Buddha Amitābha in the Western Land of Ultimate Bliss. His
name, which is Sanskrit, is often translated as Observer of the
Sounds of the World. It can also be interpreted as meaning Contemplator of Self-Mastery. (Also Guan Shi Yin, Kuanyin).

Bhagavān: (Skt.) World-Honored One (See ten titles for the Buddha)

bhikṣu: (Skt.) The technical designation for a fully ordained Buddhist
monk, one who leads a pure and celibate life and who upholds the
basic 250 monastic regulations.

bhikṣunī: (Skt.) The technical designation for a fully ordained Buddhist nun, one who leads a pure and celibate life and who upholds
the 348 monastic regulations.

Bodhi: (Skt.) Refers to enlightenment. There are many levels of
enlightenment on the path to full awakening. Bodhi is usually
reserved as the designation for the ultimate enlightenment.

bodhimaṇḍala: (Skt.) The site of awakening. (Note: Compare to
bodhimaṇḍa, which means the seat or throne on which one becomes
awakened.)

Bodhisattva: (Skt.) Bodhisattva (*bodhi* = enlightenment *sattva* = being)
can be interpreted in two ways: One, the Bodhisattva is an enlightened one among sentient beings, and two, he enlightens sentient
beings. A Bodhisattva is someone who has resolved to become a
Buddha and who is cultivating the Path to becoming a Buddha.

Brahmā: (Skt.) The god of the Brahmā Heaven, the god worshipped by
Hindus. The Brahmā net in the Brahmā Net Sūtra refers to the
enormous net of jewels that is hung in the palace of the god
Brahmā. It is used as a metaphor for the practices of purity, i.e.
upholding of the Bodhisattva precepts.

Brahmā conduct: Refers to "pure deeds" and the practice of upholding precepts purely.

brahman: (Skt.) Sometimes written *brāhman* or *brāhmaṇa*; the priest caste of India. They practice fire-worship. It is rendered in English as "brahmin."

Buddha: (Skt.) the "awakened" or "enlightened one." It is a title that is applied to those who have reached perfect enlightenment (*anuttarā-samyak-saṃbodhi*) and who have perfect wisdom and universal compassion. The Buddha of the present historical period is known as the Buddha Śākyamuni. There were also Buddhas prior to his time; there were and are Buddhas in other worlds; and there will be Buddhas in the future, both in our world and in others.

dhāraṇī (Skt.): Interpreted as "unite and hold." A *dhāraṇī*, is the chief, the head, and the origin of all *dharmas*. *Dhāraṇīs* unite all *dharmas* and hold limitless meanings. (See mantra)

Dharma: (Skt.) Refers to the teachings of the Buddha and is one of the Three Jewels.

dharmas: (1) A generic term for all the various kinds of things or entities that exist in the world, including both physical and mental phenomena (e.g. wholesome *dharmas* refer to wholesome deeds); (2) methods.

Dharma-door: A Dharma-door is an entrance to the Dharma, described in the teachings as a way or method of practice leading to enlightenment.

Dharma Image Age: (See Three Ages)

Dharma Prince: Buddhas are called Dharma Kings. Dharma Princes are Bodhisattvas, because they are next in line for Buddhahood. Mañjuśrī Bodhisattva is often called the Dharma Prince because he is the senior Bodhisattva.

dragons: Dragons are related to snakes and worms. They have the power to change their size and form, and they are responsible for the changes in weather. (See eightfold division/pantheon and *garuḍas*.)

eightfold division/pantheon: Gods, dragons, *yakṣas*, *gandharvas*, *asuras*, *garuḍas*, *kinnaras*, and *mahoragas* make up eight categories of beings that are not ordinarily visible to the human eye;

however, their subtle bodies can be clearly seen by those with higher spiritual powers. Each is discussed under its separate entry.

eighty subtle characteristics: These are the secondary physical attributes of all Buddhas. (See also thirty-two features)

five rebellious acts: These are five of the most serious violations of which it is very difficult to repent. They are (1) patricide, (2) matricide, (3) killing an Arhat, (4) spilling the Buddha's blood, and (5) destroying the harmony of the Sangha.

four continents: The four inhabited continents of every world system. They are situated north, south, east and west of the central mountain Sumeru. In the east is Pūrvavideha; in the south is Jambudvīpa; in the west is Aparagodanīya; and in the north is Uttarakuru.

four kinds of kindness: There are four kinds of kind people to whom living beings owe a debt. They are: (1) mothers and fathers, (2) teachers, (3) rulers, and (4) benefactors. Also, the kindness of: (1) mothers and fathers, (2) teachers, (3) living beings, and (4) the Buddha.

Four Noble (Holy) Truths: 1) The truth that there is suffering in the world; 2) the truth that there is an accumulation of afflictions due to desire and attachments; 3) the truth that a cessation of these afflictions can be realized; and 4) the truth that there exists a Path to end this suffering.

gandharvas: (Skt.) "Incense-inhaling spirits," musicians in the court of the Jade Emperor. When the emperor wants some music, he lights some incense and the gandharvas all come to play music.

Ganges River: The major river in northern India. Also known as River Gangā, it is sacred for the Hindus.

garuḍas: (Skt.) Great golden-winged birds. They have a wingspan of about 3000 miles. When they flap their wings, the ocean waters part, and all the dragons at the bottom of the sea are exposed as potential meals. The dragons have no time to transform into anything. They are gobbled up on the spot by the *garuḍas*, who eat them with the same relish as we eat noodles.

gods: Gods, according to Buddhist teaching, live in various heavens. They are not immortal or omnipotent. They do have long life spans and various spiritual powers. Anyone can be reborn as a god by generating the appropriate good karma; however, gods have not attained the enlightenment of the sages. They eventually die and are reborn in lower realms according to their karma.

Great Vehicle: (See Mahāyāna)

Guan Shi Yin (py): (See Avalokiteśvara Bodhisattva). Also Guanyin, Guanyin Pusa, Kuanyin, Contemplator (Observer) of the Sounds of the World, One Who Hears the Cries of the World.

Hearer: (See *śrāvaka*)

karma: (Skt.) Refers to "deeds" or "what is done." Karma can be good, evil, or neutral and is created by the body, mouth, and mind. Seeds of karma are stored in the eighth consciousness and transmigrate with it until the appropriate rewards or retributions are undergone for those deeds done.

karmic hindrances (obstacles): Obstructions or hindrances from past deeds which hinder us on the path to attaining enlightenment.

King Yama: Lord of the underworld; the judge of karma determining where beings are reborn.

kinnaras: (Skt.) Another kind of musical spirit (see *gandharvas*) with a single horn on their head. The Jade Emperor enjoys having them play music in his palace so the gods can dance.

koṭi: (Skt.) The highest number in the older system of numbers (or ten million).

kṣatriya: (Skt.) Refers to the ruling and warrior caste of India. The Buddha's clan, the Śākyas, was a member of the *kṣatriya* caste.

Lesser Vehicle: Also refers to the Two Vehicle. Those who follow this path aspire to become Arhats (Hearers) and Pratyekabuddhas (Those Enlightened to Conditions).

Lion's Roar: The Buddha's voice is called the Lion's Roar because all must listen to him when he speaks, as must the other animals when the lion gives his roar.

Mahāsattva: (Skt.) A "great being;" the title of a great Bodhisattva.

Mahāsthāmaprāpta Bodhisattva: (Skt.) "Great Strength Bodhisattva," Dashizhi (py), the third of the three Sages of Amitābha Buddha's Pure Land. The others are Amitābha Buddha and Avalokiteśvara Bodhisattva.

Mahāyāna: (Skt.) It means "great vehicle" because it teaches the Path of the Bodhisattva, which leads to Buddhahood. The Mahāyāna is also called Northern Buddhism because it is normally found in northern Asian countries such as China, Korea, Japan, and Tibet.

mahoragas: (Skt.) Huge snake spirits.

Maitreya Bodhisattva: (Skt.) Also known as Ajita, one of the great Bodhisattva-disciples of the Buddha. He is foremost in the perfection of patience, and in a future age he will become the next Buddha.

Mañjuśrī Bodhisattva: (Skt.) Mañjuśrī is interpreted as "wonderful virtue" or "wonderfully auspicious." Of all the Bodhisattvas, Mañjuśrī has the greatest wisdom and is known as "The Greatly Wise Bodhisattva Mañjuśrī."

mantra (Skt.) Mantras are phrases of sound whose primary meanings are not cognitive, but on a spiritual level transcend ordinary linguistic understanding. (Also *dharani*)

Nirvāṇa: (Skt.) Nirvāṇa is interpreted in various ways: (1) cessation, or extinction, referring to the elimination of afflictions at the time of enlightenment or to the ceasing to be of the *skandhas* when an enlightened person at death chooses to be reborn no longer; (2) freedom from desire; and (3) no longer either coming into being or ceasing to be.

Pratyekabuddha: (Skt.) Pratyekabuddhas are holy sages enlightened to conditions. When there is a Buddha in the world, they are called "those enlightened to conditions." When there is no Buddha in the world, they are called "solitary enlightened ones," because they are able to reach a level of enlightenment by themselves.

precepts: Moral rules laid down by the Buddha for his disciples to follow. They are described as being as brilliant as vajra, the original source of all Buddhas, the original source of all Bodhisattvas, and the seed of the Buddha-nature.

[sacred] prominence (on top of the head): (Skt. *uṣnīṣa*) Refers to the flesh protuberance on top of the Buddha's head. It is one of the thirty-two features of a Buddha.

Sahā World: (Skt. *sahāloka*) "The world that must be endured," the name of the world we live in. Sahā (Skt.) means "can be endured."

Samantabhadra Bodhisattva: One of the four great Bodhisattvas, he is considered foremost in practice. He rides on an elephant with six tusks. A pond appears in the curves of said tusks, and singing maidens reside in the pond. (Also Universal Worthy Bodhisattva).

Sangha: (Skt.) The monastic community of Buddhist monks (*bhikṣus*) and nuns (*bhikṣunīs*). They are the transmitters of the tradition and the teachers of the lay community. The Sangha is the third of the Three Treasures.

śīla: (Skt.) The moral precepts within Buddhism.

śrāvaka: (Skt.) Another name for Hearer or Arhat. Translated as "one who hears or listens" and refers to one who "hears the sound of the Buddha's teaching on the Four Noble Truths and awakens to the Path." *Śrāvakas* belong to one of the Two Vehicles, the other vehicle being Those Enlightened to Conditions. (See also Pratyeka-buddhas)

Six Paths: The Six Paths of Rebirth are divided into the three wholesome paths of (1) gods, (2) humans, and (3) *asuras*, and the three lowest paths of (4) animals, (5) ghosts, and (6) hell-beings.

skill-in-means: Refers to provisional teachings or wise, expedient methods. Skill-in-means can also be explained as meaning "exclusive *dharmas*." They are not restrained by any fixed standards, therefore, they are "expedient." In teaching beings, Bodhisattvas devise various kinds of methods according to the situation at hand.

sūtra: (Skt.) Discourse spoken by Buddhas, Bodhisattvas, or other qualified sages.

ten directions: North, south, east, west, northeast, southeast, north-west, southwest, above, and below make up the ten directions.

ten titles for the Buddha: A Buddha may be referred to by ten names which are: (1) Thus-Come One (Tathāgata), (2) One Worthy of Offerings, (3) One of Proper and Equal Enlightenment, (4) One Perfect in Clarity and Conduct, (5) Well-Gone One, (6) Unsurpassed Knight Who Understands the World, (7) Regulating Hero, (8) Teacher of Gods and Humans, (9) Buddha, (10) World-Honored One (Bhagavān). Another list has: (1) Tathāgata, (2) One of Proper and Equal Enlightenment, (3) One Perfect in Clarity and Conduct, (4) Well-Gone One, (5) One Who Understands the World, (6) Unsur-passed Knight, (7) Regulating Hero, (8) Teacher of Gods and Humans, (9) Buddha, (10) Bhagavān.

ten good deeds: Abstention from (1) killing, (2) stealing, (3) sexual misconduct, (4) duplicity, (5) harsh speech, (6) lying, (7) irrespon-sible speech, (8) greed, (9) anger, and (10) foolishness.

thirty-two [heroic] features: The primary physical characteristics that all Buddhas possess. They are the karmic result of a hundred kalpas of cultivation on the Bodhisattva Path.

Those Enlightened to Conditions: (See Pratyekabuddhas). Condi-tions refer to the Twelve Links of Conditioned Causation.

Three Ages: The Three Ages are (1) the Proper Dharma Age, (2) the Dharma Image Age, and (3) the Dharma Ending Age. The era when the Buddha dwelled in the world was called the Proper Dharma Age. At that time the Buddha taught the Dharma, and there were genuine Arhats and great Bodhisattvas; the sages were dwelling in the world. The Proper Dharma Age lasted for one thousand years. The Dharma Image Age began after the Buddha entered Nirvāṇa. During this period, people who practiced on the Path were few; those who were attached to external appearances were many. Peo-ple stressed the creation of Buddha images and many were made, but genuine cultivators were few. During the Dharma Ending Age, the last of the Three Ages of Dharma, the understanding and prac-tice of the Buddha-dharma gradually declines and disappears.

Three Paths: (See Six Paths)

Three Realms: Refers to the realm of desire, the realm of form, and the formless realm. Living beings within the realm of desire still have desire—greed and lust. Living beings within the realm of form do not have such heavy desire; however, they still have a physical form and appearance. They are still attached to appearances, and therefore they are not apart from the marks of self, others, living beings, and life spans. Living beings of the formless realm are without form or shape, yet they still have consciousness, and they are attached to that consciousness.

Thus-Come One (Tathāgata): (See ten titles for the Buddha) In Sanskrit, it means both Thus-Come One and Thus-Gone One.

Three Treasures: Also called the Three Gems or Three Jewels. They comprise: (1) the Buddha, (2) the Dharma, and (3) the Sangha. They are Buddhism's greatest treasures. For further information, see the individual entries for each.

upāsaka: (Skt.) Translated as "a layman who is close to work," working closely with the Three Jewels, a Buddhist layman.

upāsikā: (Skt.) The feminine counterpart of *upāsaka*, a Buddhist laywoman.

vaiḍūrya: (Skt.) lapis lazuli.

Vaiśālī: (Skt.) An ancient kingdom and city in India north of present-day Patna.

wang liang (py): A kind of malevolent ghost.

Western Land of Ultimate Bliss: Amitābha Buddha's pure land. By the power of his vows, Amitābha Buddha leads all beings to rebirth in his country, where they realize Buddhahood. This power attracts living beings to the Western Land of Ultimate Bliss, just as a magnet attracts iron filings. Amitabha Buddha vowed that he would not realize Buddhahood unless he and his Pure Land could bring beings to Buddhahood. Since he realized Buddhahood, he is able to help beings do the same.

yakṣa: (Skt.) Interpreted as "speedy ghosts." They are fierce and get around very fast. There are ground-traveling, space-traveling, and water-traveling *yakṣas*. Some specialize in sapping people of their energy; some drink human blood; and some eat people's essence. They come in many varieties.

Yashodhara: The Buddha's wife. She became pregnant and the Buddha left to cultivate in the mountains. Due to suspicions about infidelity, the Buddha's family was going to burn her alive. But because she had been faithful to the Buddha and so had upheld the precept of no sexual misconduct, the fire could not burn her.

THE DHARMA REALM
BUDDHIST ASSOCIATION

Mission

The Dharma Realm Buddhist Association (formerly the Sino-American Buddhist Association) was founded by the late Tripitaka Master Hsüan Hua in San Francisco in 1959. The Association aims to disseminate the teachings of the Buddha throughout the world, and thus is dedicated to translating the Buddhist Canon, propagating orthodox Dharma, and promoting ethical education.

The Founder
Tripitaka Master Hsüan Hua (1918-1995)

Tripitaka Master Hua, twentieth century Buddhist monastic reformer, was one of the first Chinese masters to teach a large number of Westerners. During his long career he emphasized the primacy of the monastic tradition, the essential role of moral education, the need for Buddhists to ground themselves in traditional spiritual practice and authentic scripture, and the importance of respect and understanding among religions. To attain these goals, he focused on clarifying the essential principles of the Buddha's original teachings, on establishing a properly ordained monastic community, on organizing and supporting the translation of the Buddhist Canon into English and other languages, and on the establishment of schools, religious training programs, and programs of academic research and teaching.

Born in 1918 into a peasant family in a small village south of Harbin, in northeast China, the Master was the youngest of ten children. His father's surname was Bai, and his mother's maiden name was Hu. His mother was a vegetarian, and throughout her life she held to the practice of reciting the name of the Buddha Amitabha. When the Master formally became a Buddhist, in his mid-teens, he was given the Dharma name *Anci* (Peace and Compassion). And after becoming a monk, he was also known as *Dulun* (Liberator from the Wheel of Rebirth). Upon granting him the Dharma-seal of the Weiyang Lineage, the Elder Chan Master Hsu Yun, also Xuyun (1840-1959) bestowed upon him the Dharma-transmission name Hsüan Hua (Xuanhua — to Proclaim and Transform).

When the Master was a child, he followed his mother's example, eating only vegetarian food and reciting the Buddha's name. When he was eleven years old, upon seeing a dead baby lying on the ground, he awakened to the fundamental significance of birth and death and the impermanence of all phenomena. He then resolved to become a monk and practice on the Buddhist Path, but he acquiesced to his mother's request that he not do so until after her death. When he was twelve, he obtained his parents' permission to travel extensively in search of a true spiritual teacher.

At the age of fifteen, the Master went to school for the first time, and when he was sixteen, he started lecturing on the Buddhist sutras to help his fellow villagers who were illiterate but who wanted to learn about the Buddha's teachings. He was not only diligent and focused but also possessed a photographic memory, and so he was able to memorize the Four Books and the Five Classics of the Confucian tradition. He had also studied traditional Chinese medicine, astrology, divination, physiognomy, and the scriptures of the great religions. When he was seventeen, he established a free school, in which, as the lone teacher, he taught some thirty impoverished children and adults.

At the age of eighteen, after only two and a half years of schooling, he left school to care for his terminally ill mother. He was nineteen when she died, and for three years he honored her memory by sitting in meditation beside her grave in a hut made of sorghum stalks. During this time, while reading the **Avatamaska Sutra,** he experienced a deep awakening. Subsequently, while seated in deep meditation, he had a vision of the Sixth Chan Buddhist Patriarch Huineng (638–713 CE). In his vision, Master Huineng came to visit him and to give him the mission of bringing Buddhism to the Western world.

At the end of his period of mourning, the Venerable Master took as his teacher Chan Buddhist Master Changzhi, and he entered Three Conditions Monastery as a novice monk. Chan Master Changzhi subsequently transmitted to him the Dharma of the Jinding Pilu Chan lineage. During this time, the Master devoted himself not only to meditation but also to the study of the Buddhist scriptural tradition and to the mastery of all the major schools of Chinese Buddhism.

In 1946 the Master began the long journey to the south of China. In 1947, he received full ordination as a monk at the Buddhist holy mountain Putuoshan. In 1948, after over two thousand miles of travel, the Master arrived at Nanhua Monastery and bowed to Chan Master Xuyun, China's most widely revered enlightened master. From him the Master received the mind-seal transmission as verification of his awakening, and later a more formal transmission of the Dharma of the Weiyang Lineage of the Chan School.

In 1949 the Master left China for Hong Kong. There he taught meditation, lectured on the Buddhist sutras, and sponsored their printing. He also commissioned the making of images of Buddhas and Bodhisattvas, and he aided monastic refugees from mainland China. He also built Western Bliss Garden Monastery (*Xile Yuan*), established the Buddhist Lecture Hall, and rebuilt and renovated Flourishing Compassion Monastery (*Cixing* Monastery).

In 1962, he traveled to the United States, at the invitation of several of his Hong Kong disciples who had settled in San Francisco, and he began lecturing at the San Francisco Buddhist Lecture Hall, which had been previously established as a branch of the Buddhist Lecture Hall in Hong Kong. As the community at the Buddhist Lecture Hall in

San Francisco grew, both in size and in diversity, the institution's name was changed, first to the Sino-American Buddhist Association and then to the Dharma Realm Buddhist Association. In 1976 the Venerable Master established the organization's first branch monastery – Gold Wheel Temple in Los Angeles – and he established a new headquarters as well, the City of Ten Thousand Buddhas, in Ukiah, California.

In the summer of 1968, the Master began the intensive training of a group of Americans, most of them university students. In 1969, he astonished the monastic community of Taiwan by sending there, for complete ordination, two American women and three American men whom he had ordained as novices. They were the first Americans of that period to become fully ordained Buddhist monks and nuns. During subsequent years, the Venerable Master trained and oversaw the ordination of hundreds of people, both Asians and Westerners, from among the multitudes who came to California from every part of the world to study with him. These monastic disciples now teach in the twenty-eight temples, monasteries and convents that the Venerable Master founded in the United States, Canada, and several Asian countries.

The Venerable Master was determined to transmit to the West the original and correct teachings of Buddhism, and he categorically rejected what he considered to be corrupt practices that had become widespread in China. He guided his disciples in distinguishing between genuine, scripture-based practices that were useful and in accord with common sense, as opposed to ritual superstitions that were unwholesome cultural accretions.

Among the many reforms in monastic practice that he instituted was his insistence that his monastic disciples accord with the ancient practice of wearing the monastic robe or precept-sash (kaśāya) as a sign of membership in the monastic Sangha. He himself followed, and he required that his monastic disciples follow the prohibition against eating after noon. He considered a vegetarian diet to be of paramount importance. He encouraged his disciples among the Sangha to join him in following the Buddha's beneficial ascetic practices of eating only one meal a day and of never lying down. Of his monastic disciples he required strict purity, and he encouraged his lay disciples to adhere to the five precepts of the Buddhist laity.

Although he understood English well and spoke it when necessary, the Master almost always lectured in Chinese. His aim was to encourage his Western disciples to learn Chinese, so that they could help to fulfill his wish that the Buddhist Canon be translated into other languages. So far, the Buddhist Text Translation Society, which he founded, has published well over a hundred volumes of translations, including several of the major Mahayana sutras with the Master's commentaries.

As an educator, the Venerable Master was tireless. At the City of Ten Thousand Buddhas, he established formal training programs for monastics and for laity, elementary and secondary schools for boys and for girls, and Dharma Realm Buddhist University. From 1968 to the early 1990's he himself gave lectures on sutras at least once a day, and he traveled extensively on speaking tours. Responding to requests from Buddhists around the world, the Venerable Master led delegations to Hong Kong, Taiwan, India, Southeast Asia, and Europe to propagate the Dharma. He also traveled to Myanmar, Australia and South America. His presence drew a multitude of the faithful everywhere he went. He was also often invited to lecture at universities and academic conferences.

The Venerable Master was a pioneer in building bridges between different Buddhist communities. Wishing to heal the ancient schism between Mahayana Buddhism and Theravada Buddhism, he invited distinguished Theravada monks to the City of Ten Thousand Buddhas to share the duties of full ordination and transmission of the monastic precepts, which the two traditions hold in common.

He also insisted on inter-religious respect and actively promoted interfaith dialogue. He stressed commonalities in religious traditions, above all their emphasis on proper and compassionate conduct. Together with his friend Paul Cardinal Yubin, who had been archbishop of Nanjing and who was the Chancellor of the Catholic Furen University in Taiwan, he established the Institute for World Religions in Berkeley.

In 1990, at the invitation of Buddhists in several European countries, the Venerable Master led a large delegation on a European Dharma tour, knowing full well that, because of his ill health at the time, the rigors of the trip would shorten his life. However, as always he considered the Dharma more important than his very life. After his return, his health gradually deteriorated, yet, while quite ill, he made another major tour, this time to Taiwan, in 1993.

In Los Angeles, on June 7, 1995 at the age of 77, the Venerable Master entered stillness. When he was alive, he craved nothing, seeking neither fame nor wealth nor power. His every thought and every action were for the sake of bringing true happiness to all sentient beings. In his final instructions he said, "After I depart, you can recite the *Avatamsaka Sutra* and the name of the Buddha Amitabha for however many days you would like, perhaps seven days or forty-nine days. After cremating my body, scatter all my remains in the air. I do not want you to do anything else at all. Do not build me any pagodas or memorials. I came into the world without anything; when I depart, I still do not want anything, and I do not want to leave any traces in the world....From emptiness I came; to emptiness I am returning."

Buddhist Text Translation Society

The Buddhist Text Translation Society (BTTS) is dedicated to making the principles of the Buddhadharma available to Western readers in a form that can be directly applied to practice. Since the early 1970s, the Society has been publishing English translations of sutras, instructional handbooks on meditation and moral conduct, and biographies. Many of the Society's sutra translations are accompanied by contemporary commentary, based on lectures spoken by Tripitaka Master Hsuan Hua.

The accurate and faithful translation of the Buddhist Canon into English and other Western languages is one of the primary objectives of the Dharma Realm Buddhist Association (DRBA), the parent organization of the Buddhist Text Translation Society.

When Buddhism first came to China from India, one of the most important tasks required for its establishment was the translation of the Buddhist scriptures from Sanskrit into Chinese. This work involved a great many people, such as the renowned monk National Master Kumarajiva (fifth century), who led an assembly of over 800 people to work on the translation of the Tripitaka (Buddhist canon) for over a decade. Because of the work of individuals such as these, nearly the entire Buddhist Tripitaka of over a thousand texts exists to the present day in Chinese.

Now the banner of the Buddha's teachings is being firmly planted in Western soil, and the same translation work is being done from Chinese into English. Since the 1970s, the Buddhist Text Translation Society has been making a paramount contribution toward this goal. Aware that the Buddhist Tripitaka is a work of such magnitude that its translation could never be entrusted to a single person, BTTS, emulating the translation assemblies of ancient times, does not publish a work until it has passed through four committees for primary translation, revision, editing, and certification. The leaders of these committees are bhikshus (monks) and bhikshunis (nuns) who have devoted their lives to the study and practice of the Buddha's teachings. For that reason, all of the works of BTTS emphasize the application of the Buddha's teachings in terms of actual practice.

Dharma Realm Buddhist University

Dharma Realm Buddhist University (DRBU) was founded in 1976 and is located on the monastic grounds of the City of Ten Thousand Buddhas in Ukiah, California. It is dedicated to liberal education in the broad Buddhist tradition—a tradition characterized by knowledge in the arts and sciences, self-cultivation, and the pursuit of wisdom. DRBU aims at educating the whole person and thus strives to nurture individuals who see learning as a lifelong endeavor in the pursuit of knowledge, self-understanding, and the creative and beneficial application of that learning to every sphere of life.

DRBU currently offers a BA in liberal arts which emphasizes an integration of the seminal texts of both Eastern and Western traditions and an MA degree in Buddhist Classics.

The Institute of World Religions

Founded in 1994, the Institute is located near the University of California at Berkeley. The purpose of the Institute is to study the truths of religion in harmony with other religious groups, without rejecting or opposing any religion. The six principles of the City of Ten Thousand Buddhas serve as guidelines for the Institute. Propagating the spirit of the City of Ten Thousand Buddhas with expansive open-mindedness, the Institute invites members of various religions to give presentations, deepening understanding of their ideals and practices. The Institute holds meditation twice daily and presents evening and weekend programs that foster conversation between religions, the sciences, and the humanities.

DHARMA REALM BUDDHIST ASSOCIATION BRANCHES

World Headquarters
The City of Ten Thousand Buddhas
2001 Talmage Road
Ukiah, CA 95482 USA
Tel: (707) 462-0939 / Fax: (707) 462-0949
www.drba.org

U.S.A.
California
Berkeley
Berkeley Buddhist Monastery
2304 McKinley Avenue
Berkeley, CA 94703 USA
Tel: (510) 848-3440
Fax: (510) 548-4551
www.berkeleymonastery.org

Burlingame
International Translation Institute
1777 Murchison Drive
Burlingame, CA 94010-4504
Tel: (650) 692-5912
Fax: (650) 692-5056

Long Beach
Blessings, Prosperity, and
Longevity Monastery
4140 Long Beach Boulevard
Long Beach, CA 90807 USA
Tel/Fax: (562) 595-4966

Long Beach Sagely Monastery
3361 East Ocean Boulevard
Long Beach, CA 90803 USA
Tel: (562) 438-8902
www.longbeachmonastery.org

Los Angeles
Gold Wheel Monastery
235 North Avenue 58
Los Angeles, CA 90042 USA
Tel: (323) 258-6668
Fax: (323) 258-3619
www.goldwheel.org

Sacramento
The City of the Dharma Realm
1029 West Capitol Avenue
West Sacramento, CA 95691
Tel: (916) 374-8268
Fax: (916) 374-8234
http://cityofdharmarealm.org

San Francisco
Gold Mountain Monastery
800 Sacramento Street
San Francisco, CA 94108 USA
Tel: (415) 421-6117
Fax: (415) 788-6001
http://goldmountainmonastery.
org

San Jose
Gold Sage Monastery
11455 Clayton Road
San Jose, CA 95127 USA
Tel: (408) 923-7243
Fax: (408) 923-1064
http://www.drbagsm.org

Maryland
Avatamsaka Vihara
9601 Seven Locks Road
Bethesda, MD 20817-9997 USA
Tel/Fax: (301) 469-8300
www.avatamsakavihara.org

Washington
Index
Snow Mountain Monastery
PO Box 272
50924 Index-Galena Road
Index, WA 98256 USA
Tel: (360)799-0699
Fax: (815)346-9141

Seattle
Gold Summit Monastery
233 1st Avenue
West Seattle, WA 98119 USA
Tel: (206) 284-6690
www.goldsummitmonastery.org

Canada
Alberta
Avatamsaka Monastery
1009 4th Avenue
S.W. Calgary, AB T2P OK,
Tel: (403) 234-0644
www.avatamsaka.ca

British Columbia
Gold Buddha Monastery
248 East 11th Avenue
Vancouver, B.C. V5T 2C3,
Tel: (604) 709-0248
Fax: (604) 684-3754
www.gbm-online.com

Australia
Gold Coast Dharma Realm
106 Bonogin Road
Bonogin, Queensland AU 4213
Tel: 61-755-228-788
Fax: 61-755-227-822
www.gcdr.org.au

Hong Kong
Buddhist Lecture Hall
31 Wong Nei Chong Road, Top Floor
Happy Valley, Hong Kong, China
Tel: (852) 2572-7644
Fax: (852) 2572-2850

Cixing Chan Monastery
Lantou Island, Man Cheung Po
Hong Kong, China
Tel: (852) 2985-5159

Malaysia
Dharma Realm Guanyin Sagely
Monastery
161, Jalan Ampang
50450 Kuala Lumpur, Malaysia
Tel: (03) 2164-8055
Fax: (03) 2163-7118

Prajna Guanyin Sagely Monastery
Batu 51, Jalan Sungai Besi
Salak Selatan
57100 Kuala Lumpur, Malaysia
Tel: (03) 7982-6560
Fax: (03) 7980-1272

Fa Yuan Monastery
1 Jalan Utama
Taman Serdang Raya
43300 Seri Kembangan
Selangor Darul Ehsan,
West Malaysia
Tel: (03)8948-5688

Malaysia DRBA Penang Branch
32-32C, Jalan Tan Sri Teh Ewe
Lim
11600 Jelutong
Penang, Malaysia
Tel: (04) 281-7728
Fax: (04) 281-7798

Guan Yin Sagely Monastery
166A Jalan Temiang
70200 Seremban Negeri Sembilan
West Malaysia
Tel/Fax: (06)761-1988

Taiwan
Dharma Realm Buddhist Books
Distribution Society
11th Floor, 85 Zhongxiao E. Road,
Sec. 6
Taipei 115, Taiwan R.O.C.
Tel: (02) 2786-3022
Fax: (02) 2786-2674
www.drbataipei.org
www.fajye.com.tw

Dharma Realm Sagely
Monastery
No. 20, Dongxi Shanzhuang
Liugui Dist.
Gaoxiong 844, Taiwan, R.O.C.
Tel: (07) 689-3717
Fax: (07) 689-3870
www.drbataipei.org/drm/index.
htm

Amitabha Monastery
No. 136, Fuji Street, Chinan
Village, Shoufeng
Hualian County, Taiwan, R.O.C.
Tel: (03) 865-1956
Fax: (03) 865-3426
www.drbataipei.org/am/index.
htm

Subsidiary Organizations

Buddhist Text Translation Society (BTTS)
City of Ten Thousand Buddhas
4951 Bodhi Way
Ukiah. CA 95482 USA
www.buddhisttexts.org
email: info@buddhisttexts.org
catalog: www.bttsonline.org

Dharma Realm Buddhist
University

City of Ten Thousand Buddhas
4951 Bodhi Way
Ukiah, CA 95482 USA
www.drbu.org

Dharma Realm Outreach
City of Ten Thousand Buddhas
outreach@drba.org

Instilling Goodness and Developing Virtue School
City of Ten Thousand Buddhas
2001 Talmage Road
Ukiah, CA 95482 USA
www.igdvs.org

Institute for World Religions
2245 McKinley Avenue, Suite B
Berkeley, CA 94703 USA
www.drbu.org/iwr
email: iwr@drbu.org

Religion East & West (journal)
2245 McKinley Avenue, Suite B
Berkeley, CA 94703 USA
Tel: (510) 848-9788
www.drbu.org/iwr/rew

Vajra Bodhi Sea (magazine)
Gold Mountain Monastery
800 Sacramento Street
San Francisco, CA 94108 USA